Twayne's United States Authors Series

Sylvia E. Bowman, *Editor*

INDIANA UNIVERSITY

Wright Morris

WRIGHT MORRIS

---

by DAVID MADDEN

Kenyon College

Twayne Publishers, Inc. :: New York

To
DAVE AND GINGER VAN VACTOR
AND
FOR C. P. LEE

Preface

M ANY REVIEWERS and critics who have long been impressed with Wright Morris rank him high among serious novelists. Some believe he is one of America's few finest writers, certainly one of her most original. Among those who have praised him are Mark Schorer, Leslie Fiedler, Lewis Mumford, Harry Levin, Thomas Mann, Walter Van Tilburg Clark, Harvey Swados, Benjamin De Mott, John W. Aldridge, Wayne C. Booth, Ihab Hassan, Saul Bellow, Malcolm Cowley, Granville Hicks, Harvey Curtis Webster, and Arthur Mizener. In view of this critical acclaim, and considering that since 1942 each of Morris' fifteen books has marked a progression in quality and maturity rare among American writers, it is difficult to account for the fact that he is one of the most neglected writers of our time.

Why the neglect? In my examination of Morris, the reader may detect certain features of his novels which tend to frustrate even the most literate reader. Why is there so little action or narrative? Why is it so difficult to acclimatize oneself to Morris' seemingly simple style so that one knows what he is talking about? For instance, why the use of so many sentence fragments, and especially the conscious use of so many clichés? Why the techniques that require such effort from the reader and seem to be appropriated from Joyce, Woolf, and James, although, admittedly, adapted to Morris' own purpose? Why isn't he clearer as to whether his attitude is one of satire, irony, paradox, comedy, burlesque, or tragedy? Is he as nihilistic as he appears? Is he nostalgic for or nauseated by Nebraska and the view of America he sees there? These are among the questions with which this book attempts to deal.

Regarding Morris' future among both readers and critics, optimism is justified. It is becoming less pertinent to begin a review of a Morris novel with a long reprimand directed to the American reading public for its consistent failure to give him the attention his work deserves. His short stories and articles have appeared in many quality publications, his novels have been translated into several languages, and paperback editions of four of his books are selling well. One of the purposes of this book is to persuade the reader to explore Morris' early novels.

Critical response to Morris consists mainly of admiring but of usually unenlightening, often misleading, reviews in newspapers and periodicals, many of which lack both critical perspective and interpretive comment. Until *Critique's* special issue on Morris (1962), Wayne C. Booth's essay (1957) was the only significant study of the author's canon. Morris is so unique that many reviewers, lacking as they often do adequate preparation for understanding him, are aware of his qualities as craftsman but fail to discern his intentions. It is as true of Morris as it is of Faulkner that full appreciation and understanding require a thorough reading of all the novels, which are connected by a single vision and design; each book evolves organically out of preceding ones; and his short stories and articles explore aspects of this development. As the first full length study of Morris, this book emerges from a thorough reading of the complete published works of the author.

In view of the sales figures for the author's books, I have assumed that the reader has read few of the novels of Morris. Since the early works are out of print, I have quoted extensively in an attempt to convey a sense of these books. And since one of Morris' achievements is his refinement of a unique "voice," I have quoted liberally from several of the later novels to demonstrate the continuing development of this style. I discuss his book of literary criticism, *The Territory Ahead,* only as it illuminates his own work. To avoid distracting the reader from the discussion of his novels, I trace the relation of his short pieces to his over-all vision in the annotated bibliography.

Since Morris' province is the American character and scene, chapter one introduces his characters and his landscapes. It also examines the special influence upon his work of the Midwest, the region that provided his basic raw material. Efforts to place Morris in a particular literary tradition, group, or school result in more of a loss than a gain; in the course of this book, I only suggest his place in American fiction, with specific reference in chapter one to his relation to the history of the Midwest and to some of its literature. Recognizing Morris' insistence upon maintaining the privacy of his personal life, I provide only the basic facts.

My main purpose in this study is to examine each novel closely in the approximate order of appearance. I discuss the various elements in his work as they find their most important illustration in particular books. Chapters two through four deal with six of Morris' early "plains" novels: *My Uncle Dudley, The Man Who Was There, The Inhabitants, The Home Place, The World in the Attic,* and *The Works of Love.* Morris' unique style and his techniques are analyzed in chapter five. Although it appeared before *The Works of Love, Man and Boy* is discussed with another "urban" novel, *The Deep Sleep,* in chapter six. *The Huge Season,* discussed in chapter seven, and *Love Among the Cannibals* and *What a Way to Go,* discussed in chapter eight, belong to a group of novels which explore the American character in a non-regional context. But in chapter nine two more recent "plains" novels are discussed, *Field of Vision* and *Ceremony in Lone Tree.* In *Cause for Wonder,* examined in chapter ten, one encounters many elements from previous novels. Much of the general pattern of relatedness among the novels the reader will discover for himself; he will perceive that most of the elements discussed in reference to a specific book function in others as well, and require repeated examination from new angles. Since Morris has processed his raw material as though each book contained pieces of a puzzle, the quasi-chronological approach enables the reader to see how Morris' themes and methods develop from novel to novel.

DAVID MADDEN

Kenyon College

Acknowledgments

In writing this book I have benefited from the critical comment and assistance of generous persons. I am grateful to Leonard Wolf for reading my first efforts at Morris criticism in graduate school; to Karl Shapiro for publishing my first article on Morris in *Prairie Schooner;* to Allan Hanna for inviting me to write for *Critique's* special Morris issue; especially to Virginia Faulkner who read, word by word, and commented on the manuscript in its 800-page version, amassing a two-inch stack of correspondence; to Bernice Slote for reading the long version; to Wayne C. Booth, the first Morris critic, for interrupting his work on *The Rhetoric of Fiction* to read my book; to Jonathan Baumbach for his very helpful comments; to Cratis Williams and John Lee Jellicorse for their perceptive reading of selected chapters; to Harry Ford for his sympathetic interest in the progress of the work; and to Stanton J. Linden for his assistance in the bibliography. Mary Ellen Morris kindly made available to me certain materials which would not otherwise have come into my hands. Granville Hicks has been most helpful in his comments on the book and in his strategic advice. A generous research grant from Centre College enabled me to finance a summer's concentration on the book. I doubt whether Wright Morris, from his first letter on, could have been kinder in offering certain information and responses. My wife, Robbie, was there in San Francisco when it all began.

For permission to quote from the following works by Wright Morris, I wish to make special acknowledgment:

To Charles Scribner's Sons for permission to quote from *The Man Who Was There, The Inhabitants, The Home Place, The World in the Attic,* and *The Deep Sleep.*

To Harcourt, Brace and Company for permission to quote from *My Uncle Dudley,* copyright 1942 by Harcourt, Brace and Company; *The Field of Vision,* copyright 1956 by Wright Morris; *Love Among the Cannibals,* copyright 1957 by Wright Morris; *The Territory Ahead,* copyright 1957, 1958 by Wright Morris.

To The Viking Press for permission to quote from *The Huge Season.*

To Alfred A. Knopf for permission to quote from *The Works of Love,* copyright, 1951, and *Man and Boy,* copyright, 1948, 1951 by Wright Morris.

To Atheneum Publishers for permission to quote from *Ceremony in Lone Tree* and *What a Way to Go*.

I also wish to make special acknowledgment to:

Mrs. Thomas Mann for permission to quote from a letter to Wright Morris from Thomas Mann.

Ginn and Company for permission to quote from *The Great Plains* by Walter Prescott Webb.

Wright Morris for permission to quote from his letter to the author, from the Amherst Lectures, from his National Book Award Acceptance Speech, and from various articles and books for which he holds copyrights.

Contents

Chronology

1910	January 6, Wright Morris born in Central City, Nebraska.
1910-1919	Lived in Central City, Schuyler, Kearney, and other towns along the Platte.
1919-1924	Lived in Omaha; two summers on Uncle Harry's farm in Norfolk, Nebraska.
1924-1927	Lived in Chicago, near Lincoln Park, worked at Larrabee "Y".
1927-1929	Cross-country jaunts with father; lived on Uncle's farm in Texas.
1930-1933	Adventist College in California (5 weeks); Pomona College, Claremont, California. Wrote prose poems and Chicago gang pieces.
1933	Began European *Wanderjahr:* Vienna, Schloss Ranna in Wachau.
1934	Italy, Germany, Paris. Returned to Claremont. Married Mary Ellen Finfrock, of Cleveland, Ohio. Began first novel.
1935-1938	Wrote two novels, volume of prose pieces (*Inhabitants* sketches) and began photography of American artifacts.
1939	Summer: Wellfleet, Massachusetts. Work in photo-text medium: further work on *The Inhabitants.*
1940-1941	15,000 mile jaunt around the States, expanding *Inhabitants* photos. Los Angeles; wrote *My Uncle Dudley.*
1941	Lived in Columbia Heights, Brooklyn. Finished *The Inhabitants.*
1942	Returned to California via Norfolk, Nebraska. Guggenheim fellowship. *My Uncle Dudley* published.
1942-1943	Wrote *The Man Who Was There.*
1944	Moved to Haverford, Pennsylvania.
1945	*The Man Who Was There* published. *Man and Boy,* first draft.
1946-1947	*The Inhabitants* published. Early drafts of *The Works of Love.*

1947   Guggenheim for *The Home Place*. Returned to Norfolk for photographs.

1948   *The Home Place* published. New draft of *The Works of Love;* wrote *The World in the Attic*. Moved to Wayne, Pennsylvania.

1949   *The World in the Attic* published; *Man and Boy* revised.

1950   Completed final draft of *The Works of Love*.

1951   *Man and Boy* published.

1952   First draft of "How They Put in the Time," early version of *The Field of Vision. The Works of Love* published. Wrote *The Deep Sleep*.

1953   Writing *The Huge Season. The Deep Sleep* published.

1954   Received third Guggenheim. *The Huge Season* published. Spent fall and winter in Mexico. Began *The Field of Vision*.

1956   *The Field of Vision* published. National Book Award. Wrote *Love Among the Cannibals*.

1957   *Love Among the Cannibals* published.

1958   *The Territory Ahead* published, Summer: Lectures at University of Southern California. September: Europe. October: Amherst Lectures. Winter: Mexico, working on *Ceremony in Lone Tree*.

1959   Venice for six months. Finished *Ceremony*. Greece, then back to U. S. and Mexico.

1960   *Ceremony in Lone Tree* published. Lived in Pacific Palisades, California. National Institute of Arts and Letters Award.

1961   Divorced first wife. Married Josephine Kantor. Taught at Los Angeles State College.

1962-
1963   Returned to Venice for summer. *What a Way to Go* published

1963   Returned to California, now teaching at San Francisco State College.

1964   *Cause for Wonder* published.

Wright Morris

CHAPTER 1

Wright Morris' House of Fiction

IN THE LIFE of Wright Morris there has been no paucity of raw material. Of life as literature, he says in *The Territory Ahead:* "Raw material, an excess of both material and comparatively raw experience, has been the dominant factor in my own role as a novelist. Before coming of age—the formative years when the reservoir of raw material was filling—I had led, or rather been led by, half a dozen separate lives. Each life had its own scene, its own milieu; it frequently appeared to have its own beginning and ending, the only connecting tissue being the narrow thread of my *self.* I had been *there,* but that, indeed, explained nothing." Precisely *where* is a question that the landscape and the characters—rather than the particulars of the author's life—will determine. "In an effort to come to terms with the experience, I processed it in fragments, collecting pieces of the puzzle. In time, a certain over-all pattern *appeared* to be there. But this appearance was essentially a process—an imaginative act of apprehension—rather than a research into the artifacts of my life." Of literature as life, Morris says, "I seek to make my own what I have inherited as clichés."

Very little biographical material is available. Not a public figure, Morris insists on privacy. (For the basic facts, see Chronology.) But the "transitory, elusive facts" of his life may be viewed, imaginatively transformed and processed, through the windows of his house of fiction.

I *Landscapes, Houses, Inhabitants*

In his preface to *The Portrait of a Lady* Henry James wrote: "The house of fiction has ... not one window, but ... a number of possible windows not to be reckoned ... every one of which has been pierced, or is still pierceable, in its vast front, by the need of the individual vision and by the pressure of the individual will."[1] This is particularly apt as a description of the works of Wright Morris: each of his novels is a window in his house of fiction, twenty years abuilding. Morris' fiction is a fiction of landscapes, of houses, and of characters.

The composite landscapes—inscapes as well, in a sense, since *place* shapes character in Morris' field of vision—form a single locale: the Nebraska plains, the navel of the world. Struggling between the conflicting tensions of time-past and time-present, his characters may be found in Indian Bow, Lone Tree, and Junction, Nebraska; on the West Coast, the land of milk and honey, sitting in Pershing Square, lying on the Hollywood beach, attending a small California college; on the East Coast, living in the untamed station-wagon suburbs of Main Line Philadelphia, or teaching in small colleges near New York City. His characters are also lying on the Mexican beaches, sailing the Atlantic seascapes, sitting in Paris cafés, riding gondolas down Venice canals, gazing at the beaches and the ruins of Greece, or waiting out the snow in the Lower Alps of Austria. Much of this ground is covered in cars, which demand of us the kind of attention accorded the characters who drive them: Uncle Dudley's Marmon touring, Horter's sports car, Lawrence's Bugatti, Uncle Harry's Model-T, Bud Momeyer's Hupmobile, Boyd's Plymouth.

Many houses and places to hide form a single fictional house in which the characters are usually engaged in homecoming, reunion, funeral, or christening ceremonies. Some of these houses are firmly in this world; others seem out of it. At one extreme is the home place in Lone Tree, the farms of Uncle Harry and Uncle Ed; in Junction, there is Bud Hibbard's house, and in various other small towns along the Platte, the houses of Will Brady. At the other extreme are the urban houses of Gussie Newcomb in California; of Mrs. McKee in Lincoln, Nebraska; and of Mrs. Ormsby and Mrs. Porter along Philadelphia's Main Line. These are all set so firmly in this world, the province of Mother, that the inhabitants, especially the males, often take refuge in a place where they can feel suspended, neither in nor out of this world. Under the porches, in the garages, in the attics, and in the basement and the outdoor johns, the orphans, young and old, of the matriarchal society may be found. Along with the roaches and the flies, the spic-and-span habitation is made uninhabitable for its inhabitants.

Between the two extremes are many other places where the characters feel more or less both in and out of this world: in Tom Scanlon's mythical Lone Tree Hotel and in Monsieur Dulac's loony bin, the castle Riva near Vienna; on the open road, living on wheels, with Uncle Dudley; on a dirt farm in the panhandle with Uncle Fremont; in Agee Ward's garage apartment; in hotel lobbies with Will Brady; at the sandpit with Boyd and McKee; on the beaches; along the canals of Venice; on ships at sea with Soby and Cynthia; in Caddie Hibbard's house in Junction; in the switch tower in Chicago with Will Brady; and at the bullring in Mexico with

Boyd and the folks from Nebraska. In many of the houses, the reader encounters the imperishable artifacts or the transitory possessions of the inhabitants: objects which evoke revelations and buried emotions.

When one looks at the mere number of fully drawn characters Morris has created, carrying some, in various disguises, from book to book, one is forcibly struck with the truism that the reason one approaches a house of fiction is to meet the inhabitants. Morris' house is well inhabited with a fascinating assortment of characters who span four generations.

The author's sensibility assumes various disguises: unemployed hero, beguiled witness, sometimes cautious lover. Imparting conceptual form to most of the novels, this perceiving intelligence passes through many mutations. When the reader first meets him, he is The Kid, at the wheel of the Marmon, seeing America first; he relates the exploits of his hero, Uncle Dudley. Missing in action, The Kid turns up as artist Agee Ward in the minds of various witnesses in California. As Clyde Muncy, writer, he revisits the Nebraska home place with his city kids and his cynical wife, Peggy. In the next book, he moves on to Junction, where he rummages in the world in the attic, the world of his childhood, responding to the last magnetic charge of Caddy Hibbard. Having made a brief appearance as Will Brady's adopted son, he shows up along Philadelphia's Main Line as the artist Paul Webb, trying to make sense of the life and death of his beloved father-in-law; his wife, Katherine, is sister in spirit to Peggy Muncy. Peter Foley, teacher and writer, who bears an unjustified resemblance to Lindbergh, tries to recapture the essence of the 1920's in his novel and in his memories of the heroes and heroines of that epoch.

We next meet The Kid as Gordon Boyd, hero, lone wolf, fool, successful failure, seeing his past through the ritual of a bullfight. From The Kid to Earl Horter there is a more direct line. As a writer of popular lyrics, Horter lies on the Hollywood beach, soaking up the clichés of American culture. Exposing himself to a girl named the Greek, he learns to be a cannibal lover. The Foley mask shows up again on Arnold Soby, who feels a kinship with Mann's Aschenbach; on a sabbatical to Venice and Greece, set adrift on a ship of fools, he learns the wisdom of the body. The latest manifestation of The Kid is Warren Howe, television script writer and novelist, who returns, thirty years later, to the scene of a memorable experience in Austria and discovers the nature of time. The field of vision through each of the windows in the house of fiction changes as the central character evolves, each manifestation producing a new facet.

Either at his side or from afar, an assembly of witnesses, friends, and schoolmates follow the adventures of this recurring character. Private Christian Reagan, recalling the childhood days of the missing Agee and his effect on Grandma Herkimer, experiences a vision; Peter Spavic keeps an album record of Agee's European tour; his vicarious experiences via cryptic postcards and outlandish photographs are so intense as to shape his life. Foley is only one of several of Charles Lawrence's witnesses: another is Jesse L. Proctor (who is a great deal like Gordon Boyd), Jewish writer and salvager of human beings, who wrecks his life trying to imitate Lawrence. Babbitt of the Megaton Age, Walter J. McKee is captive in the past he shared with the hero, Boyd. The man who writes the sentimental music to Horter's lyrics is Macgregor, a beach fixture, who ends up emotionally bankrupt with his Million Dollar Baby, Billie Harcum. Wolfgang Prutscher, a girl-shy, skinny Austrian, took Warren Howe to a madman's castle in the Lower Alps; Sol Spiegel, rotund, romantic junk collector, accepted Howe's invitation to join him; Charles Horney (a version of Peter Spavic), head of a progressive school, stayed home in an unsuccessful attempt to resist Howe's influence as an old-fashioned romantic exploring Europe. These characters, often comic, provide effective contrasts to the central figures.

One of the most beguiling groups of characters is what might be called the fools who persist in their folly to the verge of wisdom. Heroes, transformers, improvisers, mythic figures, they are audacious and unpredictable. They are all aspects of a similar inspiration. In the beginning, we encounter Uncle Dudley, clownish con-man, first seen leading a caravan of fools and mavericks across the desert toward a vaguely projected Eldorado, but ultimately into an Arkansas jail. He is the wild uncle nobody wants to claim but everyone remembers. Contrasting with Uncle Dudley's creative form of audacity is Furman, recurrent jailbird; whenever he is faced with a "basterd," he spits in his eye. The reader gets glimpses of Dudley as Agee's Uncle Kermit, "a man with grass stains on his pants," who lures Agee onto the open road. He even turns up as Mrs. Ormsby's Uncle Dwight on a Texas dirt farm. In the latest book, he is Fremont Osborn, first to forsake the home place and its gods, first to break the virgin soil of the dust bowl, and one of the first to live on wheels in the new boom towns of the Uranium Age in Quartzite, Arizona.

The Kid's father, Hank Ward-Will "Chicken" Muncy-Will Howe, has much in common with Uncle Dudley. Railroad station agent, egg candler, a man of few words, blighted victim of the American Dream, and a wanderer, he always seems "in cog-nee-toe" to his acquaintances. He has his fullest expression in Will Jennings Brady;

a man of inarticulate loves and dreams who builds an empire in the chicken business, he begins in a soddy at Indian Bow and ends, dressed as Santa Claus, in a Chicago canal. A figure in a worn carpet, Uncle Harry Ward-Muncy stays put on the farm in Lone Tree; in him, many of the Dudley-Brady characteristics are blended. Tom Scanlon, who sometimes confuses himself with Buffalo Bill, stays put, too; in the lobby of the deserted Lone Tree Hotel, he gazes out at the ruins of a town that once faced the heroic West; he is a fossilized remnant of the mythic past. A quite different audacious bewitcher is Charles Lawrence, tennis star of the 1920's; a Gatsby figure, he is a magnet who demagnetizes himself when he discovers that he can't be the perfect hero to Foley and Proctor, among others. Monsieur Etienne Dulac, too, is in a class by himself, although he reminds us of both Uncle Fremont and Tom Scanlon in their most extreme moments. At eighty, behaving like a Don Quixote who refuses to surrender to time and space, he still gives his guests "cause for wonder."

A cadre of handymen possess characteristics in common with the uncles, fathers, and mythic characters. Lemuel Purdy, the first one encounters, takes care of Aunt Angie and Caddy Hibbard in Junction. Like the more interesting Carl Parsons, who is employed by the Porters in the suburbs of Philadelphia, Purdy tries to take care of people who can't take care of themselves. Purdy and Parsons know more about the inhabitants than anyone else. The wildest handyman of all is George, peasant-lover and mad prankster of Schloss Riva, who shovels snow onto visitors from the roof of the castle; when the snow melts, he paints everything white, including the inhabitants.

Along with these "oddball" males, should be noted the prevalence of audacious females. The original impulse comes from Grace. Mother of the Agee-Howe character, she died the year he was born. A lyrical presence in the early novels, she emerges most clearly in the latest one as an audacious pioneer girl who resembles Annie Oakley. Imported from southern Indiana, Caddy Hibbard is a romantic figure who brings a current of liveliness and creative energy to Junction, an influence doomed to blight. A mildewed spinster, Gussie Newcomb experiences a rejuvenation in her post-humous relationship with Agee Ward; missing, he turns up in her unpredictable behavior. In his search for love, Will Brady encounters Mickey Ahearn, a pugnacious teen-age prostitute, who sends him her illegitimate infant, and "The Girl," who beguiles him across a cigar counter in the lobby of an Omaha hotel. In bed, "The Girl" talks for hours, and it seems to Will that the point of his being there is to listen.

A different sort is Montana Lou Baker, who looks like Garbo; a bohemian of unrealized talent, she roared through Foley's life in the 1920's. The most audacious female of all is the voluptuous Greek, a natural, beneficent, overflowing fountain of sensuality who transforms Horter. Etoile Momeyer, adolescent bursting into womanhood in Lincoln, Nebraska, anxious to get on with being a lover and a mother, resembles the Greek. She is actually a trial run for the more important character, Cynthia, who plays as many parts as there are men with ideal female images to project (Eve, Nausicaä, Botticelli nude, Lolita). The latest "far out" female is Kitty Brownell, who resembles Montana Lou Baker; she says and does what she thinks; she mortifies Wolfgang and Warren Howe, but she enchants the madman, Dulac.

Setting in sharp relief the antics of these wise fools is an assortment of characters who range from half-wits to maniacs. Sixteen-year-old Manny Plinski hides turtles in Will Brady's pockets as a token of affection; even though Manny speaks gibberish, he and Will communicate as much as they need to. A senile version of Manny, Mr. Erskine collects the razors of acquaintances who have died. Dressed as a woman, Paula (Paul) Kahler once killed a man who molested him; he then withdrew from the male world, and the reader discovers him dressed as an old maid, knitting at the bull ring, seeing nothing. *Ceremony in Lone Tree* is full of typical Morris "kooks," who sum up, at one extreme, the human predicament: Le Roy Momeyer, who releases his frustrations through the twin exhausts of his eerie hotrod, which he finally uses to slaughter his tormentors; Bud Momeyer, mild postman who also delivers eggs in a Hupmobile discarded by the fire department and who stalks stray cats with a bow and arrow; Hyman Korpman, man of two lives, one in his apartment, the other in the street below, who finds himself most at home among the blind in a garden secluded from the world. Madame Dulac, with the body of a toad, and the voice of an angel, lives in a room shut off from the rest of the castle with her senile, mange-ridden dog.

Responding to conflicting currents of influence, the small fry, the little monsters, in Morris seem to belong somewhere between the half-wits and the wise fools. In a hallucination caused by her contact with Private Reagan, Annie Mae jumps into Grandma Herkimer's grave; on the home place, Cally May, exposed to Agee, acts as though she is subject to forces beyond her control (these girls seem early versions of Etoile and Cynthia). Peggy and Bobby, normal children who get flypaper stuck in their curls, are bemused by Uncle Harry's method of education. Will Brady's boy; Ormsby's boy, Virgil; and Judge Porter's boy, Roger—all are cut from the same confused pattern: faced with the jig-saw puzzle of their lives, they bolt. Contrasting with these boys is short, behelmeted Private Lipido, audacious debunker from Texas, who shows Ormsby the kind of child Virgil would like to have been in order to cope with a weak father and an awesome mother. Little Gordon McKee, in a Davy Crockett coonskin cap, responds to the magnetic charges of both Scanlon and Boyd; but, in the end, he is bewitched by his grandmother, Lois McKee, much as Lipido is won over by Mrs. Ormsby. Trying to keep his affinities with Le Roy under control, Calvin McKee, a stuttering, nascent he-man of the old Western style, finds himself constrained by women in a matriarchy.

We encounter most of the rural matriarchs at a time when they are regarded more as grandmothers and aunts than as mothers and wives. Agee's Aunt Sarah (as Muncy's Aunt Clara) survived the clearing of the plains, and then fought grasshoppers and boredom in a place where the only thing to hide behind was an apron flung over her face. Aunt Angie is a mean-spirited sort who resents any change; like Scanlon, she shuts out anything not associated with the venerable past; she sits, judges, and abides. Though some end un-willingly in the suburbs, Morris' crew of fabulous, leathery grand-mothers came from the plains. At ninety-two, Grandma Herkimer despises the new, also, but she is young enough to respond to the life-giving audacity of Agee Ward. On the home place, Grandmother Cropper, a shoe box full of memories in her lap, reminds Agee and Muncy of the qualities of the old breed. Moody and quarrelsome, Mrs. Ormsby's mother, like Judge Porter's, likes to shock with vulgar expressions or unpredictable behavior, such as eating a whole quart of ice cream or a whole four-pound box of chocolates.

In the small towns, Adalaide of Colvin, California, and Adaline of Lone Tree, Nellie Hibbard of Junction, and Ethel Bassett of Calloway, Nebraska, are typical, ad-created, new-style housewives who keep their husbands' emotions too well supervised and their houses filled with the contraptions of the Disposal Age. With her urban aspirations and cliché concept of family and position, Nellie threatens what little traditional farmer's independence Bud has managed to retain. In the urban areas, the female pillars of society stand even more firmly on the bowed necks of their men-folk. Violet Ormsby, a block of ice, keeps her house as neat as the North Pole; a bird watcher, she keeps a keen eye on her husband, Warren. It seems that Judge Porter's wife, Millicent, buries him without re-morse; but something about her exacting and exasperating regimen brings out the best in the men who depend upon her. Lois McKee has never forgotten the kiss on the front porch that told her forcibly, for the first and last time, what it was like to be a real woman;

but her life seems dedicated to denying what she had discovered. Warren Ormsby is as domesticated as a white rat, Judge Porter runs the country but is an exile in his own house, and Walter McKee realizes the hopelessness of improving on the impression Boyd's kiss made on Lois. In her tight-corset character, Mother seems monstrous; but a moment always comes when she rises to the occasion and once again bewitches the male.

Some of the women are more caretakers than wives; Frau Dulac, who brought the ailing Dulac back to the castle after the war, would "make a good housemother at Auschwitz." Miss Mathilde Kollwitz, an old-maid teacher, adopts various strangers and soon reminds them of the blessings of orphanhood. But her friend, Miss Winifred Throop, forsakes this female image and attempts to live spontaneously, responding to the cues of the flesh. As mother and wife, Maxime Momeyer refuses to become the rigid, pressure-boiler of emotions her sister Lois is. She knows that to be taken advantage of is something no girl, including her daughter, Etoile, should miss.

In contrast to these models of rectitude, both willing and reluctant, are the Amazonian or vulgar women. Opal Mason, a friendly, frank-speaking harlot, introduces Will Brady to sex. Mrs. Dinardo is an ample and splendid example of the female who has taken on the purely physical characteristics of the defunct male. Señora Eroza is a fertile mass of Mexican flesh who sits like an idol in her doorway, watching her uninhibited brood moil in the yard. Pretending, with her peroxide hair and coy femininity, to be the image of proper Southern womanhood, Billie Harcum is perhaps the most vulgar of all.

Morris' occupational characters are fully drawn and memorable. Eddie Cahow (or Mr. Beggs), Lone Tree barber, who appears in four of the early books, can tell one who he is and where he came from, even though he has been away thirty years and his folks are long dead; Eddie's head is an archive, his tongue ready with the record the moment someone walks in the door. Mr. Moody in Junction and Mr. Bayard in suburban Pennsylvania are a good deal alike: they are, as friends of the deceased, eager to arrange the burial with a minimum strain on the survivors, and to adhere strictly to the conventions of the funeral ceremony. Reverend Horde of California and Reverend Barr of Pennsylvania are understanding and impressionable. Reverend Horde helps to trigger Private Reagan's moment of vision, and Reverend Barr fumbles earnestly among the bereaved, encouraging Grandmother Porter to tell her off-color Civil War joke to put the mourners at their ease with death.

Morris has a particularly comic facility for rendering the broken dialects of Old-World professors and humbugs. Dr. Liszt, a soulful old phony, "titches muzic" and also teaches The Kid, indirectly, the inadequacies of outmoded Old-World attitudes. Dr. Lehmann, an amateur psychoanalyst and a more interesting version of the German soul-and-psyche-searcher, attempts to mend the lives of both Paula Kahler and Gordon Boyd. On the ship, Soby meets: Mr. Lipari, an Italian who is to have an audience with the Pope but whose faith is tested severely by the gods of the sea; Señor Pignata, a painter who is driven almost insane by the fickle gods of the flesh who caper in Cynthia; Dr. Hodler, an amateur archaeologist who is dedicated to resurrecting Nausicaä and Odysseus in the living; and Herr Perkheimer, the audacious little man bestrapped with cameras which seek the rear view of every cliché.

The characters who inhabit Morris' house of fiction, the actual houses, and the landscapes on which both may be found, testify to the pleasures of reading Morris. A tour of the house seems an appropriate prelude to a careful analysis of its structure and purpose.

II *The Great Plains*

One senses in Morris' novels the abiding presence of his Nebraska childhood. That the dust caked his teeth, that the wind lashed his youth, his characters are not allowed to forget. That he spent only his first nine years on the Great Plains attests to the immensity of their effect upon him. "The character of the plains," he says, "has conditioned what I see, what I look for, and what I find in the world to write about."[2] In "Our Endless Plains," he comments, "I have spent most of my life puzzling over the lines on the map of my childhood. In what sense, it might be asked, have I been away? The high plain lies within me." Earlier, he suggests the nature of his vision: "Where there is almost nothing to see, there man sees the most."[3] In *The Crack-Up*, Fitzgerald, anticipating Camus' absurd man, suggests the double perspective that focuses Morris' field of vision: "the test of a first rate intelligence is the ability to hold two opposed ideas in the mind at the same time, and still retain the ability to function."[4] It is to this test that Morris subjects himself in his work.

It is necessary to point out that Morris is neither a regionalist nor a local colorist. While the Great Plains provide vivid counterparts for every aspect of his work, even in what might be called the urban novels, Morris renders the past only in its effects on the present; and he writes about Nebraska only as it represents conflicting extremes in American land and character. An impression of the special importance of the Great Plains to America may suggest why Morris has found that region rich in levels of raw material, symbolism, and concept.

In his "frontier hypothesis" of 1893, Frederick Jackson Turner dramatized the importance of the frontier when he contended that "the existence of an area of free land, its continuous recession, and the advance of American settlement westward, explain American development" and American character.[5] Walter Prescott Webb, in his influential study of the Great Plains, describes the contrast between the grasslands and the region east of the 98th Meridian. The plains brought about "a marked change in the ways of pioneering and living. For two centuries American pioneers had been working out a technique for the utilization of the humid regions east of the Mississippi River." They solved their problems and conquered the frontier "at a steadily accelerating rate." The Great Plains was "an environment with which they had had no experience."

> As one contrasts the civilization of the Great Plains with that of the eastern timberland, one sees what may be called an institutional *fault* (comparable to a geological fault) running from middle Texas to Illinois or Dakota, roughly following the ninety-eighth meridian. At this *fault* the ways of life and of living changed. Practically every institution that was carried across it was either broken and remade or else greatly altered. The ways of travel, the weapons, the method of tilling the soil, the plows, and other agricultural implements, and even the laws themselves were modified. When people first crossed this line they did not immediately realize the imperceptible change that had taken place in their environment, nor, more is the tragedy, did they forsee the full consequences which that change was to bring to their own characters and to their modes of life. . . . Their plight has been stated this way: east of the Mississippi civilization stood on three legs—land, water, and timber; west of the Mississippi not one but two of these legs were withdrawn,—water and timber,—and civilization was left on one leg—land. It is small wonder that it toppled over in temporary failure.[6]

According to Webb, six forces, each shaping its characteristic heroes, transformed a wilderness into the world's granary: the trails, the railroads, barbed wire, the harvesting machine, the windmill, and the six shooter.

The myth of the Great American Desert produced an even greater myth, the Garden of the World. First the availability of free land disappeared and then, after a gradual process of waste and exploitation, the land itself vanished: the fabled high plains became the Great Dust Bowl of the 1930's. Standing in the wasteland of the present, dreaming of a heroic past, some men became victims of "the poison of the Great American Myth." Having studied the

American frontier boom, Webb, referring to the four-hundred-year boom Western civilization has experienced, recently wrote that mankind is searching for "a new frontier which we once had and did not prize, and the longer we had it, the less we valued it; but now that we have lost it, we have a great pain in the heart, and we are always trying to get it back again.... If the frontier is gone, we should have the courage and honesty to recognize the fact, cease to cry for what we have lost, and devote our energy to finding the solutions to the problems now facing a frontierless society."[7]

These historical forces figure as some of the most important symbolic and raw-material elements in Morris' novels. He makes of them a metaphor for comments on the American Dream and character. His books compose a kind of *Crack-Up* for America. Fitzgerald may have spoken for the America Morris depicts when he said of himself: "I began to realize that for two years my life had been drawing on resources that I did not possess, that I had been mortgaging myself physically and spiritually up to the hilt. What was the small gift of life given back in comparison to that?—when there had once been a pride of direction and a confidence in enduring independence" (72). The pioneers went West to realize a dream, but, ironically, they overcame great hardships to conquer a land that future generations, especially artists, left as soon as they could to seek the fruition of the dream in the East (Fitzgerald) or in Europe (Hemingway). Except for that which one may find imaginatively transformed in his books, little of the history of the plains is relevant to a study of Morris.[8]

III *Fact and Fiction*

What is fact and what is fiction? "Lifted from the road one Fourth of July to ride in the saddle, gripping the horn, with a white-bearded old man who was known in those parts by the name of Buffalo Bill," Morris must have pondered this question early.[9] Webb points out that, as a creature new in Western civilization, the Westerner was an impressive image who appealed strongly to the Romantic imagination from the beginning. He asks whether we might not say that the 98th Meridian "separates the literature which Bill Hart interprets from the literature of Hamlin Garland?... that the novels and stories of the Prairie Plains are essentially and predominantly realistic, and that the fiction of the arid plains is—Wild West literature, if you please—almost entirely romantic?" (482). In *Ceremony in Lone Tree* Morris suggests much the same idea: "The emptiness of the plain generates illusions that require little moisture, and grow better, like tall stories, where the mind is dry. The tall corn may flower or burn in the wind, but the plain is a metaphysical landscape and the bumper crop is the one Scanlon sees through the flaw in the glass."

The glass through which the Midwestern writer has scrutinized his world is flawed in such a way that his vision is split. Some writers exploited the melodramatic unreality of the frontier (Harte, Cooper); others recognized it as a focal point in American character (the contrasting views—success and failure—of Crevecoeur and Garland). Midwestern literature has reflected both of the two broad traditions in American literature: that which derives from England and Europe and that which interprets the American scene. The small town in fiction, chiefly a development of the Midwest, was a late phase of local-color literature, which had lost popularity when Morris began to write. Small-town fiction may be divided into two general types: the Romantic, which depicts a kindly, democratic world, or the prairie in terms of its victors (James Whitcomb Riley, Harte, Meredith Nicholson, Tarkington, Dorothy Canfield Fisher); and the Realistic, which depicts a petty, competitive world, or the prairie in terms of its victims (Masters, E. W. Howe, Rolvaag, Edward Eggleston, Joseph Kirkland, Sinclair Lewis, Sherwood Anderson).

In the Midwest there existed, says Garland, "a life that was unlike any ever seen on earth, and which *should* [italics mine] have produced its characteristic literature, its native art chronicle."[10] Perhaps in the following Midwestern poets and fiction writers, together with those already named, it *did*: T. S. Eliot, Carl Sandburg, Vachel Lindsay, Paul Engle, Floyd Dell, Zona Gale, James T. Farrell, Theodore Dreiser, Glenway Wescott, Louis Bromfield, Ring Lardner, Frank Norris, Willard Motley, Nelson Algren, Saul Bellow. Although Morris may not be the greatest writer to come out of the Midwest—a region that produced Fitzgerald, the Romantic, and Hemingway, the Realist—he is the most thoroughly Midwestern; but, at the same time, his work remains universal. By symbolic and other means he recalls and recasts, probably unconsciously, the vast Romantic and Realistic tradition of Midwestern literature to which he brings his own unique qualities.[11]

What is Morris' field of vision? Bringing into focus a representative part of America, he has sought the meaning of the legends, myths, and realities of America as they survive and prevail today in the minds of common men; the uncommon exist for the edification of the common. We are conditioned to think of action when we think of the West. Born when the short-lived era of action, the conflict with the Indians and such, had passed away, Morris became interested in what he observed himself—the monotony of everyday life. He conveys only a sense of the history of his region, and it is in his writing about the Great Plains that he creates the strongest sense of *place;* there is very little immediate description of the past and of certain Nebraska phenomena, but one becomes aware of the effect upon Morris of the rich raw material. Usually, what interests him is the impression left on the imagination—the internal rather than the external drama. Still his work is "rooted in our folkways," as Lewis Mumford said of *The Home Place.* Even in the novels with urban backgrounds, one encounters some of the most authentic Americana of recent years.

In *The Field of Vision* the question is posed: Did one live on the plains in spite of the fact that the conditions were terrible? "No, one lived there *because* of it. Only where fools rushed in were such things as heroes bred." These conditions, says Morris, produced "the power to transform. . . . The budding hero found it more than enough." In what sense might one say that the land was the first hero? In Morris' early books the reader may perceive that the plains, despite their adverse effects, produced a breed of men both positively and negatively charged.

In the attic of his personal past, Morris contemplates the world. Central City and other towns in which he grew up lie in a kind of transition zone. In the days when a lone cottonwood tree (now petrified into a monument) served as a landmark for travelers who followed the great trails that passed along the Platte Valley, then as a stopping place for the Overland Stagecoach and as shade for the Pony Express rider, and still later as a station for the Union Pacific, Central City was known as Lone Tree, a small town that looked both to the East and to the West. While Morris uses many Nebraska place names—sometimes for his characters—few direct correlations exist; and the geography doesn't always jibe. This inaccuracy suggests that the names are meant to be evocative.

In his National Book Award speech in 1957, Morris noted that one of his advantages as a writer was "the fact that I was born near the navel of the world"—near the geographical center of the United States. To one born and reared astraddle the 98th Meridian, polarities came spontaneously to mind. In the middle of the West, Nebraska itself is half West, half Midwest; and it exemplifies within its own boundaries the great division based on land and climate. Morris quite naturally uses the magnet concept to explain the effect of his heroes upon other characters.

In Lone Tree, the American Dream and the American East-West conflict have become fossilized. Boyd, the returning artist of *Ceremony in Lone Tree,* sees Lone Tree as a place where "the future still hung in balance, the moonlit plain was like the stormy Atlantic, something to be crossed, a stage in a journey, with the gold fields the great good place at the end. Lone Tree, like the *Spirit of St. Louis,* was up there in the wild blue yonder, the cuckoo-land between the end of your dreams and wherever you are from." With its imagination responding to the magnet of the fabled West, the frontier that no longer exists, and its back turned toward the industrial East, Lone Tree is a perfect manifestation of an American tendency to build great technological complexities but to gaze in the direction of dreams. "There never was a people who tried so hard—and left so little behind as we do. There never was a people who traveled so light—and carried so much" *(The Inhabitants).*

Lone Tree and its environs are becoming something like Faulkner's Yoknapatawpha County. But Morris does not build up the kind of complex social relationships that exist in Faulkner. Although Morris' novels seem more autobiographical, and lack the vast, intricate cultural construct and the more consistent historicality of Faulkner's work, perhaps Morris' microcosm, being Midwestern, is more representative of contemporary America, more evocative of the dynamics of its history, of the nature of its land and its character.

Leslie Fiedler says that Morris has been trying in all his books "to convince his readers that Nebraska is the absurd hell we all inhabit."[12] On the arid plains, man may have achieved intuitively a kind of existential knowledge. Where he fronts nature stripped to essentials and is forced to live on essentials alone, man, reduced to what he is, standing on the frontiers within—often as empty as a private Hiroshima—must face sooner or later the imperfections of his dreams, and end in either suicide or stoic endurance—the Kierkegaardian gambit. Destructive and creative, rather than ethical, forces are loose in Morris' world. He does not seem to cast blame. How does one blame a cyclone or a dust storm, or the land for being flat and obdurate? He observes effects in a quiet way that suggests Camus' idea of the absurd. It is appropriate for a god to roll a huge rock up a mountain, and for a man to roll grains of sand around on his tongue.

Such is the "mystic world" to which Morris "returns again and again," the "navel of experience from which the author has never departed, and now uses as a magnet to order the iron filings of his separate lives." It is made up of "holy provinces, and within them lies what we come to recognize as the author's field of vision. . . . The writer, using fragments of disorder, seeks to impose order on the world around him, that otherwise immense panorama of futility and anarchy" (NBA). The Great Plains demanded new techniques if its raw material were to be mastered. And Morris has dealt with the task of transforming that raw material in his art.

In *The Territory Ahead,* a critical book, Morris focuses on what he conceives to be the major fault in American writers of genius and in their imitators: the inability to transform through imagination, technique, and conception the raw material of experience, with the result that the writer becomes trapped in a mythic past, unable to move on to the territory ahead—the living present.[13] Morris himself has processed "in fragments an experience ... so wide and so varied that the fragmentary approach seems almost compulsory to me."[14] Thomas Wolfe's problem was that, in his effort to *possess all* of experience, "Nostalgia took the place of imaginative possession: reminiscence took the place of apprehension." It was Henry James who demonstrated that "technique and raw material are dramatized at the moment that the shaping imagination is aware of itself," for "the final act of coherence is an imaginative act." In the faults of the masters whom he discusses, Morris recognizes his own: "The realization that I had to create coherence, conjure up my synthesis, rather than find it, came to me, as it does to most Americans, disturbingly late."

"It is the territory behind that defeats our writers of genius, not America," because the opposing idea of the present, "has been excluded." Huck Finn's last words, "I got to light out for the territory ahead," express a refusal to be immersed in the past to the point of immolation. "In a way my books show the development of an escape from nostalgia." In the first six books discussed in this study Morris is immersed in the raw material of his past; in the others, he is moving toward the territory ahead. Even in the early novels, of course, there is a conscious movement in that direction.

"It is the *nature* of the future, not its extinction, that produces in the artist such foreboding, the prescient chill of heart of a world without consciousness." But he who can live in his own present lives in both the past and the future. As Camus said in *The Rebel,* "Real generosity toward the future lies in giving all to the present." But what constitutes the present? "Since he must live and have his being in a world of clichés, he will know this new world by their absence. He will know it by the fact that he has not been there before. The true territory ahead is what he must imagine for himself." In Morris' latest book, *Cause for Wonder,* Warren Howe makes a discovery already expressed by the author in *The Territory Ahead:* "It seems to be the nature of man to transform—himself, if possible, and then the world around him—and the technique of this transformation is what we call art.... Both talent and imagination are of little value" without the conception that transforms.

CHAPTER 2

The Hero and the Witness

I N FORM, two novels could hardly differ more radically than
Wright Morris' first two, *My Uncle Dudley* (1942) and *The
Man Who Was There* (1945). The first is simply told; the field of
vision in the second is more complex than in any other of Morris'
works. But both develop some of the same characters and themes
which pass through various transformations in *all* the novels. Both
draw on his Nebraska childhood, his Chicago years, and the Pomona, Los Angeles, and other California backgrounds. In both,
Morris disregards chronology as he manipulates his experiences for
fictive purposes. "My own fiction," Morris says, "has tampered with
my own facts."[1]

I My Uncle Dudley:
A Gasoline Raft Afloat on the Asphalt River

My Uncle Dudley is a wryly humorous chronicle of an odyssey
which The Kid—the unnamed adolescent narrator—and his Uncle
Dudley make across country in an old Marmon touring car with
seven men who share expenses. The events occur in the mid-1920's,
"the Homeric phase of the gas buggy era." The novel has neither
the tone nor the scale of the Homeric epic, but it conveys the
quality Clyde Muncy (a later projection of The Kid) talks about
in *The Home Place:* "An epic is how you feel about something." In
the context of American fictional heritage, the passengers float
down the Big Muddy on the raft, refugees from the world of
Aunt Sally.

Dudley and The Kid, and even the car, are archetypes—the Uncle
one had, or wishes one had had; the Huck Finn some were and all
would like to have been; and the car most would like to have
"tooled" down the open road. A semi-orphan Nebraskan, The Kid
has traveled a little on his own, read a few great works of literature,
and worked on his uncle's farm. Straight man to Dudley's vaudevil-
lian antics, he tells the story with a subdued sense of comic wonder.

The black sheep of a Nebraska family, Dudley likes to "get out and go." An embodiment of many American clichés—"he looked a little bit like all the characters you ever saw," he, nevertheless, has distinctive qualities of his own. Widely traveled, gregarious, a former Texas dirt farmer, he has a Will Rogers-Sandburg-Lincoln wisdom and wit. A man who might believe that "the shortest way to heaven is right smack through hell," he is a common-sense disbeliever in God. A "voice" in *The Inhabitants* describes him well:

> All he ever heard was wagon wheels in the dust somewhere. Every night was a Saturday night and everything he saw had the look things have when a band is passing by. All he ever saw in people was what they were meant to be. . . . What he saw wasn't the people so much as something over the people, like the smell of leaves burning or the dust that hangs over the square. Like the harvest moon, he saw everything bigger than it really was. I can't tell you what he saw—but I can tell you it was something he could love.

The novel opens with Dudley and The Kid sitting in Pershing Square, homesick for Chicago's Lincoln Park in the spring. "'You had enough milk and honey?' he said. 'I guess I've had enough,' I said." Nostalgia is one of the prime motives behind the trek. The seven passengers, whom one meets in "The Roundup," have different destinations but a common strong desire to get away. Cut from archetypal patterns, each has characteristics representing various aspects of, and attitudes in, American character and culture. A subdued hilarity permeates The Kid's and Dudley's maneuvering of the nostalgia of the other homesick men they encounter that morning.

Dudley meets each on his own ground, improvising, with his considerable rhetorical powers of persuasion, on the thing that is basic with them all—the longing to re-establish some kind of connection: "'We're leavin this wonderful land—this sunshine. We're goin home.' 'Bygod,' said the man, 'I sure wish I was too.' He was a tall man and used to wearing overalls. His thumbs kept feeling for the straps, scratching his chin." Lost in the land of milk and honey, the man in the imaginary overalls is still in the territory behind, where the straps are. The mind does what it can to maintain connection with the past, with the feel of things as they were; but the hand reaches to take hold.

Having collected passage money in advance, Dudley and The Kid purchase an old Marmon. In *The Man Who Was There*, a picture of the car, or one like it, turns up in an album belonging to Agee Ward: "It will not let you forget where it has been. For it is not a car any more; it is a character."

After "The Roundup" comes "Passage"; the titles of the sections suggest a westering parallel. During the course of the journey, the long series of flat tires and the other mechanical malfunctions are physical correlatives of the various personal crises among the characters. One by one, the "paying guests" leave; only Red—a young sailor with whom The Kid has partially identified himself as an adolescent in transition—is around for the concluding episode in the Arkansas jail. Red has survived contact with the land and responded fully to Uncle Dudley.

In the wagon treks West, survival of the fittest was physically determined; but this spiritual journey of The Kid and Dudley is primarily a matter of moral survival. There are, says Morris, "no easy trails across the Eldorado landscape of the heart."[2] In the spirit of the westward trek, this is the landscape Dudley and The Kid traverse. Witnessing the interaction among them, with the personality of Dudley as a controlling, evaluating force, The Kid participates in a spiritual westering; he is at the physical controls of the car (his prairie schooner), but Dudley is his spiritual guide.

II The Relationship Between the Hero and His Witness

Especially important in *My Uncle Dudley, The Man Who Was There, The Huge Season* and *The Field of Vision*—a central, recurring theme in Morris' novels, around which many other themes revolve and through which his vision is often focused—is the relationship between the hero and his witnesses.[3] The hero is the character with whose effect on the other characters most of the novels are concerned; usually he is not the main character in the ordinary sense and his is not the dominant point of view. The witnesses are those characters who become in some way transformed as a result of their relationship with the hero.

The hero exists as hero only in the lives of the witnesses. Only the essentials about him are presented; he has almost no identity except as hero; he *is* only what he does. The witnesses exist as witnesses only as their lives are substantially altered by contact with the heroes. Usually the witness, through whose point of view the novel is rendered, is presented more fully and in relation to things other than his role as witness. Since Morris is primarily a comic writer, the relationship is more that between Don Quixote and Sancho Panza than Lord Jim and Marlowe.

Of the few general critical essays about Morris, Wayne C. Booth's formulation of an initial interpretation, "The Two Worlds in the Fiction of Wright Morris," is most pertinent. A concern in all the novels, Booth says, is with the problem of determining what is real and what is phony. The so-called real is not real. One must go beyond what seems real, beyond oneself to a reality that is both in and out of this world (a cliché expression that in Morris rings true). According to Booth, the novels dramatize three main ways of achieving this victory: (1) Heroism: the moment of real action, usually a foolhardy act of unmistakable physical courage. (2) Imagination: the moment of truth, a sense of the human meaning of things, conveyed by visual reality. (3) Love: the moment of compassion, when one discovers reality in love as admiration or as pity. Morris' novels focus, Booth concludes, upon these moments which, occurring in the stream of so-called real time, are acts of timelessness in a world of change.[4] It is in the first sense that Uncle Dudley is a hero.

III   *The Hero's Powers:*
Audacity, Improvisation, Transformation

In a world of transience, the important thing is to transform; in a world of impermanence, some men seek permanence of a kind. On the street corners of the cities, where the clichés of the American character congregate, Dudley puts these clichés, his raw material, through a series of spontaneous transformations; from the captivity of the cliché—from the phony—he liberates the real McCoy. One of the qualities of the hero is his ability to transform fact into fiction: to give motion to the inert, vibrancy to the dull, an aura of the exotic to the commonplace, to revive the cliché by turning it upon itself. Himself a blend of fact and fiction, Dudley takes his cues from clichés and creates new "facts."

If Dudley is mostly fiction, The Kid is mostly fact, raw material; and his uncle takes on the job of processing him, of getting the best blend. The idea of a father-substitute has become a literary cliché; real enough in the relationship between The Kid and Dudley, Morris makes no symbolic fuss about it.

In addition to a magnetism that attracts witnesses, the hero, to effect transformations, must be audacious; and he must have the kind of spontaneity that generates improvisation. In the pioneer sense Dudley is audacious when struggling on a Texas dirt farm and later, in the usual Morris sense, in his manner of living. When the "caravan" enters Tucson, Dudley's transforming audacity comes into play. The car and its passengers are not described: the reactions to their appearance are revealing enough. A cop on foot leads the car to the police station. But Uncle Dudley beats him to the draw. Walking briskly into the station, he soon emerges with the Chief, who apologizes. " 'Only thing I notice,' he said, turning back to Uncle Dudley, 'is maybe you overdone it a bit.' Uncle Dudley looked at all of us again. 'Best types I could find,' he said. 'All modeled on life itself.'" What story did Dudley improvise? In respecting the reader's imagination, Morris creates an aura of magic around the hero. Eventually, Dudley infects most of the passengers with audacity, for the whole journey has an air of uncertainty—an air congenial to audacity.

The audacious act may take its cue from the cliché, but only because its intention is to negate the cliché by making it new. Mr. Liszt, a German-immigrant music teacher representing the spiritual idealism of the Old World, tries, like Uncle Dudley, to get more out of a thing than it really has; but he never quite makes it because he repeats rather than rejuvenates the cliché and misses the real thing—a blend of fact and fiction in the hands of an improviser, a transformer. When he wanders from the road into the desert to stand alone and gaze Byronically at the sky, the Old World Romantic response to "beauty" in nature gets stuck on the cockleburs of the real American scene. He is captive in his clichés. Liszt's response to beauty is sky-oriented; Dudley's Whitman-Sandburg-Chaplin response is earthy, grounded in the commonplace.

If one is audacious enough to confront the real thing, one runs the risk of being abandoned by the safe cliché. The real McCoy is what one has after the cliché has been sheared off. In Oklahoma, when two of the passengers, solitary old men, make off in the night with all the luggage and valuables, those remaining find they are stripped down to the real thing—themselves. Some feel a profound freedom; others panic. Even in the harshest material circumstances, Red, Dudley, and The Kid have inner resources which the circumstances themselves sustain. But Liszt is one of those who fails to get into the spirit of the gratuitous turn of events whereby new elements of risk and uncertainty are constantly introduced.

When the car breaks down, as it frequently does, The Kid and Uncle Dudley don't. Trouble is part of the situation they have chosen to be in, and the situation, like the country, is there to respond to, not to be gotten through. Above all, trouble offers an opportunity for audacity, improvisation, and transformation. The Kid, who is young and confronts experience freshly, displays his improvisational ingenuity in repairing the breakdown-prone car; but Uncle Dudley, a man of the world, is free to transform the situation.

I had just time to see a brick courthouse and a man standing there. Then all hell broke loose and dragged at the rear. My foot went to the floor on the brake, but we didn't stop, nothing happened— just more hell than ever hanging on behind. Doors opened and people ran out and stared. We came to the tracks and just like in Kansas City, whatever it was caught there, we couldn't go on. There was a sick, gritty crunch—then that was all. The people just stayed where they were; the road was clear. Uncle Dudley got out and crossed the street, bought a cigar.

The climactic breakdown of the car, caught on the tracks where a train would soon be coming through, an awed crowd—and Uncle Dudley simply crosses the street and buys a cigar. His timing, in the droll style of W. C. Fields, and his buying the cigar seem more impressive than the breakdown.

In the audacious crossing of succeeding frontiers, the American found that nowhere more than on the Great Plains was he called upon to develop his ability to *improvise;* today this trait rules with greatest authority in California. What began as an adaptive need, dictated by the nature of land and climate, becomes a way of responding to life as it comes in Dudley's travels, a way of transforming clichés and undesirable realities. Life with Dudley, that "early master of making-do," is "life played by ear," a schooling in the "Art of Improvisation." Taking his cues from Dudley and others, The Kid, captivated by the quality of style, improvises on his own character. "The contagious elements in style evade formulation. They are creations, rather than fashions, and arise out of organic impulses and hungers."[5]

Who transforms Dudley? Himself. "Character, as I never tire of saying, is primarily an imaginative act, a fiction, to which the flesh in incurably responsive. It is the fiction that shapes the fact" ("Made," 483). Life as fiction shapes The Kid into the fiction of Agee Ward. In one way or another, Morris renders this process in every book.

IV *Campfire and Jail:*
Two Views of American Land and Character

Like the street corner, "the wide open spaces" around the campfire is a good place to transform clichés; and a small-town Arkansas jail is a good place to test and evaluate them. Where the night talk "seems to be sayin more'n it's sayin," one seems able to create, or re-create, one's life as well as America itself. Both around the campfire and in the cell the world is represented in miniature, stripped—just as the Marmon, after the final breakdown, is stripped by Negroes in the night. In each place one is both in and out of this world. The long, rambling, philosophical bull sessions provide The Kid with further means of contrasting the empirical teachings of his uncle with the ideas and ways of life of other men. For instance, around the campfire, Dudley discusses the way trouble makes a man: "You got to be mighty smart to know what trouble to take away."

The final and most important transformation is set up in the pestiferous Arkansas jail, where the odyssey ends. If the campfire is the most appropriate place for talk about America, the second exploration of the human situation—which has a more social context—occurs no less appropriately in a jail crowded with local derelicts. Coming from the environment of the open road where individuality operates in a social vacuum amid natural severity (allegorically, America's frontier past), the Kid enters a new environment which epitomizes social malfunction.

Dark though the picture looks, Uncle Dudley attempts to transform the dirty facts of life into good, clean fun. But he is out of his element. Though his wanderings have broadened his outlook and made him more pliable and tolerant, primarily Dudley is a product of the pioneering spirit of the plains; in him, verbally if not actively, live the real and abiding values of the past. Voluble around the campfire, he takes no part in the nocturnal male talk at the jail. Though they are countrybred, these outcast Southerners are rooted in the decadence of a fallen aristocratic society; they live by rebellious values and notions about which Dudley can make no comment that would show his insights as superior to theirs.

As The Kid listens to the night talk, he recalls the early phases of his association with his uncle on Dudley's dust farm in Texas. This section presents interesting shifts of time and place, contrasts between what The Kid is remembering and what the men are saying, just as there is a contrast between the cell and the open land of Texas. Weaving these memories into the line of present action also helps to suggest that, for The Kid, Furman, the jail's almost permanent inmate, and Dudley are blended. It is now that The Kid first attempts an evaluation of what is going on and of the past. He has a revelation about his life in Texas: that there's a reason for everything, "though it didn't follow that I'd find it out. It only followed that there was a reason there to find. And for both me and my Uncle Dudley that was enough." Although the reader is given very little of what The Kid learns, he may assume that The Kid will sharpen his field of vision. However, as one of the men says, "You gotta come back two, three, four times before you know. You gotta forget half the things you learn before you know."

In a situation where the undercurrents are evil and the overtones are grim, The Kid responds to another kind of teacher, another kind of audacity. Furman's purpose in life is to spit in the eyes of people whose vocation or avocation is to foster falsity and malice either by brute force or by a tyrannical, corrupt approach to life—a purpose which, needless to state, continually lands him in jail. Even some of the bums do not approve of Furman's seemingly self-destructive audacity, but the boy does. Yet for the men, too. he is a kind of hero; they are awed and admiring witnesses: "'Furman only man I know who really more somethin than what he ain't.'" Unlike themselves, Furman has a reason for being in jail: "'Spittin in eyes is just what I been called on to do, an what a man really called on for he must.'" Furman *is* what he *does* to the extent that one of the men comments, "'You say that you in and out but the thing about you—you out while you in.'"

In the light of Furman's way of dealing with what is phony, the boy for the first time finds his uncle wanting. Realizing this, Dudley improvises on a new method of teaching. He knows that it is no longer enough to continue in his *quiet* way to behave in a manner deserving The Kid's emulation; and it would not be good simply to imitate Furman. He must inspire The Kid with a gesture whose significance may bewilder him, but whose audacity will support him on the solitary journey of his own westering.

Because of their insolence, Red and Furman are held in jail when Dudley and The Kid are released—the only two who remain in the original caravan. None of them, ironically, reaches his great good place.

> "Well, Kid—" he said, "we'd better spit up."
> "Spit up—?" I said.
> "Split up," he said.

They plan to meet later in Chicago at the Larrabee Street Y. "I got out and stood in the ditch grass and he leaned on the running board. He just stayed there looking at Cupid and once Cupid looked at him." A brutal pervert, Cupid is the only cop into whose eye Furman has not spit.

> "O. K.—now beat it!" Cupid said. . . . He [Dudley] tipped his head and winked at Cupid with his good eye. Cupid thought that was pretty funny and winked back at him—then he closed one eye and opened the other one wide. And right when he did Uncle Dudley spit him, full flush in that eye. The juice spattered all over his face and dripped dark brown on his front—but he didn't move. . . . Then suddenly he reached for the gun, but Biscuit had it. . . . He made motions with it for Uncle Dudley to get in. . . .
> Uncle Dudley turned and spit the rest in the road, hitched up his pants. He didn't look at me but climbed inside and closed

the door. . . . They went along with a wheel in the road grass like we had come. . . . On the turn my Uncle Dudley put out his hand.

With this humorous gesture the book ends. Though Morris' humor is almost slapstick at times, it is never gratuitous. This incident evokes both theme and character. The seemingly superficial and folksy humor, along with the dry wit and subtle lyricism, ultimately serve (as is characteristic of Morris) to reveal the book's basic seriousness of concept and intent.

Humor and tone are important in Morris. The plainsman's humor, Webb comments, grew "out of suffering." Out of the endless grubbing for water and the grim struggle with climate and soil developed a deadpan, ambiguous, and macabre humor that probably helped the farmer maintain his sanity. Morris' quiet humor blends with its own unique flavor such borrowed ingredients as the Chaplinesque touches noted by Harvey Swados. Morris' temperament is basically humorous; his intentions are basically serious. It is perhaps because of the tension between the humorous and the serious, comedy and horror, that some readers are not quite certain whether Morris' tone is warmly intimate or coldly distant. If one fails to sense a warmth *in* the novels, a reader familiar and saturated with Morris' view comes to feel or know a warmth *behind* the novels. One must note at this point Morris' denial of a primary intention to teach a moral: "The notion of a message was never part of my experience at the conscious level." Certainly, however, the blend in his work of irony, satire, and "divine" comedy evokes compassion.

From the navel of the world, the Nebraska plains, that desolate way station between the industrial East whence the exodus began and the Far West where it ended, The Kid has made a long journey. This trip began in Los Angeles, where the adventurous westward movement was forced to halt at the sea and where its spirit died amid the transplanted Eastern industrialism that engulfed the West. It ended in Arkansas, where the decline of Southern values had hit cultural rock bottom and where even industrialism had failed to flourish. With his uncle as mentor, The Kid has moved through present-day American civilization on his way to a realization of some moral, esthetic vision by which he can live. Having discovered the land and a few of its heroes, he can now set out alone in search of one of its products—himself.

Though this first book ends with no dramatic moment of truth, there is a strong implication of hope, of belief in the boy as a witness capable of benefiting from exposure to the heroic. That he has told the story shows that he has imagination and insight, and his vision of his uncle is sharpened by genuine love. Although he does not yet conceptualize his raw material, he begins in the jail to process it.

The witness may live in the everyday world of the "phony" and the cliché, but, in his relationship with the hero, he encounters the real McCoy; he experiences the moment of compassion or of imagination, or both, or even the moment of heroism. These are means of achieving self-transformation, release from the realm of mundane reality into a greater, truer reality. In a world of transience such moments are permanent because of their enduring effect on the characters.

Usually, the hero does not experience the moment of love or of imagination. He does not benefit from his own actions, although in the moment of heroism he knows he creates substantial reality. The hero and the witness are for each other what neither can be alone. The heroic act cannot occur without the witness. Without the hero, the witness cannot experience the moment of love or of imagination. Just as the facts bear witness to the verisimilitude of the fiction, The Kid's presence causes Uncle Dudley to behave as he does.

Thus, the essence of Morris' vision is presented in his first, seemingly simple book. I fully agree with John W. Hunt, Jr., who declares in "The Journey Back: The Early Novels of Wright Morris," that Morris' "early books are not mere apprentice pieces, trial runs of a major literary imagination. They are finished, rewarding novels which justify in their own right... careful critical attention."[6]

V   The Man Who Was There:
Compassion and Imagination

Uncle Dudley, the original man who was there, is a hero in the realm of action. In *The Man Who Was There*, Agee Ward (alias The Kid) is a hero in the realm of the imagination. The romance of the open road, the hero-witness relationship, the act of improvising, the taking of risks, the transformation, the function of the cliché—these themes and elements are reasserted in *The Man Who Was There*, which begins to pick up pieces of the puzzle *My Uncle Dudley* sets down. As Agee Ward, The Kid's role is now reversed from that of witness to hero. The evolution of The Kid through many of Morris' novels,—sometimes as hero, sometimes as witness—exemplifies the process of metamorphosis that functions in this novel.

Bewildered reviewers complained when the book first appeared, of its lack of form: for them, Agee, "the man who was there," was missing. Certainly it is true that the complex design is difficult to follow if the reader fails to perceive the thematic, organizing principle and the fugal quality of the structure. The seeming chaos of characters, points of view, time sequences, and incidents actually is given form and impetus in the hero-witness relationship and in the concept of transformation.

Transformation, intricately revealed in character relationships, is the book's theme. Its organizing idea is the hero's power to cause transformations in others. Transformations are of two kinds: spontaneous, temporary ones, and those which have had a long, complex buildup and are permanent. By the very nature of his behavior, Agee, himself a product of transformations, creates a chain of transformations whose effect is most notable in the lives of the two major witnesses, Private Reagan and Gussie Newcomb. Transformation becomes a compassionate, imaginative act in which fact and fiction blend. Because of the transforming aspect of the hero-witness bond, the characters are often both in and out of this world. Along with comments on the book's structure, transformation and its variants will be, therefore, the particular object of this discussion.

The novel is divided into three main sections, in each of which an important transformation occurs. Southern California is the setting, and the time is 1943, or thereabouts. The first section, "The Vision of Private Reagan," is an account of events on the funeral day of Grandma Herkimer, who knew Agee Ward when he was a boy. Another boyhood friend of Agee's, Private Reagan, attends the funeral. En route he learns that Agee has been reported missing in action. During the service at the grave, Reagan has a vision, and both Agee and Grandma Herkimer are resurrected in him. Preceding the major transformation, minor ones occur in several of the many characters. The point of view shifts quickly and frequently.

The four-part middle section, "The Three Agee Wards," relates events which occurred before Agee was reported missing; and it opens and closes with "Album" sequences. The first look at Agee is in a chronological series of photographs from an album found among the belongings in his California apartment. With his Uncle Kermit (Dudley), Agee sees America first; then comes a year in college, a European *Wanderjahr*. Pictures, post cards, and drawings take the reader to the point at which Agee succumbs to nostalgia and leaves Paris to return to his home town, Lone Tree, Nebraska. The point of view is strictly Agee's in "The Ward Line" and "The Osborn Look"—the homecoming sequences—in which he visits his father's family on the home place and then wanders around Lone Tree. In them Agee is primarily a witness, acted upon and transformed.

[42]

The closing album sequences, presenting a photo of Agee with other army inductees, provides a link with the preceding Reagan section and leads into the final section, "The Ordeal of Gussie Newcomb." The rejuvenation of Gussie under Agee's influence, but operating obliquely, is the third of the book's three major transformations. Except for a brief segment near the end narrated in first person by Mr. Bloom, a friend of Agee's who becomes Gussie's suitor, the point of view remains Gussie's.

VI   *The Missing Hero: Three Views*

It will simplify the following discussion, if instead of following the author's order, the reader begins with "The Three Agee Wards," in which he will find the sources of the series of transformations that affected Agee and, through him, the others.

In the beginning were the land itself and the way of life of the inhabitants. Since leaving Lone Tree, Agee has become not only the painter Dudley wanted to be but also a writer. He has roamed back and forth over America and Europe; but, in every sense that matters, he has never left home. " 'Where you're from is where you're goin',' said Eddie Cahow [the Lone Tree barber], 'and where you're goin' is where you're from.' " Incomplete himself, Agee cannot complete his paintings of Lone Tree, "Journey's End" and "The Journey Out."

In Agee's album are his drawings of typical artifacts on the home place: a pump, a privy, a Monkey Ward catalogue, one chill egg. These farmyard clichés of American culture are real enough to lure him from Paris. It is the connection made long ago that the artistic, sophisticated Agee Ward wants to check, renew, and evaluate. And perhaps he feels the need to return to the real thing, to move again in a world where things are their essential selves: "Everything spaced, evenly spaced, the chairs, the table, the icebox, the couch—everything with its own proper identity.... There were no *arrangements,* no groupings of any kind.... Nothing was done to make it look more, or to make it look less than what it was."

But the prodigal has difficulty recognizing the country, and the natives have difficulty recognizing him. During his years away Agee has, in a sense, lost connection with the land. But the land is losing connection with itself because the new generation of inhabitants is losing connection with *it*. Agee's Uncle Harry Ward is anxious about the fact that Agee is unmarried: "Me and him ... is the last of the line." The process of metamorphosis must continue; it has reached a transitional stage on the home place. Uncle Harry, refusing to change, represents the old way of life; his "aggie" college-educated son, Will, represents the new agrarian way. Aunt Sarah laments the cutting down of the trees; now the land is as it was when Uncle Harry first came and planted the trees himself: "'I was the first—and now I'm last.'" But he knows that "'He ain't a farmer... who thinks what he plants ain't liable to die.'" Will, however, is continuing the cycle by planting trees to replace those his father had to cut down; it is Adaline, Will's wife, who exemplifies the transition in her desire for and emulation of urban things.

In the homecoming passages Morris creates a mood in which one expects magic powers to function. Agee begins to exert upon others the same power that the home place exerts upon him—the power which comes from having had connection with things that have a kind of holiness. Of the people who effected transformations in Agee, his mother, who died the year he was born, was the first; she is resurrected in him, she sets the magical form his life is to achieve.[7] When Agee visits her grave, the headstone "looked new, terribly new, but beneath the name was the date—1910." (Most of his major characters and some of the important events date from this year when Morris was born). The epitaph reads: *She died so that he might live.* "Some defect in the stone, and the slanting light, seemed to stress the word *he*." An old cliché, made new. The stone seems new because Grace's effect on Agee is still new. And if Agee, reported missing in action, is in fact dead, he has died in terms of the patriotic cliché so that others might live; but in reality he has given people more by having been the man he was before the war than by being killed during it.

At the end of the nostalgic return, Agee attempts an evaluation. Like The Kid, he still feels there's a reason for everything; the problem is to find it. Agee simply exposes himself to things as they are, letting them make their quiet impact on him, neither pointing out the clichés nor digging into the reality underneath them. But, as in Agee's painting, a beginning is made. *The Journey Out* lies somewhere in the territory ahead. In its thematic design, "The Three Agee Wards" constitutes both a sequel to and a recapitulation of *My Uncle Dudley: roundup* of Agee's identity, *passage* with Uncle Kermit, *one man* (Agee) *on a horse*. In its depiction of a nostalgic return, it anticipates *The Home Place;* and, in its delineation of the transmutation of nostalgia into nausea, *The World in the Attic.*

The technique used in the album sequence—the photograph-description approach to character, event, and meaning—was new at the time, insofar as I know. A technique that anticipates *The Inhabitants* and is used in varying ways in all his novels, is this condensed, impressionistic rendering of material which enables the author to cover much ground in comparatively few pages. A number of the photographs give the strange feeling that Agee always seemed somewhat out of the physical picture—out of this world. In a class photo, for example, "a girl named Stella Fry had waved her hand right in front of his face. . . . and the shutter clicked." It is as though reality were conspiring to blot him out of the picture.

"The Album" presents the past as it is alive in the described pictures; "The Ward Line" presents the *natural*, primitive process of transformation or metamorphosis on the land, coming to an end in Agee; "The Osborn Look," in its "that-he-might-live" motif, suggests the spiritual, metaphysical, or mystical realm of transformation, the sphere in which Agee's powers predominantly operate—he leaves his spirit behind. Although as a person Agee is unfinished, he continues to take shape through a series of transformations in others. Lacking connection with the past, he creates a future in other unfinished people; and he thus transcends the hell of impermanence.

VII *Vision and Ordeal: The Hero Resurrected*

In "The Vision of Private Reagan" and "The Ordeal of Gussie Newcomb" Agee does nothing extraordinary to the characters, but his effect, subtle and circuitous, is strong enough to contribute some sense of meaning and wonder to their lives.

In both cases Agee's effect operates by remote control, but the transformation process in "The Vision of Private Reagan" is the less complex of the two. For Reagan, Grandma Herkimer is a kind of hero. Partly because Agee bewitches her, she bewitches Reagan; thus, through her, Agee, too, bewitches him. On the morning of her death, Grandma Herkimer sat up in bed and called twice for Agee Ward. Did Reagan himself hear her? At the funeral service— which he senses would strike Grandma as phony—his bewitched behavior affects others, among them the minister, who unwittingly helps to precipitate Reagan's vision. He speaks of the divine trinity of conception from man through woman to God. " 'This is the Resurrection,' he said, 'that a man should die so that he might live, that he should go so that thereby he might come again.' " Here is the signal for which Reagan has been waiting. He yells: " '*He has come again!*' There being nothing else to do, Reverend Horde raised his hand in an attitude of blessing." Grandma Herkimer had called for Agee who showed up in Reagan, with the result that she is buried as she would like to have been, unceremoniously.

The satirical tone Morris uses in rendering the funeral preparations is appropriate. Satire and the sacred, fact and fiction, the idea of being both in and out of this world are interwoven. The comedy supports the audacity that transforms. In the realm of transformation, the characters are moved to compassion and revelation. It is appropriate, too, that the funeral ritual forms the incident nexus of this section. It recapitulates the cycle of birth, life, and death; and it enhances the mystical quality of events, of character changes, and of shifts in point of view.

"The Ordeal of Gussie Newcomb," the book's final section, is presented with relative clarity; and the reader is able to follow the complex transforming process almost chronologically. No blood relationship exists between Agee and Gussie Newcomb, but she becomes his spiritual next of kin. The ordeal to which she is subjected results in her transformation and in a resurrection in her of Agee Ward. "I'll be back," he had told her.

Tracing the progress of the transformation, the reader sees that the first shock is the telegram informing her Agee is missing. Next of kin? She hardly remembers him, even though he has been keeping up the rent on his garage apartment. The change in Gussie begins with the sudden descent upon her of people who knew Agee. They want to rent the apartment, or at least to look at his things, probably imagining that they retain the magical effect of his touch, and hoping that through contact with his possessions they can re-establish connection with the hero. Although at first skeptical of Agee's power thus revealed, Gussie baffled and fascinated, moves into the apartment herself.

If Agee is really dead, he already is resurrected in Peter Spavic, who kept up his albums for him while he was traveling. Peter doesn't believe that Agee is missing, and neither does Mrs. Krickbaum with whom Agee used to discuss art and the "human predicament." According to what Mrs. Krickbaum tells Gussie, Agee "didn't believe . . . that if you were alive you were ever really missing. He said that anything really alive just went on and on."

Through her contact with Peter, Mrs. Krickbaum, and the others, and by communion with Agee's personal effects, Gussie most completely absorbs his personality into her own. The album and the paintings inspire thoughts analogous to those Agee had about the home place and the inhabitants. As she sheds her old-maidish ways, a rejuvenated Gussie begins to emerge. Dressed in some of Agee's outlandish costume pieces, she goes on a hip-wiggling promenade, plays a pinball machine, and is the life of the party at a neighbor's. Never having taken a drink before, she overdoes it, spouts witticisms picked up in her posthumous relationship with Agee, and winds up in the bathroom in a clothes hamper.

Now she is more doubtful even than Peter Spavic that Agee is missing. Becoming young again, she begins to hear an inner music, and things seem to say more than they are saying. Her suitor, Mr. Bloom, no longer can be sure whether he is courting her or she him. Gussie almost proposes to him, speaking in the same breath of the child they will have. But Mr. Bloom, influenced by Gussie, has become Agee; he asserts his dormant masculinity and puts her in her place with a blunt command.

On the day Gussie is to elope with Bloom, Peter Spavic finds her sitting in her apartment in the dark, as Agee used to sit. Between them, they split Agee up: Peter's child will be named Ward; hers, Agee (boy *or* girl). Peter says: " 'He thinks he's missing—but boy, did we fox him!' " Just the way Agee would have put it. Gussie feels a kind of power. Transformed herself, does she have the power to transform?

When the novel ends the reader still has not been told, officially, whether Agee is missing or dead. The book's title refers to a feeling the witnesses have that Agee never seemed to be there. The irony is that the witnesses are not "really there" except as Agee's effect on them brings their own lives into focus; and, in a sense, Agee is real only in his effect on his witnesses. The man who was reported missing is the man who was and will always be *there* in the people in whom he left himself behind.

The journey in search of meaning, of roots, of values, always leads back, ends where it began, at the home place, where, as in Agee's painting, one side of life remains in darkness while on the other side there is light. When he leaves Lone Tree, having begun to see it in perspective, Agee is no longer followed in quite the same way by his shadow—his old self, shaped by Nebraska, that has followed him across America and Europe. "The shadow of a man had to pass from morning to evening by going before him—not by lapping at his back. For when he turned, it turned, and the shadow had foreshortened until he stood upon himself, shadowless, here in the street." But both Agee and the author are still too infatuated with the home place to keep the past sufficiently under control.

In 1948 Morris said that the American creative writer "is now engaged in an endless and heartbreaking search for an unstated myth." Applicable to Morris at this point in his career, the observation is true as well of Agee, a man passionately in search of a myth. Agee tries to escape captivity in the nostalgia of the past by processing the past, by transmuting it as myth into the formal, conceptual realm of art. Agee's creator is engaged in the same task.

CHAPTER 3

Return of the Native

I F "an epic is how you feel about something," the episodes, names, and dates in Morris' books are part of one great epic—the epic of the American consciousness: the only wide-open spaces we have left. Like The Kid and Agee Ward, Morris attempts to discover America first, to enter into the "collective memories of the pioneer American past," as Frederic I. Carpenter says. The pattern developed in *My Uncle Dudley* and in *The Man Who Was There* is recapitulated: from the mythic elements, to the individual's confrontation of the past as it survives in the present, to the attempt to find meaning. In *The Inhabitants* the emphasis is on the artifacts inhabited and on the land; in *The Home Place*, on the inhabitants themselves; and in *The World in the Attic*, on what the land and the people signify to one man: Clyde Muncy (alias The Kid and Agee Ward), writer and self-exiled Nebraskan, who is nearing middle age. Though the approach is mainly comic, a tone of Romantic pathos pervades the three books, the second and third of which are told in the first person by Muncy.

Morris asks Crevecoeur's "disquieting and perennial question": What is an American?[1] De Tocqueville, the sensitive foreigner, tried to answer it; James's attempt in *The American Scene*, Morris feels, is the only successful one. But de Tocqueville dealt more with the outward and James with the inward manifestations, while Morris is concerned with both. For Morris the answer lies somewhere in the small towns of the Midwest, roots of American strength that flower in the East.

"I went back to Nebraska," says Morris, "with the idea of seeing, after a long absence, the life that I remembered, but saw very poorly as a boy. I wanted really to see this life, so to speak for the first time."[2] Photography offered a means of making a fresh, immediate contact with his raw material. It is not unsureness but his profound search for meaning that dictates experimentation and explains the changes in Morris' method. Vision is always the means of order. Alan Trachtenberg has said: "Morris' craft of vision focuses upon the community of men in America searching for a way to convert the loss of pastoral innocence into a gain of personal integrity. Vision itself is both the instrument and the substance of this transformation."[3]

I The Inhabitants: *Voices and Artifacts*

Originally, Morris planned a series of five, photo-text volumes dealing with the movement of American life from the farm and the small town to the city. Only *The Inhabitants* and *The Home Place* use this technique; *The World in the Attic* appeared without the photographs. Readers of the first two had been confused as to the proper relationship between pictures and text. They expected a journalistic relationship; the author intended a poetic one. These books should have been combined into a single volume, in which *The World in the Attic* would probably have been the most successful blend of fiction (novel) and fact (photograph).

The Inhabitants, a large book which measures 1'1" by 9½", is structured on three levels. On the left, one reads: (1) an "I"'s improvisations on an answer to the question, What is an inhabitant? (2) the "I"'s remembrance of the past in the voices of inhabitants he has known in his travels over America. On the right (3), one looks at stark photographs of churches, farmhouses, beached boats, porches, barns, grain elevators, graveyards, privies, doors, hotels, stores, factories, windows, steps, sidewalks and street fixtures, adobes, back fences, which are rich with associations now that they are abandoned. The pictures are representative of most regions in the United States, enhanced by suggestions of various land forms and weather conditions, with an emphasis on rural and small-town architectural detail. The relation between the memory or passage of dialogue and the visual statement is not always apparent; it is never obvious. The form of the whole is very fluid; to avoid any indication of strict sequence, Morris doesn't even number the pages.

The prose voices are like Joycean epiphanies: "the sudden 'revelation of the whatness of a thing,' the moment in which 'the soul of the commonest object ... seems to us radiant. ... a sudden spiritual manifestation' either 'in the vulgarity of speech or of gesture or in a memorable phase of the mind itself.' ... It claims importance by claiming nothing."[4] Thus, Morris epiphanizes blind Uncle John: "My cane has the carved head of a dog, smooth hollow sockets are his eyes. Walking, I keep my fingers there. I can feel him check me at a rise and lead me where objects fall away. Space is a thing we lean upon." By the nature of his way of life, John inhabits the look and feel of the sepulchral white barn with its thin, soft shadows pictured opposite his "voice."

Through the medium of photography Morris tried to lay his hands on the object itself, "the *ding an sich*." And he does create the illusion that it is purely the artifact itself that one sees. But the resources of photography alone are limited: "Reality is not a *thing* but a *conception*, and the camera cannot cenceive. I tried to overcome this limitation by a marriage of sensations in the mind of the beholder."[5] Wherein lies the book's organization and form? It is created by the perceiving sensibility that makes relationships and finds meaning: the fusion occurs in the reader rather than on the page, and the various elements join together, as they do in Blake's illuminated printing, into a "supreme metaphor."

The book carries an epigraph from *Walden:* "What of architectural beauty I now see, I know has gradually grown from within outward, out of the necessities and character of the indweller, who is the only builder.... it is the life of the inhabitants whose shells they are...." Thoreau's comment and Morris' reply suggest the theme of the book: "Thoreau, a look is what a man gets when he tries to inhabit something—something like America." Morris looks beneath the cliché "you look like a man who grew up around here." "What there is around here grew up in you.... you're the one that's inhabited."

The pictorial focus is wholly on the artifacts, which were "ready at hand, like coined phrases." No human beings appear, but they are there in the things they inhabit, in objects worn and preserved by many generations—the objects themselves are inhabited. The visual aspect of the material things among which the inhabitants live and die reveal their nature, way of life, values, and spirit. Wear conveys not only a peculiar charm to Morris but a fundamental truth—imbued with elements of the personalities of the inhabitants by daily contact and use, the enduring objects become, in a sense, holy.[6] "I found these objects beautiful because of their saturation with experience ("Privacy," 53). New structures, new artifacts, make no such statements.

In a letter to Morris, Thomas Mann, a European observer, wrote, "What these courageous pictures show is the harsh beauty of ugliness, the romanticism of the commonplace, the poetry of the unpoetical." Behind the "slang-like anti-rhetoric, the anti-aestheticism of its texts," he sensed "a social and spiritual democratic tendency."

In his treatment of things as they are on the American scene, Morris tries to convey the "anonymous air of permanence." Everything transitory must be processed out. Although it is strongest in being what it is in all its whatness, the typical transcends itself into the archetypal and the mystical. The mysticism in his concept of *things* as being holy, of empty houses as being inhabited, lies in the kind of response that certain minds, like Muncy's, make to the perceived thing.

In *The Home Place* and in *The World in the Attic*, Muncy under-takes the voyage of discovery, returning to the home place in search of his cultural roots. Through Muncy's witnessing intelligence and sensibility, Morris articulates the inarticulate agrarian spirit of Nebraska. Uncle Dudley did not need to return because he had taken with him the essential, sustaining qualities. But Morris-The Kid-Muncy, a later generation, are living in a period of transition. Uprooted, exiled, drifting, they have to go back because they have that in them which made the pioneers go West—a questing spirit, an urge for westering into the interior of oneself. It is as if Huck Finn were to go back to re-evaluate what he ran away from. The territory ahead keeps referring him to the territory behind, and the point is to try to find out where he is. With the general question, "What is an American?" Morris links Muncy's specific question, "Who am *I?*"

II The Home Place: *Going Home Again*

Nostalgia brings Clyde Muncy (more sophisticated than Agee) to Lone Tree, Nebraska, where he experiences a prodigal's impressions of what Harry Levin calls "the complicated and unobtrusive patterns of American life." As in the homecoming segments of the Agee novel, Muncy's visit lasts a morning and an evening of one hot sum-mer day. Against the background of his past, he responds sensitively to a series of minor events, typical for one who revisits a rural home place. The book has no narrative line. Like much of Morris' work, it is composed of moments, of impressions that harmonize with the whole. This novel is almost entirely one of sensibility, of character. Unity lies in viewpoint, attitude, and overall mood. The effect of the rural environment on the city Muncys gives rise to a humor that depends upon the quiet collision of ways of life going in opposite directions.

In *The Home Place*, as in the other two books, Morris is concerned with our "appalling and visible freedom to be blighted." Having himself made the shift from rural childhood to urban adulthood, Morris depicts the contrast. He merely implies the negative aspects of American urbanization, but in his comments on James's *The American Scene*, Morris' own viewpoint is explicitly stated: "James does not want things as they were, he asks only that the process of becoming should finally become something of value, not just one more thing to tear down, in order to put something else up." Like James, Morris observes "a principle of waste that feeds on itself" in a civilization whose "motto might be *Let Nothing Stand*, since all things stand in the way of Progress" (*Territory*, 211-12). Amid such transience, "it is virtually impossible to describe the *state* of things. . . . Anyone who has looked for the house where he was born, the empty lot where he played, the porch where he wooed his sweetheart, will know the singular paralysis that grips the heart to find these landmarks gone" ("Made," 492). Without the concrete symbols it is difficult to maintain even a stifling tradition.

Although the rural way of life is narrow, it seems to win, at least, on its own ground, represented by the old folks. The old rural way is what Americans are losing. Before it goes, they need to look at it and to assimilate the best of it.

The Muncys represent the urban way in which "the new is obsolete on its appearance," for "early obsolescence is a built-in characteristic of a wide range of products." The inhabitants represent a way in which *enough* things are permanent. In the character relationships, the contrasts and conflicts are presented between Muncy and Uncle Harry (as in the Agee novel) and between Peg, Muncy's wife, and Aunt Clara (alias Aunt Sarah); the children, Bobby and Peggy, absorb and reflect the adults' behavior and moods. As husband and father, Agee-Muncy's field of response is enlarged; as an outsider, Peg, who mocks him probably because she suspects him of sentimentality, provides skeptical counterpoint. Within Muncy, contrasts in attitude and emotion are created by his ambivalent response to the old man and to Clara. What he feels about the beauty of the past contrasts with what he comes to think of the inhabitants in the present, and the ensuing ambiguity imparts tension to the simple incidents.

III   *Artifacts: Connection With the Past*

The rural-urban *conflict* centers around familiar farm and small-town clichés. More important are the *contrasts* in character and sensibility. They arise out of the manner in which Morris develops his concept that rural artifacts are inhabited and holy. Many Morris characters attempt to maintain connection with the past through artifacts—what a man uses to keep a grip on the connection.

In his photographs, Morris catches in the permanence of art the same worn, talismanic objects that Agee drew on postcards from Paris. The only human in the series is Uncle Harry, among his artifacts: at the beginning, standing in a doorway, face in shadow; in the middle, standing casually with his back to the camera; in the end, going back through the doorway. Although the photographs are excellent, their relation to the text is more literal and less interesting than in *The Inhabitants*.[7]

Daily, through talk and private feeling, the uncomplicated inhabitants subtly connect with the present and reconnect with the past in their effortless, unconscious response to permanent artifacts which tell them who, what, and where they are. In their routine seasonal and daily relationship with nature and man-made objects, they are so much a part of their environment that they do not concern themselves, as does the intellectual Muncy, with the *why* of being. But aware of his destructive compulsion to evaluate his emotions, Muncy learns how to make the feeling "contain the whole works."

There are communal and family artifacts. For the inhabitants, the town itself is permanent. For instance, the white grain elevator, a communal source of connection and a tribal symbol, is a monument that testifies that "the place is still inhabited." The present and the past, the spirit of the family, is kept alive in the parlor at evening by family legends and magic. Grandmother Osborn's cane-bottom chair is holy because of the series of transformations it has undergone. When she went West, the cane-bottom became her connection with the life she left in the East. "Her kids grew up with their bottoms on it," and it seems to have supported more than their bodies. Grandmother Cropper, an old fool with her shoe box full of junk and her head full of memories, strives for permanence by talking unceasingly of the past. In her, history is just as immediate as the moment is for Muncy. It is only through recalling artifacts that Aunt Clara can touch Muncy's roots in her own life.

And there are personal artifacts, such as Uncle Harry's Model-T. A new artifact will enable him to maintain connection with the transient children. When they get flypaper stuck in their hair, their curls have to be cut. To hide their raw, shaven heads, he buys straw hats for them—and one for himself, which he adds to his large collection. Uncle Harry is not particularly aware of the connections that sustain him. Muncy looks at the worn Axminster rug: " 'If you're lookin' for the figure—' Clara said, 'you're just about ten or twelve years too late.' " Uncle Harry is not certain he ever noticed it himself. For a moment he thinks it's too late now, but looking through the screen at the road helps him make the connection: " 'No, come to think I did look at it,' he said. 'It was nice.' " In the end, Muncy, watching him enter the barn, observes that the figure is in Harry: "The figure on the front of the carpet had worn through to the back."

Time was when Muncy too communed with rural artifacts. As a boy, he did most of his thinking in the three-seater privy, "the rural chapel, where a man puts his cares in order, or forgets his cares and turns his mind to other things." On 53rd Street there is "no privy, with a view of the valley, no unhinged door, no sun on your knees ... no a-loneliness, nothing but the damned tiled privacy. Places to worry, that is, but no place to think."

The farmer exemplifies the sanctity of individuality and privacy, themes which reach their most heightened expression in the scene in Uncle Ed's house. In the modern world the idea has grown that at the root of privacy there is something suspect; the private, therefore, is meant to be exposed. Privacy is so rare today, Morris believes, that there is a quality of holiness about it. In photographing the house, Morris himself had the revelation Muncy experiences. Morris photographed a bed, symbol of privacy. Under it was a chamber pot. "In the honest guise of telling the facts, this photograph ended up lying, since in such a context the larger statement ... the revelation could not be heard above this shout" ("Privacy," 54). Shock "is the technique of invasion, and it marks a signal failure of art," the purpose of which is to *reveal*. Here is a typical instance of Morris' refusal to exploit the more sensational details. He re-shot the bed, without the pot. The details harmonized with the conception in the second photograph, a portrait not of a habit but of a way of life, an eloquent expression of the atmosphere and the meaning of privacy.

Muncy wants to take his family out of the city and to live in the house that belongs to Uncle Ed, who is dying in the hospital. A dispute arises because the place is a farm and Muncy is no farmer. That evening, Aunt Clara, perhaps intuitively knowing what they will find and feel, suggests that Muncy and Peg have a look at the house. Even as they enter, they know what Eddie Cahow, the town barber, meant when he said: " 'Makes a big difference ... whether you know the people or not. ... you get the feeling they're still on the place.' " Muncy himself feels that "any house that's been lived in, any room that's been slept in, is ... forever occupied."

Peg's gaze falls upon a bed. "As if she saw someone in the bed," she flinches and steps back—an invader of Ed's privacy. As Muncy and Peg move through the rooms, they examine the artifacts, laughing at some; but their attitude slowly changes. Muncy feels he is committing a violation against something sacred: "Was there, then, something holy about these things? If not, why had I used that word?" At one moment he feels what he expects a thing of beauty to make him feel: "to take me out of my *self*, into the selves of other things." "That kind of holiness, I'd say, is abstinence, frugality, and independence—the home-grown, made-on-the-farm trinity."

Little Peggy runs into the house, yelling that they can move right in because Ed has died. But Peg, who early in the novel said, " 'I'm not going to budge until he's really dead,' " feels that Ed still occupies his home place. Muncy puts things back where they were before his camera eye intruded: "I felt like a man whose job it was to close up a church. . . . that was the word for a man's house. The citadel, the chapel, of his character."

Throughout most of the book, Muncy is outside the clichés, looking in, unable to perceive the blend of superficiality *and* validity. But he proves to be the man James is talking about in the book's epigraph from *The American Scene:* "To be at all critically . . . minded—over and beyond an inherent love of the general many-colored picture of things—is to be subject to the superstition that objects and places, coherently grouped, disposed for human use and addressed to it, must have a sense of their own, a mystic meaning proper to themselves to give out: to give out, that is, to the participant at once so interested and so detached as to be moved to a report of the matter." Muncy has cut the physical umbilical cord, but the mystical one still connects him with the home place.

IV   *Ritual and Gesture: A Means of Connection*

If Muncy is unsure, to the extent that he is unconnected, who he is, the inhabitants have no doubts about themselves. Who one is depends on what and where one is, and is expressed by one's response to one's surroundings. The quality of the response determines the extent to which one connects with his world. " 'I'm a farmer's wife,' " says Aunt Clara, who is depicted only in typical occupations—cooking, washing, canning. "Eighty years of rural life had shaped this flesh so well there was little for the writer to do but observe it. In this book the author was both writing fiction and reporting on fiction become flesh" (Lectures). Cut from an archetypal pattern, only the clichés, the constants, the forms, and the rituals and gestures of Clara's and Harry's way of life define them.

Morris' world is one of formal and informal rituals and ceremonies, with their meaningful gestures. In a land where Indian ritual is still within memory of the older inhabitants, the isolated rural farmer lives according to personal habits which become almost ritualistic. Sometimes their only value in the novels is to provide detail and mood and to convey a quality of feeling or attitude; but often, as in their relevance to the theme of audacity, they reveal character. While some spiritual satisfaction is one effect of ritual in Morris, no formal religious ritual is depicted. Ritual in his books consists of those gesture patterns, sometimes accompanied by verbalization, that evolve out of relationships among characters or out of the routines of a way of life, and provide a means of making connection.

Gesture and speech as expressive forms of ritual are symbolic transformations of mental experiences that cannot be adequately expressed in any other modes. Ends in themselves, born of an elementary inward need rather than an outward purpose to serve social aims, they may have no specific meaning. Even for the rational man these forms of expression, revealing man's desire to transcend his practical concerns, gratify an inclination toward the magical and the mystical.

Their characteristic gestures and the ritualistic quality of their foolhardy, audacious acts, account in part for the bewitching effect the heroes have upon their witnesses. But in ordinary activities Morris' characters enact fragmentary, tentative, improvised forms of ritual and gesture which recur throughout the novels. Old men like to hold their tobacco-stained fingers to their noses, and many characters sniff whatever happens to get on their fingers. The grandmothers' laughter is inward, a slight tap of their heels being the only outward manifestation; others place their hands over their mouths when they laugh. Certain women connote rather than denote anger by tucking in their clothing. In many ways characters relate themselves expressively to their bodies. A woman's kicking off her shoes before sex is not so much an action as it is a gesture of demarcation between the stifling conventions of social reality and the real thing—sex. The waving gesture has many functions, among them a comic surprise or a slight climactic effect. It may be symbolic of connection when a man walks out of the barber shop and waves to the brakeman who is waving to him from the caboose of a passing train. This particular gesture of gregariousness has a connotative flourish which defines and enhances character. Complete moments within themselves, these gestures and rituals also suggest and reveal other things.[8]

Having encountered the many disquieting forms of transience, Muncy has come home—"where you hang your childhood"—to reconnect with the permanence he recalls. Why make connection? To achieve a mystical harmony with oneself through the environment of one's past—to transform oneself. If "you can't repeat the past," as Nick tells Gatsby, perhaps you *can* "recover something, some idea of" yourself. While he can understand it to a degree, Muncy cannot—it is too late—become part of his past world. If the creative Muncy seeks connection, the inhabitants live it.

In *The Home Place* and in *The World in the Attic* Morris insists that Americans need to go home again, and that, in order for America to come of age, they must.

VI   The World in the Attic: *Nostalgia-Nausea*

Because there has been a failure to possess the positive, genuine aspects of the past, the present consists mostly of clichés and phoniness. In the present, the dead past is given a semblance of life by characters who are captives of the past.

What was only suggested to Muncy in *The Home Place* is further developed, although not entirely resolved, in *The World in the Attic*. Returning to New York from Lone Tree, the Muncys pass through nearby Junction, where Clyde spent some years of his childhood. In Part One, "The World," Muncy revisits the scene and the inhabitants. The Muncys bring the sophisticated urban point of view to Junction. Clyde's childhood friend, Bud Hibbard, and Bud's wife Nellie, go-getters of the town's new generation, represent the rural world in transition. Combined, the Muncys' and the Hibbards' views make up the present world. In Part Two, "The Attic," Muncy enters the legendary house of Clinton Hibbard, Bud's uncle. In the house live Aunt Angie, Clinton's mother, and Miss Caddy, his widow. The next morning, Caddy, once the town's most provocative and lively citizen, is found dead. Muncy helps to arrange the burial. Having moved in the past as a recollecting observer, he becomes seriously involved in the town's present.

By his greater control over theme, structure, diction, and incident, Morris indicates that he has learned to process his raw material with greater freedom from "the apparatus of nostalgia." He achieves the kind of objective conceptualization that is characteristic of his best novels. The first half of the book is impressionistic, a series of reminiscences like *The Home Place;* but the second half has a novelistic narrative line. "The Ward Line" and "The Osborn Look" (sections of *The Man Who Was There*) and *The Home Place* are episodic, direct confrontations out of which no apparent pattern evolves. But in the Junction where past and present meet, Muncy's confrontation guides him in a definite direction and he achieves the insights Agee failed to reach. In Lone Tree, the past, saturated in the immediate present, is merely alluded to. In Junction, however, the past is specifically and dramatically related to the present.

Muncy obviously tries to make the fiction of nostalgia become, through the nausea of actual contact, something real. The forces of nostalgia and nausea function in most of Morris' novels. Drawn back by nostalgia, an idealized blend of past and present, Muncy reacts with nausea. When that blend confronts the actual complex of present experience, past and present react violently to each other in nausea, and the only catalyst is the conceptualizing intelligence. What is home-town nausea?

I can get it in a lunch room like this, or at the bend of a road, any country road, where a telephone pole tips out of a clutter of dust-heavy weeds. . . . This sickness is in your blood, like a latent fever, a compound of all those summer afternoons, all those fly-cluttered screens, and all those Sunday papers scattered on the floor. The idle curtains at the open windows, the heat over the road like a band of light, and the man on the davenport, with his pants unbuttoned, the comics over his face. . . . Everything is there, in abundance, to make life possible. But very little to make it tolerable. Any one of these things, at a time, is nostalgia—but taken together, in a single lump, it is home-town nausea—you are sicker than you think. You had better sit down.

Muncy lacks connection with the town. It has broken for him mainly at those points where it has broken for the town itself. The novel is partly about the death of a small town, and thus of the past, of the pioneer American dream, of the promise of the frontier; it is a recollection and a recognition, a requiem for a way of life that is vanishing. Nostalgia-nausea and the death of a way of life are linked themes that are conveyed to Muncy in "The World" and conceptualized by him in "The Attic."

Impelled by a nostalgic remembrance of the *promise* of that way of life, Muncy tries to make connection with the living and the dead and with the town. Wandering about Junction, making random observations and evaluations, he encounters many artifacts, places, and people who remind him of the past and who testify to his identity. In the cemetery he recalls three "bearded giants" who saw the promise flower, then dry up on the arid plains. One of these, his own father, is Will "Chicken" Muncy, who was both a "go-getter" in the egg business and a railway station agent. Standing before Will's gravestone, Muncy feels that he never really saw his father "until brought here, face to face with the stone, the dried flower wreath, and the fact that this huge piece of granite was tipped." His father, too, "suffered from home-town nausea."

Muncy's father used to tell him the story of another "giant," Tom Scanlon. In a room facing west on the top floor of the New Western Hotel, Scanlon slept in his clothes, the nightpot by his side full of cigars. In winter, he pulled his bed over by the window and looked out on the spur of the Main Line tracks. Where there was nothing to see, Scanlon saw plenty. "For reasons of their own all kinds of men, with a bottle in their hand and one in their stomach," sensing that the promise dissolved imperceptibly into failure, "figured there was no finer place in the world to walk than the ties." To get away from what they had on their minds, they walked "right down the middle, to Kingdom Come." When Scanlon died "in bed, a cigar in his mouth, a good many men would have felt cheated—except for the fact that he sat the nightpot on his head." He didn't have time "to die like a man" on the tracks, but "he did what he could." Scanlon's audacious gesture, like Dudley's spitting in Cupid's eye, is a comment on life as he has seen it.

Even before Muncy was born, Grandfather Osborn, another "giant," found it too crowded around Junction. For him, as for Daniel Boone, "Neighborliness ... was a good day's drive." He was "mad all his life with the incurable vagueness, the receding promise, of the next frontier." In his will "divided among his children, were the splintered fragments of three frontiers—Paradise won, Paradise lost, but never regained."

Muncy is also moved to remember his dead mother, Grace Osborn, whose charm still casts a spell. Grace and Caddy Hibbard symbolized the world these men and Clinton Hibbard tried to build out of almost nothing. In contrast is the world of Nellie and Bud Hibbard. While Nellie is still enough of a country woman to have no false modesty and to covet Caddy's house without pretense, and while Bud (whose antics once reminded Muncy of Huck Finn) is still close enough to the land to remind Muncy now of the universal kinship of rural men, they cause Muncy's nauseated reflections on the transition from the old to the new. Bud's house is full of the clichés, the artifacts of the temporary urban culture. The living room reflects its inhabitants and, in a sense, all Americans: "It looked like the difference between our fathers and ourselves. This difference is the measure we have taken of the new world, and made it ours, or it is the measure of the extent that we have failed."

From pioneer frugality issued an abundance which has created the unfortunate attitude that the young must be spared what the older generation endured: "What was that? What made men of them? What made *that* kind of man, anyhow, and perhaps there was more than a casual connection between that kind of man and what we call our way of life." Bud and Nellie intend to *give* their children what older generations had to work for. Men of caliber, it seems, produce everything but men of caliber: "Had we been victimized by the fact that abstinence, frugality, independence were not the seeds of heroes, but the roots of the great soft life?" The irony is that Americans strive to erase the very conditions which made them great, while sustaining many of the conditions which constitute failure.

The Bud Hibbards may acquire all the modern conveniences, but it will be a long time before their point of view becomes urbanized and sophisticated. In Bud's basement sanctuary Muncy reminds him of the two lovely Swedish girls whose light could once be seen down the road. Bud reacts as though the mention of them would "corrupt Nellie's home," although "nothing had happened." The green light is faint, but Gatsby Hibbard's "unutterable dream" still lingers about the house. Twenty years later the breeze that was redolent of the various scents of promise still blows through the basement windows.

Muncy has no intention of entering the home-sweet-home of the *mythic* past until Bud and Nellie encourage him to visit Aunt Angie. He finds Aunt Angie talking to herself, "carrying on a discussion with worthy people who were not there." As she moves about the room, she seems to have "an abiding trust that things were where she had left them, and unchanged." Ignoring the presense of Muncy, she goes into herself where the past is preserved and makes connection with the little Muncy boy.

Purblind and deaf, representing the staid spirit of the town, Aunt Angie takes delight in nothing; she lives in the kitchen downstairs, shut off from the rest of the old house. Miss Caddy, after Clinton's death, was "more and more inclined to do her living in bed." From the strange girl who brought life and romance to Junction, she has become an old woman wasting away in a room near the attic. Angie despises Caddy for failing to give Clinton children, making him last of the line; she rejects Bud for having those urban characteristics which estrange him from the old breed.

Later, in the room in Bud's house where Muncy sometimes slept as a boy, Peg informs him that *her* contact with relics of his childhood has been a run-in, brought on by city-country conflicts, with "the finest creature on God's green earth," as Bud once called the girl he married. As Muncy looks out on the railroad tracks, Peg, voicing the attitude of many a self-exiled Midwesterner, heaps her city sarcasm on top of his mixture of nostalgia and nausea: " 'I told her I lived in New York because Junction was like this.' " Muncy had hoped she would listen to him, but neither his wife nor his children share his feelings, as they had somewhat in Lone Tree. Although he has rejected much about the city and exalted certain aspects of the country, he has to agree in part that Junction is "a god-forsaken hole."

At the end of "The World," Muncy ponders what he has observed. Junction is "a house divided, the old town facing the west and Horace Greeley, but the once up-and-coming part of town facing the east. For the east was ... the way to leave." It is "a row of stores facing the burned ditch-grass—and nothing else. Like a row of old men with blinded eyes" who face "the firing squad, the careening globe, and the impending flood." Since morning, Peg has sarcastically interrogated Muncy as to the connection between the

past and the present, the old and the new. That night, she answers
herself. " 'Maybe you're the connection.' "

Nostalgia equals the promise of the past; nausea, the present
failure of the dream. Muncy's memory of men and women of the
past and his encounter with men and women of the present cause
the discord in nostalgia that results in nausea.

VII *The Promise of the Past: A Magnet*

A kind of hero-witness relationship focuses some of the book's
themes and motifs. In a series of moments illuminated by the light
of Caddy's death, Muncy, the discerning witness, better understands her, her witnesses in the town, and himself. Caddy transformed her witnesses by her manner of assault on the present. Like
the house, she had a strange, imported aura in the up-and-coming
town of Junction. She could be expected to do the unexpected, the
audacious; perhaps Muncy alone always knew that that explained
why Clinton had married her. The frontier of Romanticism was
still alive in Caddy, "the cloak of light with the red sprinkling can."
Now for her the past is really dead, for only the present as she
lived it from one magical moment to another was real. Even in her
last days and after her death, she represents that kind of immediacy
to the townspeople.

When the town's promise was young, there seemed to be an
"unseen force" around which they all arranged themselves "in an
orderly manner." Unique and exciting, Caddy once personified that
force. But both her effect on the town and the town itself never
panned out. Across from her house there is a dump now, "right
under the light at the end of the road." That light seems at the
heart of the dilemma; it signifies the reverse of what the green
light at the end of Daisy's dock meant to Gatsby. "Right now
waving over the dump, but when I was a boy—when we were all
boys—pointing to the new world a-coming, the brave world we
all had in mind." Caddy, like the dream, led a man "to think and
to feel what he might not have been led to think or to feel at all."
"Then one day, overnight almost, you miss something." Perhaps a
jerkwater town can't sustain the dream of marble stairs and elegant
girls. What did it mean then to boast that one was born and reared
in the Midwest? "It meant my compass was set. That however the
world or the poles shifted, my needle still pointed toward the house
on the corner. . . . A magnet . . . supplying the town with energy
and direction, like a dynamo. . . . One could string up a wire to
this force and be alive."

Bewildered as to what to do with the charge Caddy gave off, the town missed its chance at "the real McCoy." Only the life of the imagination, as exemplified by Aunt Angie, seems to endure among these people. For her, as for Muncy in a different way, the present was never alive until dead; no transformer, she embalms the past.

Of the townspeople, Purdy, a neighbor who looks after Caddy and Angie, is a major witness. In Caddy's house, he and Muncy quietly improvise upon a relationship in which Muncy communes with the spirit of his father; for Purdy and Will Muncy are a great deal alike. Purdy, who has been forty-five years under Caddy's spell, feels as though he were born and reared in her house. Perhaps others felt a similar, intimate connection and kept it just as secret. But after Clinton's death, only Purdy is to blame for his failure to reveal his love. During the day of her death, he does what he can. He communes with Caddy through artifacts, becoming her husband by wearing Clinton's clothes.

As the Muncys leave town, the lights in the houses they pass are out. But Caddy's house, (as brilliantly lighted as it was years ago for the parties), appears to be burning, "at the end of the road" near "the smoking dump." Muncy almost expects to see Caddy on the porch. Most of the people came to the parties from nearby towns—imported, like Caddy herself. But, as in Faulkner's "A Rose for Emily," the townspeople get their chance. They come in droves not only to view her body more closely than when she was alive, but to go upstairs, a place foreign to most of them, and to touch her belongings.

Peg wonders if a wedding is being held. In the "lightblind rooms" the town, having missed the wedding, is attending its own wake. "Life—with a capital—was not what it used to be . . . Once, if one could somehow believe it, they had been in love." With the current off, the doomed town, like Aunt Angie, is more dead than alive; without "a past or a future," it is "just passing the time until one of these prospects came along."

Aunt Angie, "an old bear at the front of her cave," enters the room, "from the old world, that is, into the new one." The ghost of the townspeople's folly, haunting, reproaching, mocking them, even for regretting what they have not done, she feels "again what she had known all the time. The folly of it. They were witless. And now they were dead." Even when Muncy was a kid, Angie imagined that the Dead Wagon (once a prairie schooner) often passed her window; in a wishful ceremony, Caddy and the other foolish elements in the town went, bit by bit, to the graveyard. But perhaps Caddy wins a partial victory. Now that she is dead, her light may burn feebly in those who couldn't stand the glare when she was alive.

During the previous evening, Muncy had failed to see Caddy alive; and, as a boy he never really saw her face, for it was always withdrawn, Pan-like, into one of her flowered hats. Although the magnet seems to have lost its power, Muncy is the witness most fully charged. But now he is afraid to look upon the corpse of the promise of the past: "For I knew that more had died, upstairs, than I had reckoned with. I had also died, and the gist of my life was to be born again"—in the territory ahead, in the present. It is appropriate that the day of Caddy's death and of Muncy's return coincide.

As he turns from the window, the past in Muncy now casts a shadow in the future. He tips his "rear-view mirror to keep the light out of it," a gesture symbolizing his rejection of the captivity of the past. The light that matters is in him, not behind him in the attic. But the "magic" glass ball on the sewing machine is broken. Bud and his line will inherit and prevail. He will perhaps relate to his children the incidents of the past, but he will fail to grasp their significance. And he will live in Caddy's house, but fail to know its holiness. However, Clyde Muncy, being both in and out of this world, will cherish and constantly repossess, as he moves in the world, the heroic essence of what he has discovered in the attic. In the beginning, Muncy confronted both the unprocessed past and the present reality of the town. In the end, through the ceremony of Caddy's death, nausea results in compassion and revelation, and in a beginning of order and meaning.

In both homecoming novels, there is pathos in Muncy's realization that the old, which holds at least a nebulous promise of sustenance even for the exile and which has lured him back in search of its essential meaning, is passing; with the new generation, those very urban things from which he is trying to escape are creeping into the country. But past and present blend and become assimilated in Muncy. Having observed life on both sides of the meridian, he consciously transforms with imagination what he sees and thus escapes being crippled by the past. He keeps the best of it alive in the archetypal forms of art, which, shorn of clichés and inessentials, live forever. Although his life lacks harmony, he has the will to unity. There is a mythic lyricism in his confrontation of the past, and the resulting compassion is almost heroic. But Muncy cannot go home again because only the shell remains; the indweller has shriveled and all but dissolved into dust. Freedom from nostalgia is freedom to what? That question Muncy has yet to answer.

CHAPTER 4

Emotional and Mystical Works of Love

D RAWING HEAVILY from the store of memory common to the first five novels in which Will Brady is prefigured in Dudley, Will Ward, and Will Muncy, *The Works of Love* is a symbolic narrative that gives mythic expression to most of the previous themes and elements. Although some critics regard this book as a failure, I agree with those who feel it is one of Morris' most convincing.

The Works of Love is a pivotal volume in the author's grapple with his raw material and his developing sense of craft. A manuscript of more than 300,000 words was reduced to aproximately 80,000. The result is perhaps more in the nature of a tone poem than a novel, introducing elements and characters that give rise to later books.

Near the turn of the century, William Jennings Brady was born in Indian Bow, Nebraska. After the death of his parents, he quits his job with the station agent and strikes out for civilization. Thus begins Will's involvement with a series of jobs, towns, houses, women, and with an adopted boy. Will is night clerk in the hotel at Calloway, builds an empire in the chicken business, becomes a sorter of waybills, and finally impersonates Santa Claus for Montgomery Ward. In Calloway, he is a lover of a middle-aged prostitute and befriends a younger one; he marries his boss's widow who leaves him when she discovers that he has been seen with a young cigar-counter girl in Omaha. He marries "the Girl." When she runs away, Will wanders the streets, talking to children. Although "the Girl" returns, she has changed. Will leaves her in Los Angeles and goes to Chicago. One day, in his Santa Claus costume, he half-intentionally stumbles into the canal and drowns. "A man who headed no cause, fought in no wars, and passed his life unaware of the great public issues—it might be asked: why trouble with such a man at all? What is there left to say of a man with so much of his life left out?" His might be the story of "the man who was more or less by himself."

In Sherwood Anderson's fiction, Morris probably recognized his own flesh. Will Brady is like Hugh McVey of Anderson's *Poor White;* he is also patterned to an appreciable extent after Morris' father.[1] The styles, the characters, and some of the themes of the two authors invite comparison. Anderson's effect on Morris is most evident in *The Works of Love,* which is dedicated to him. But Morris wrote his novel before reading Anderson's "The Triumph of the Egg." "The small, small world, the large, *large* egg," Morris explains (Letter). He often explores the territory Anderson pioneered.

The novel is narrated in the third person from Will's point of view. Although Morris, in using the clichés of Will's life and outlook to define him, may seem to use them against him, Will is Morris' most compassionate character study. The pervasive tone of detached humor, sometimes compassionately satirical, saves the novel from either morbidity or sentimentality; even in lyrical moments the humorous tone creates balance and distance.

Three major themes in *The Works of Love* are: (1) the "blighting" effect of a single-minded pursuit of the American Dream of Success; (2) the consequent frustration of various emotional works of love whose failure may lead one to a limited success in (3) mystical works of love. An examination of these themes may provide a close look at the American character as revealed in the life of Will Brady.

I *The American Dream: Real, but Hollow*

In the Great American Desert, the American Dream of Success both flowered and withered: "In the dry places, men begin to dream. Where the rivers run sand, there is something in man that begins to flow." Men like Brady, who thrive on dreams, often welcome ready-made ones. In one view of the American dream, anything and everything is possible for everyman. But since the Nebraskan and the American past are both mythic and real, the concept of the American dream, based on the clichés of the past, conflicts with the often nightmarish realities of American life. Contrary to reality, Will succeeds as easily as the myth promises. But Morris shows that, once translated into reality, the dream becomes like the "giant brooding" statue of Abraham Lincoln himself—soft green with corrosion.

During the westward trek, excess baggage had to be shucked. In Nebraska, the navel of the world, part of that excess got dumped; and some people were content to stop and live on it. Individuality, not abundance, was what the pioneers craved. Will does not witness the real heroism out of which the storybook idea of success was fabricated, an idea which is worshiped by men who seek compensation for their own emotional and spiritual lacks. In Will Brady, Morris has created an archetypal character who symbolizes the American myth of the dream of success, an outgrowth of the myth of the pioneer spirit. He exemplifies the American character and spirit as it has failed; but, in the manner of its failing, it has somehow succeeded.

If there was for young Will a world east of the prairie, it had no reality. Had Will not been stirred by the look of the people in the dining cars of trains that passed quickly through Indian Bow, he might have stayed put. Emotionally starved, he reached out not for what they *had* but for what he thought they *were*—connected through each other to something grand. He goes to Calloway to make such a connection. Although he moves easily into potential love situations, they never pan out. However, when business opportunities come along, he never fails to respond spontaneously. In the absence of love, he responds to the romance of big ideas as to a magnet. Ironically, the innocence and sense of wonder, which foster emotional and spiritual love, contribute instead to his almost accidental material rise with the Midwest itself.

Married, a father, and living in a fine house among the finer things, Will is enticed by the American dream as personified by T. P. Luckett, prototype of the go-getter, the booster. "Will Brady had never thought of himself in such terms. Whether he was an up-and-coming man, and ought to be up-and-coming with the east, or whether what he was doing or not doing was wasting his time. He simply did it. That was the end of it." Like so many men who are persuaded the rainbow cliché has them in mind, Will would just as soon *not* do what is necessary to become a man of caliber. There is a double pull at the heart of Midwestern character: complacency in the backwash of the flood of Westward expansion and imitation of Eastern go-getterness. As Will tells Luckett, " 'In a way, I like it here' " in Calloway.

But infected by Luckett with the go-getter virus, Will begins to come under the spell of such bewildering terms as "carriage trade" and the magic of the American sell. The egg business involves a kind of magic that appeals to his solitary and dreamy temperament. A clumsy man, he responds to eggs with a gentle touch, perhaps because he senses in them the miracle of life rather than their ability to feed men and make money. However, having tasted of finer things, his family's appetite will grow. So the consumption of cars, clothes, and houses begins; but Will's spirit and his emotions remain where they always were—nowhere.

Too busy making a fortune to live a life, Will neglects his

family, for whom, presumably, he has built the business. Always an outsider, even in relation to his own material success and failure, he feels no connection with anything in the life his fortune has wrought. Related to each man's dream of success is the dream of "the finest house money can buy." But a theme in most of Morris' novels is the inability of a man to feel at home in his own house. Will was reared in a sod house "such as a prairie dog might have made" where there was "nothing but the sky that pressed on the earth with the dead weight of the sea." In Calloway he lives in the Merchant's Hotel where he works. He envies his boss's home, but after he marries his widow, the view of the tracks, the semaphores, and the trains become the greatest source of peace the house has to offer. Will repeatedly acts on the "ad"-world illusion that another house, another town, will bring himself and his family closer together. He buys a fine house in Murdock for the first wife and an even finer one in Omaha for the second, but he is a stranger to most of the rooms: "Homelike? Well, that was said to be the word for it." He "sometimes marveled at this strange fellow . . . known all over the state as an up and coming man of caliber. A man who lived in the basement of his fine new thirteen-room house," so as not to disturb anyone, especially himself.

Will senses the irony and futility of his life. One who has arrived, he is bewildered by a feeling that he is nowhere. His compass watch tells him "as nothing else would, about where he was." One day, like Sherwood Anderson, Will simply walks away from his empire. But it is not a willful, traumatic severance, since nothing was ever in a true sense his—neither the houses he owned but did not live in, the wives he married but could not love, the child (not really his) whom he never knew, nor the business that was the dream come true but that had nothing of the truth in it. Only the undiscovered world of the spirit, where something may yet happen, is his.

It is that world toward which he is always tending. He leaves the West to Tom Scanlon, "fixed in the mythic past," and he strikes out upon the always open road of promise, "toward an intolerable future." In pursuit of love, he cuts himself off from roots that strangle as much as they nourish. If in Calloway it is doubtful he ever could have connected through love and imagination with the objects and the human relationships of permanence, in Chicago nothing is permanent in the quotidian sense except his hopeless and disguised feeling of loss. What did he lose? What most men lose—a chance for human fulfillment.

Unlike Arthur Miller's Willy Loman—that collective symbol of the middle-class go-getter—whom, in his responses to the clichés of success, he in some ways resembles, Will is not a victim. He simply *is* what he happens to *be;* he ends in the canal largely because he began on the prairie. But, as with Willy Loman, the symbolic stature of Will Brady gives tragic consequence to his fall. In his personal fall, the American Dream collapses. He exemplifies the American's "appalling and visible freedom to be blighted" emotionally more than materially.

II *Emotional Works of Love:*
Will Brady as Father, Lover, and Husband

The American male talks business but dreams of love on pagan islands; in business, as well as in love, he is deluded by the ideal which the American myth tells him is his for the asking. When faced with the complexities of love, Will takes refuge in business. He is never avaricious; material things merely occupy the emptiness he has no love to fill. He responds to anything that takes him out of himself into what promises to be a world better than that into which he was born, and later, to anything that takes him out of the world he has made. He fails to build with love something he can love. A man of paradoxes, Will exemplifies two major aspects of the American character: a surface gregariousness that makes for material success but works in denial of an extremely inarticulate and stunted emotional complexity.

Throughout his novels, Morris explores the various works of love among kith and kin. "The longest sustained and most explicit quest for love is that of Brady," says Wayne Booth (14). The emotional history of America comes to an impasse in Will Brady. One senses his unarticulated love-hunger on every page; the book is a ceremony of the human will to love. But, in his failure to achieve consummation, he inspires little more than pity. The reader becomes a compassionate witness to the frustrations of love, caused partly by Will's lack of a self-knowledge that can lead to an understanding of the everyday humanity of others.

In Will's life one observes the pathetic longing of Americans for roots in the permanence of love. There is a paradox in the nature of many men: a crying need for love, resisted by a fearful unwilling- ness to give of oneself and a desire for non-engagement; the result is inability to receive love. As D. H. Lawrence says in the epigraph: "We cannot bear connection. That is our malady." Will's central problem is that his willing attempts to give love are distorted by his inability to receive it. Since his abilities are limited, love is seldom offered him. He only succeeds in attracting other emotionally unfinished grotesques. Eventually, Will is thrown back in despair upon the Great American Desert in himself. He never leaves the land of his father, Adam: "He could leave it, that is, but he could never get over it."

The forms of Will's emotional loves go from his youthful lust for a whore, to a middle-aged response to young girls, to identification with movie pagan lovers. Before Will is mature enough to be a lover or a husband, chance makes of him a "father." With Mickey Ahearn, the youngest of the Calloway whores, Will for the first time makes emotional contact with a female—but as a father, not as a lover. Women are always leaving Will. She is the first, but she sends him her infant boy to raise. As for his fatherly duties, "once or twice a week he bounced the boy on his knee in a horsey manner, and let him play with the elastic arm bands on his sleeves." Once, the Boy tries to communicate with his father. In the washroom of the Paxton Hotel, he asks, "'Why are you so different?'" Will, who knew from the beginning "that talking was going to be something of a problem for both of them," turns on the water, trying to flush the question down the drain. Many fathers seem only to have adopted strangers.

In Chicago, Will connects with his "son" through strangers in the park and waitresses. By showing them the letter the Boy writes once a year from Nebraska, he endows it with a potency that will ultimately communicate more to him than the superficial words connote. What he does not know about the Boy, he makes up. "'Oh, how he must love you!'" they all say. But somehow he finds that hard to picture. In his telegraphic manner, Will writes ten or fifteen post cards, intending to mail them when he gets more homelike quarters. The last one (which appears also in *The Inhabitants* and in *Ceremony in Lone Tree*) reads: "Dear Son — Have moved. Have nice little place of our own now, two-plate gas. Warm sun in windows every morning, nice view of park. Plan to get new Console radio soon now, let you pick it out. Plan to pick up car so we can drive out in country, get out in air. Turning over in my mind plan to send you to Harvard, send you to Yale. Saw robin in park this morning. Saw him catch worm." The post card *does* reach the Boy since Will's feelings for him are based on a spiritual reality stronger than blood, a creation of will and imagination: "A man, a boy, and a dream of the ever open road" where everything is possible. For Morris, blood kinship alone sustains very little of value.

Will has more success with Manny Plinski, a seventeen-year-old half-wit, who shows his affection for Will by putting his favorite turtles in the old man's pants pocket. Manny is a partial mute whose speech is garbled, but Will seems to understand him pretty well. "They had found there was very little that needed talking about." For people like Will (and perhaps even for articulate people), the ability to speak often intimidates the free flow of love; mute, they may achieve metaphysical communication.

Will is a child to the older women in his life; a father to the younger ones. With the prostitute Opal Mason, he is a child-lover. Lover "might seem an odd way to describe a man who brought nothing along, said nothing loving, and left a good deal up to the woman, to say the least." With the widow, he is a child-husband. He would settle for *one* woman like his boss's wife, although, when she looks into his face, she never seems to see anything. Their "romance" is subtle and non-erotic; he marries her.

On their honeymoon, Will finds his wife "rolled up tight in the sheet... wrapped from head to foot" like a mummy. Something like that, he realizes, takes practice and fear. After a sleepless night, he gains less insight into his own life in the future than into the life his boss must have lived. He feels neither anger nor dislike but pity for the dead husband and for the woman, who seems ready for burial. *He* sleeps next to the wool blanket, perfect symbol of his sexual life. After several nights, he grows indifferent; and she, sensing his attitude, gives up her sheet, an act which he regards as a compliment, "perhaps the highest he had ever been paid." Only in public, their bodies brushing slightly, do they touch. He learns to do for her what her son had done: "He had discovered, in this strange way, something about loving, about pity, and a good deal about hooks and eyes and corset strings." But when they return to domestic life in Calloway, the promise of what might be, built on that nominal intimacy, fades: "The woman who spoke his name was a stranger again, his wife."

Another version of Mickey Ahearn turns up in "the Girl." In bed, "the Girl," like Opal Mason, wants to talk. To Will, listening is another form of loving, the kind women need. For "the Girl," sex is merely what brings two people together. Will marries "the Girl." Afterwards, both she and the Boy look at him "very much as if he were an impostor." His role as father and husband is confounded when both the Boy and "the Girl" are mistaken for his children. Living in a room cut off from Will, they behave as though they are.

When "the Girl" runs away and the Boy goes to live with a neighbor, Will wanders the streets to find what he has lost (but never really had). He meets a "nymphet" who sells kisses. She is a younger version of the girls he has known. During the day, he handles eggs, "but during the night there was nothing he could grasp like that with his hands." He wants to touch the little girl's silly, out-of-date hat to connect with her and with all the other women he has felt anything for. The book is full of mute human contacts and ways in which talismanic artifacts help the lover relate to the loved one.

When "the Girl," his wife, returns to him, he takes her to Los Angeles, where "they would both begin, as he had read in books, their life over again." She tells Will that she was beguiled by him because he didn't seem to know what to do with himself. "Maybe what she felt was love . . . the day that she saw that he was hopeless —or maybe what she felt was something else." Most women are attracted to Morris males by this hopeless quality.

Alone, Will goes to Chicago, where sensual love puts comfortably at a distance the love he was incapable of feeling intimately. One night he stops at the lobby doors of a movie theater to hear the love song of a pagan lover, "as if there was a crack in his world and he could see into another one." " '*Come with me*,' the pagan lover would sing, and Will Brady would. . . . What kind of love was it? The doors usually closed before he found out. He might have bought a ticket, but perhaps he didn't want to know. It was enough for him to know that the young lover was there, still doing what he could." Sometimes it seems to Will that he has died but that his eyes, looking backwards and forwards at the same time, are still open. "An old sorter of waybills and a pagan lover at the same time." And thus would seem to end the love song of Will Jennings Brady. But there is another side to the old, cracked record.

III   *Mystical Works of Love:*
From "The Wilderness" to "The Wasteland"

On the other side, the refrain is one of mystic love. The pioneers started out with what they thought were only the essentials, but they found at various stages that fewer and fewer things were needed, including themselves. In western Nebraska especially, the traveler can see what Morris saw as a boy—everything kept down to the essentials. Stripped down, like the mystic, the plainsman must have often felt, as Brady does, both in and out of this world. His perception of his environment is direct, exhibiting "the simple and steady looking-upon a thing" that Bergson calls intuition. He learns intuitively that one must go beyond what seems real, beyond oneself, to a greater reality. Uprooted from one wasteland and transplanted in another (Chicago), Brady seeks a way "to live in this world, so to speak, and yet somehow be out of it."

Morris' double vision pertains even to mysticism: while its traditional seriousness is retained, mysticism is used in an almost comic or sardonic manner in both *The Man Who Was There* and

The Works of Love. The theme of the latter book and Morris'
recurring interest in the pathetic progress of American life from
"Wilderness" to "Wasteland" are reflected in the symbolic titles of
the sections. If we follow Will's physical journey, we may see the
development of his mystical inclinations. From innocence of the
world, he is drawn through the material world in response to a general ideal; when he rejects the world, he embodies a specific ideal,
the cliché-innocence of Santa Claus. From response to the outer
world and people, he responds to and finally merges with man in
the inner world of the spirit. From the unpopulated emptiness of
the plains, he moves to a metropolis where he is compelled to make
a physical response to the mystical by leaping into the canal. He
passively idealizes what he doesn't understand. He moves in awe
through a world that is real and belongs only to others, and he is
amazed when his own relevance to it is pointed out. Will's is the
American spirit that wants to reach out, to love and be a part of
everything; but he mistakes appearances for the real thing, so that
he is often victimized by his own Romantic wonder. The dichotomy
in his nature is that he feels the reality of the spirit; but he is
persuaded, throughout most of the book, to work at the reality
of things.

In "The Wilderness" of Indian Bow, what exists for Will to
respond to Morris puts into one paragraph: "At times this empty
world seemed unreal," and he felt "he was the last real man in it."
A pure emptiness within him reflects the wide, flat plains outside
him. The landscape and the inscape blend. In some ways, this is
the story of a man who, given what he had to build on, did what he
could. In Calloway, he begins to connect with man through the
artifacts around him. Smelling the mop in the Merchant's Hotel, he
feels in harmony with his environment. The novel is redolent of the
smell and palpable with the feel of *things*.

In Murdock, Will enters "The Clearing" which the material world
has made. The smell of sick and of dead chickens on himself is
probably his first intuitive contact with the metaphysical: "It made
a man wonder, and wonder makes a religious man." His wonder
compels him to see in the thing itself something more than meets
the naked eye.

In "In the Moonlight" he is kept awake by wondering what keeps
his neighbor awake. In solitude, his imagination takes him into the
rooms of his neighbors' houses where he becomes a part of their
lives and dreams; then he becomes an explorer who ventures into
the interior of his own house. As a witness, he achieves a mystical
compassion and kinship with all lonely men. The pathos lies in his
inability to communicate what he feels, for mystical experiences

are ineffable. Ironically, he is respected as a man wise in the ways of the world. When, as a prominent citizen, he spouts clichés, men tell him, " 'Bygod, Brady . . . there you said something.' . . . Had he? Well, nothing you could put your finger on." Will Brady is the man who *wants* to say something. The dead language at his service conveys only banality.

If, in rooms made for the purpose of coming face to face with people one knows, Will finds it impossible to connect, he feels at home in places like "The Lobby." In *The American Scene*, Henry James wonders if the hotel lobby "may not just *be* the American spirit most seeking and most finding itself." It seemed to James the "realized ideal of . . . the supremely gregarious state . . . one of my few glimpses of perfect human felicity." (*Territory*, 207-9). Morris says: "It is the purpose of hotel lobbies to take you out of the life you are living, to a better life, or a braver, more interesting one. . . . There in the lobby the other life is possible." There in the crowded lobby in Los Angeles "bigger than life, was Paradise on the American Plan. A hotel lobby, that is, as big as the great out-of-doors."

In "In the Cloudland" Will sees nothing unreal about the bizarre props of the Hollywood world as compared with the real life he observes in Pershing Square. Like the pigeons, the old men there have "given up the notion of being some fancier kind of bird." One old bum feeds the pigeons morning and evening by "wetting the hard dry bread in his mouth, rolling it into a ball, then feeding this spittle to the birds" to give his own spirit flight. "Was there any man, Will Brady asked himself, who didn't understand something like that? Who wouldn't like, that is, to be fed to the birds himself?" Having begun with chickens, Will does not agree that such men are "wacky"; theirs is simply one of many ways to make love. "Put it this way: he felt right at home with them," with transformations. Brady becomes like the old man whose vision suspends him between heaven and earth and on whose face is "the rapt gaze of a holy man." The "religious" experience occurs in the moment when a character directly confronts another thing in such a way as to take him out of himself, but it is valid only for the moment.

Morris' epigraph from Blake is probably used ironically: "Grown old in Love from Seven till Seven times Seven / I oft have wished for Hell for Ease from Heaven." Will leaves the heaven of California and enters "The Wasteland" of modern civilization, completing a cycle; for in Chicago he is back in "The Wilderness" of his own soul and spirit. What other lodgers refer to as a stink in the rooms above the delicatessen, Will knows to be the smell of man coming from the canals; it often revives him. Where his spirit most expands, his body is cramped. A runner of green rat poison leads up the stairs to his tiny room, "suitable for light housekeeping." Like Will, the room has no physical identity, and he "does his living somewhere else"—in the switch tower where he works at night.

Having intuitively felt a lack of sustenance in reality, he transforms himself; he creates with imagination, like an artist, his own life as he goes along, doing what he can within his capacity. For instance, he dresses up in his best clothes, seats himself in the lobby of a fine hotel, and has himself paged—to make connection with the man he once was. But like many people in the book, he is always too much *out* of, never enough *in*, this world. He makes substitutions for the real thing until the reality of this world consists in the realness of substitutions. Certain things throw him into himself, others draw him out of himself; but the middle ground sinks beneath his feet.

In the tower in the freight yards, sorting waybills, Will feels more alive than anywhere else. At the large window facing east, smelling the lake and the canal, he feels like the man in the canal drawbridge, "in charge of the flow of traffic, of the city itself. All that he saw seemed to be in his province, under his control"; and it is, because his imagination encompasses and pervades it. In this nocturnal communion, he feels he is back "where he started from"—"the empty world in the valley" where he often felt "he was the last man in the world." As a boy, he stood outside looking into train windows; now, inside the tower, he looks out on the city and man. Paradoxically, in the tower cut off from it, he feels a part of what he sees. That something in man, in Will, that begins to flow in the dry places of "The Wilderness" comes out in the canal of "The Wasteland."

Will's ironic role as Santa Claus is a gesture of heroism, a final pathetic effort to live at once realistically and mystically among men, "to be mortal, and immortal at the same time." Booth says that Will "re-creates, re-imagines the ideal of disinterested love" (9). The effect of a sunlamp which he used to transform himself into a healthy-looking Santa Claus blinds him. He stumbles out the back door of Montgomery Ward. What he sees through his bleary eyes looks like an inferno—the smell is acrid, the air "blown to him, so it seemed, by the bellows of hell." But the odor that poisons most men is to him the breath of life. On his face is "the look of a man with a vision" as he staggers toward the water, "toward the great stench as if he would grasp it, make it his own." Found in his pockets when he is dragged from the canal are turtles and a post card to his son. His tragi-pathetic need for love and permanence could be satiated only in the canal, symbol of the decay of the American spirit and of the breakdown of the American dream.

He immolates himself in his love of humanity, in the mystical smell of mankind, in the canal, where the spirits of a multitude of other hopeless men flow everlastingly.

But Morris' mysticism is, paradoxically, a down-to-earth mysticism, a means of connecting with this world, of making the most of immediate experience, of plugging into the eternal present. Non-religious mysticism is one of the oldest kinds; Buddhism, for instance, posits no god. But though a man may not have *religious* experiences with reference to a definite creed, he may feel a connection with something sacred; such are Muncy's feelings after communing with Uncle Ed's house. Morris makes no great effort to lend absolute authority to the mystical element in his books, for he would probably agree with Walter T. Stace that even if the mystical experience "is wholly subjective, it still reveals something which is supremely great in human life. . . . [It is a] gateway to salvation—not, I mean, in a future life, but as the highest beatitude that a man can reach in this life, and out of which the greatest deeds of love can flow."

If his human emotions are stagnant, Will's spirit transforms; but he fails to transform the ordinary in *its* realm. In his infinite solitude, he becomes intuitively aware of human possibilities; but he cannot translate them into living behavior. He never becomes a part of the ordinary world of human relationships which must serve as a basis of departure—to know things beyond oneself, one has first to know oneself. Yet he does possess a wisdom that lies in the "ability to subject oneself profoundly to experience." But even the mystical response is one-way. He can respond through a conventional public symbol—playing Santa Claus to mankind—but he never achieves a reciprocal relationship.

With *The Works of Love,* Morris leaves the attic. He returns to it, however, in *The Field of Vision* and *Ceremony in Lone Tree;* in these the world directly confronts the attic.

CHAPTER 5

The Dynamics of Morris'
Style and Technique

ALTHOUGH Morris' style does not change basically, it is in refinements of technique that *Man and Boy* and *The Deep Sleep* (to be discussed in the next chapter) differ from Morris' previous works and mark an advance in his development as a craftsman. The techniques developed and the surer control of style achieved in these novels probably enabled him to return with greater control to the raw material of the plains. As one approaches the more complex novels, a few observations on his style and his structural techniques are appropriate, for they sometimes obstruct comprehension and appreciation.

I *Style as Action*

Morris is not, as he has sometimes been called, a Realist. "Anything, anything," he says, "which takes us back to realism as the *real* thing is a retrogression."[1] Realism as a *genre* cannot escape the clichés produced by the rendering of character and event in sequential time. All his books "testify to the function of verisimilitude: the life-like look that conveys" a "sense of life so real it evokes a little more than life," for "the artist's problem is to let the facts" he chooses to reveal "speak for themselves" ("Privacy," 51). Thus, the reviewer who referred to the "murderously meticulous household detail" in *Man and Boy* was simply under the impression (one the author intended to create) that Morris had recorded every realistic detail.

In 1951 Morris said, "If I once believed that there could be no peace until everything had been said, I now seem to believe that such talk would make peace impossible." Revelation, then, becomes "the problem of stating what remains unsaid" ("Privacy," 55). Morris' under-writing often results in seeming superficiality. "Underwriting—which seems to be a species of under-water swimming—

has its many disadvantages, and that is one," says Morris. "Is the pool empty? That is how it often looks" (Letter). He is overt only in the matter of evaluation; he may be explicit, as James is, about meaning.

Morris wants "to use a minimum of words for a maximum effect" (*Twentieth Century Authors*, 691). His style is simple but rich in nuance. He has remarked on the "resonant density" of James's mind; the phrase applies as well to his own. Like James, Morris uses the parenthetical phrase with masterful effectiveness as a device: to complicate, to delay, to create a humorous tone, to convey a sense of mock dignity, and to maintain a sense of objectivity. This device and the one of reversing the normal syntactical structure of sentences create subtlety or point up crucial words or phrases; they often help create a rhetorical tension that sustains interest in the absence of overt action. As he is never really out of, though never entirely in, the minds of his characters, his frequent and effective use of the sentence fragment is one of the dictates of his style.

Morris sustains a harmony of tone in his style by successfully blending his third-person narrative prose with the speech and thoughts of his characters. He knows how to make the contrast between different sensibilities engrossing and meaningful; for example, one may compare Webb's sophisticated wit and sarcasm with Mrs. Porter's telegraphic, cryptic mode of expression in *The Deep Sleep*. The overall nature of his style lends itself easily to the various levels of character sophistication. At his best, no author has seemed so much at home in his style since James and Hemingway. If the texture of Morris' prose receives the kind of close attention it demands, one experiences one of the finest sensations his novels provide.

Some readers lament the absence of action in Morris. The narrative action in *Man and Boy* and the *The Deep Sleep*, for instance, is not strong enough to support the heavy symbolic freight in the two novels. But most of the so-called dramatic events in Morris occur off the novelistic stage; onstage is enacted the drama of human consciousness. Within narrow limitations of time and place, the sensibilities of his characters, infected with "the virus of suggestion" and involved in the process of conceptualizing, actively respond to ordinary events: the active sensibility *is* action. Conflicts between inner attitudes generate internal action, rendered in such a way that external action would be distracting. Not narrative action, but relationship, revealing meaning, is important. The particular fascination is in Morris' manner of relating the outer lives and the psyches of his characters, of creating a congruence of outer and inner reality. This is essentially a triumph of style. In *Love Among the Cannibals,* the swift pace is generated more by the style than by the action it describes. In *What a Way to Go,* except for swift moments of farce or burlesque, it is style describing moments of perception that creates the amazing sense of motion.

Morris' technique for creating events does not rob his reader of emotional potential. In most novels the kinetic quality of action is depleted in the relationship between the author's raw material and his treatment of it. The manner of rendering tends to consume, *as* it is being produced, the emotional energy of dramatic event. The reader feels only the heat—he does not participate in the combustion; it has taken place in the creative act itself. But Morris' subdued style puts the relation between the already *processed* material and the reader, whose sensibility is kindled rather than passive. Morris knows that the form of violence often inhibits content and meaning, that it prohibits complexity of feeling, attitude, and response in the reader.

When the dramatic incident threatens to take over, Morris' style reasserts the pre-eminence of process over raw material. Flat expressions, rhetorical devices and clichés, carry the weight of his most important points, his highest moments, so that the ideas, the events, speak for themselves in the contrast between bland language and dynamic meaning. Such an effect I term the *impinged moment:* something more impressive or vivid than the moment, and seemingly unrelated to it, climaxes it—paradoxically *does finish* it. Morris presents the discovery of a flat tire in such a way as to make the manner of the discovering more effective than the thing itself: "A dog sniffed around like it was time. He did it on the gas pump and then he did it on the front wheel. It wasn't till then that I noticed the tire was flat." What would ordinarily amount to humorous detail here has the quality of dominant event. The moment of violence is often impinged by a sardonic gesture that mocks action. This effect reflects the nature of his quiet view of life. Morris says: "My problem as a writer is to dramatize my conception of experience, and it may often exclude, as it often does, the entire apparatus of dramatic action" (Letter).

II   *Time as Structure: "A Technique of Discovery"*[2]

Unity in some of Morris' more intricate novels depends upon an organic point-of-view structure for which time is the generative force. To understand theme, character, symbolism, and narrative sequence, the reader must follow carefully the complex operation of time. Morris' time-viewpoint technique may be found in Faulkner (*The Sound and the Fury,* for instance), and as far back as James

(The Wings of the Dove), Conrad *(Lord Jim)*, and Woolf *(To the Lighthouse)*. But the manner of Morris' variants, partly dependent upon uniqueness of style, is important.

In most of Morris, time is out of joint. Flowing, erratic, static, sometimes seemingly confused, it often operates within a single novel in several ways; time differs as the points of view of the characters differ. A relatively crude multiple-vision technique is used in *The Inhabitants*. In *The Man Who Was There*, Morris risks obscurity with his frequent shifts in point of view. In *Man and Boy*, he for the first time divides a novel into viewpoint sections that alternate repeatedly between two characters. He moves on to the greater complexity of five points of view in *The Deep Sleep*, a combination particularly suited to his talents. These novels are rendered in third person in modified stream-of-consciousness. Thematically, the five points of view combination is most effective in *The Field of Vision*. No less than fourteen points of view alternate in the immediacy of the present during a reunion in *Ceremony in Lone Tree*. A combination of the first-person and the third-person narrative technique is used, though quite differently, in *The Huge Season* and in *Cause For Wonder*. There is a single point of view in *Works of Love* and in *What a Way to Go*, both of which are told in the third person consistently. The four other novels are told consistently in the first person. Thus, Morris experiments with various points of view; and in each experiment he is confronted with new aspects of the problem of time.

Morris has created a fiction of *moments;* his photographs testify vividly to this aspect of his vision. He emphasizes the importance of seizing the immediate present in highly concentrated moments of love, audacity, or imagination, often in the hero-witness relationship. Out of a concept that sees character and time in the same light develops a complicated thematic pattern in which character and event are fragmented. Redefined from moment to moment, time is the ambience in which the novels take form. As time and character point of view function intricately together in a free-associational continuum, point of view reorganizes and structures time. For time is a creation of consciousness; it exists in and for consciousness. Passing through the evaluating consciousness, answering to psychological conditions, time becomes a frame and a quality of mind.

As the sensibilities of the characters respond from differing perspectives and attitudes to the same object, idea, event, or character, they hinge upon or merge into each other. For instance, in *Man and Boy*, Ormsby's first section *ends* with: " 'Ohhhh Mother!' he called, and waited for her to rap on the floor"; Mother's first section *begins* with: "Rapping her mule heels on the floor. . . ."

Thus, moments overlap and are recapitulated, but often at different points; for instance, the reader sees the incident at the New York train station through both Mother's and Ormsby's quite different perspectives. Present moments progress in relation to past moments. Experienced through multiple points of view, past and present fuse, become one immediacy. Since each character throws his own light on time and event, the reader's multi-vision provides him with extraordinarily rich insights into the various relationships.

When action and character are in dynamic psychological inter-play, the reader may experience action and know character simultaneously as each character reflects the same fragment of experience in a vibrant moment of consciousness. Constant reference to the past enables the characters to define their identities. Often, the flowering in the present of meaning seeded in the past constitutes the dramatic reality of the moment. This interaction of past and present results in a mystical timelessness that affects the real world of the character. One of the aims of this technique—truly "technique as discovery," for author, character, and reader—is to make one feel the transformation of raw material through concept and imagination by participating with the characters in going over and over the common experience.

To readers unfamiliar with Morris' total vision, the repetitions and what appears to be looseness of form in the early novels may seem artistic flaws. But, just as they are related in a general way by their themes, all Morris' novels are also specifically and intricately related by repetitions of and variations upon certain characters, incidents, minor ideas, motifs, gestures, artifacts, places, and forms. This relationship is less apparent in the urban novels than in those of the plains. But even the first and the most recent book are related in this way. Grown older, Uncle Dudley and The Kid (as Uncle Fremont Osborn and Warren Howe), reappear, together with many details, in *Cause for Wonder.*

No novel, no body of literary work, is without its effective details, but Morris differs from many writers in imparting to each detail an importance which makes it both a thing in itself and a piece of a complex puzzle. Although each book is an artistic whole, it has a transcendent relationship with previous and, potentially, with future books. "The last book and the book that is to come," Morris says, "are linked imaginatively so that a chain reaction seems to be taking place."

In each novel Morris approaches his raw material from a different perspective. Fresh contexts are created for pieces of the puzzle which either have not yet found their most revealing fit or which fit in various combinations. Some of the same scenes reappear and whole passages from other books are repeated almost word for word. But, although he is haunted by these fragments, he alters or combines. For instance, the new photographic approach partially dictated the reappearance of the barber shop scene from the Agee novel in a greatly altered form in the Muncy novel; in *The World in the Attic*, Muncy merely passes by, Morris having been there before and gotten what he wanted. Since his raw material is rooted in mythic ground, its features re-assert themselves and only variations are necessary. For Morris is less interested in sheer invention than in the transformation of the typical. Out of a scene that is essentially the same in both books come different transformations.

He strives to achieve an objectivity whereby he may escape the captivity of mere nostalgia and avoid immersion in his raw material. According to Morris, he did not calculate these repetitions and variations, which derive from what I call *the common memory store* of the central characters. They evolved out of his constant effort to arrange the pieces of the puzzle, which begin to fit in *The Field of Vision* and finally take shape in *Ceremony in Lone Tree*. Their cumulative effect is to give a sense of unity to the works as a whole and to reflect the nature of his vision.

Obviously, no single work can be considered artistic if it *relies* upon reference to, or build-up from, others; but none of Morris' novels has this reliance. Each is rooted firmly in its own field of vision. However, Morris himself says: "Few writers of my time write so much out of all their books, so that an exposure to all the books in a way is necessary to the book that comes next." He moves "in a kind of circular motion," touching "on the old as I roll forward toward the new" ("Point of View," 36). The result is a feeling of intimacy with the characters and events that is created by no other body of work, except Faulkner's, Wolfe's, or, more recently, Lawrence Durrell's. While the continual changing and multiple viewing explains perhaps the limited impact of some of the novels taken singly, they also explain the "house of mirrors, many-faceted sense of *deja vu*" conveyed by the books taken as a whole. A thorough assimilation of this store of memory provides the reader with a fuller understanding and with a richer perception of each novel. For instance, by the time one, going through the novels in sequence, comes to *The World in the Attic*, Muncy's memories, reactions, and perceptions are one's own.

For Morris, "the prehistoric present" is more effective than straight storytelling via narrative sequence because one of his major themes is the persistence of the past in the present. In *Cause For Wonder*, Warren Howe perceives: "The moment. The given-taken moment contained such time as there was." He has returned to the ruined European castle where George, the madman caretaker, once shoveled snow on him. At the wild close of the day of his return, Howe steps into the courtyard and suddenly panics: "... he had heard, or *thought* he heard, snow sliding from the roof. Heard the soft sibilant hiss of it across thirty years, a meaningless time vacuum. When he had put foot in the court time had picked up where it had stopped, the night the first whispering slide had buried him to the ears." Living in time with intuitive imaginativeness, Howe creates himself from moment to moment.

The process in most of the novels is to accumulate the fragments of a complexity and to assemble in the end something that the mind can comprehend. Man's desire to know himself is the universal element most actively felt in Morris. Amid all the perishables of man's existence, the one imperishable is his faculty to process, to order, to *insinuate* himself into the realm of meaning. In it he realizes that wholeness is all and that, even though that "all" is perhaps unattainable, its pursuit is what makes life meaningful and, above all, bearable; clichés make life tolerable for those who lack the stronger imaginative impulses toward the attainment of meaning. Morris' most conscious characters are faced with the dilemma of what to make of a diminished thing.

Perhaps instead of a history, a tradition, Morris has these fragments which he tries to construct into a meaningful whole. His memory is so vibrant that his characters are engaged in the same act of researching the past, and the structure of his novels is often shaped by the processes of memory. Man's present hold on his life depends upon the extent to which he is able to contract these multiple moments into a single intuitive apprehension. But Morris' prevailing conception persistently denies power to the mere reminiscing impulse in favor of an effort to create and possess coherence, to achieve permanence out of the fluctuations of impermanence. If the discerning, inquiring mind sooner or later emerges nauseated from nostalgia, it is because it naturally recoils from disorder and fragmentation, especially as they affect the past. The positive charge of the past diminishes in many respects in direct proportion to the degree to which the individual fails to make it new by transforming it. "To make new we must reconstruct, as well as resurrect."

CHAPTER 6

Two Views of
the "Great American Home"

MAN AND BOY (1951)—published before *The Works of Love*— and *The Deep Sleep* (1953) are the first of Morris' novels to depart from the persistent plains environment, although they are prefigured in earlier novels and developed in later ones. The crowded, "untamed station wagon country" contrasts with the open, untamed plains. In suburban Philadelphia, the microcosm of family and home is the focus for close observations on middle-class manners on the American scene. The family relationship, symbolic or actual, is the immediate social context for most of Morris' novels.

With the shift in setting, there is also a difference in the women. Mrs. Ormsby and Mrs. Porter of *Man and Boy* and *The Deep Sleep* are the first female forces to be observed in *direct* action. Archetypal mothers, they reject the defunct male West and "make do" in the East. But, as Philip Wylie has indicated, the influence of the "momarchs" knows no geographical bounds: "Our land, subjectively mapped, would have more silver cords and apron strings criss-crossing it than railroads and telephone wires."[1] The males remain spiritually situated over "drafty privies," each feeling like the last man on earth. In the house, run by Mrs. Ormsby's and Mrs. Porter's principles, the wilderness and the wasteland meet. Making "a frontal attack on the hideout—the Great American Home"—of the "pussy cat with a blood curdling roar," Morris "soon found he was in No Man's Land."[2]

I   Man and Boy: *Momarchy*

Present events in *Man and Boy* cover about five hours sometime during World War II in the lives of Warren K. Ormsby and his wife, whom he calls Mother. Heroically missing in action (like Agee), the Ormsbys' son, Virgil, is being honored by having a ship named after him; Mother is to christen it. Almost half the novel is concerned with the train trip to New York, during which Ormsby meets Private Lipido, a soldier, who invites himself to the ceremony. They proceed by car to the East Side slums where Mrs. Dinardo, a friend of Mother's, joins them. In the final quarter of the book, Mother, Mrs. Dinardo, Commander Sudcliffe, and his wife go in one car, Ormsby and Lipido in another to the Brooklyn pier, where the ceremony occurs. Mother has a skirmish with the navy from which she emerges triumphant.

Symbolically, the novel's form is ceremonial. The actual ceremony of greeting at the station is less important than the symbolically theatrical ceremony in the slums. The ceremony begins with the ritual of Ormsby's and Mother's simple morning routine. Every morning, Mother pulls the light cord and intones, "'Fiat lux,'" a gesture which reaffirms her status as goddess. The order of her life is reflected in this ritual: "Ready and waiting, her gloves with her purse, her purse with the eggs, the eggs with her coat, Mother picked up the receiver and dialed the number on the pad." The book is full of urban ritual and gesture, which augment style and meaning. The events, including the christening, constitute simultaneously a funeral and a rebirth ceremony. Since it is Mother who presides over this extended ceremony, one should look more closely at her and at the American male-female conflict out of which she long ago emerged victorious.

Mother stands for "social formulation, rectitude, decorum, prohibition, inhibition, permission," among other things; Latin tags and biblical maxims, distorted for her own purposes, apply to most situations and her glittering generalizations cover the ground. Telegraphic notes left all over the house are her main form of communication with Ormsby. "They sometimes had something like a conversation between the first and the second floors, but it stopped the moment one of them came into view." She talks to herself and, as events occur, mentally describes them to Mrs. Dinardo. On the telephone she is fluent, and sometimes even laughs. Her anger is quiet, but lethal. "Somehow it always took him by surprise. And after all of these times it never left him anything at all but sick." A feature editorial recently proclaimed that "Mother had, single-handed, saved a good part of the nation for the quail." But she has turned the house into a no man's land for Ormsby. His every move during the morning reveals his fear of waking her: "Carrying his shoes, Mr. Ormsby followed the throw rugs to the closet, like a man crossing a swift stream on blocks of ice." A girl of the old school, Mother "made life a little harder in some ways, but in other ways where in the world would you find a woman to match."

As a girl, Mother learned that in dealing with her mortal enemy, the male, it is best to "use the element of surprise." In dealing with Ormsby and the Boy, she employs the element of mystification. She tries to save money by using a piece of soap in a wire cage to make suds. They never appear, so Ormsby keeps a tiny bag of soap powder hidden and sneaks it into the water. " 'You see—?' Mother would say, as the water began to suds, and hold up the stale button of soap for him to admire. He always did. It was getting to be something he believed in himself." This is an example of Mother's effect in minor ways (ways which mount up) on Ormsby.

But the male has failed the female, just as the West has failed to rise above the East. The frontier has been won by male brawn and daring, and now the female manages it and the male descendants of the men who won it, according to the rules of the house. Because modern American civilization is in many ways oriented to her, Mother can best rule it. Mother's first lines are: "Rapping her mule heels on the floor she said: 'Modern man is obsolete, Mrs. Dinardo.' " But, says Morris, "as of now both man and woman are tragically duped: the Victor has no way of digesting the spoils" (Letter). Faced with what Leslie Fiedler calls "the anti-mother made flesh" and with the spectacle of his father's submission, it is little wonder that Virgil bolted from the jigsaw puzzle of his life scattered on the floor and took refuge in "the universal sanctuary of the war." Virgil "had been missing, some people would say, for a good many years."

But Virgil turns up again on the day of the christening because both Mother and Ormsby are transformers; *Man and Boy* is a ceremony of major and minor symbolic transformations. The male-female conflict is sometimes subtle indeed. It takes the form of an unconscious battle between Ormsby and Mother for possession of the Boy. Mother can live in the present because she creates it from moment to moment. Having lost the real boy of the past, she is enabled through his rebirth in the ship to possess him in the present. Because Ormsby moves so timorously in the present created by Mother, he strives to resurrect the Boy through intercourse with the past in the basement and in the attic.

Mother is a kind of heroic influence (unconsciously), and Ormsby is the principal witness. The male, the dreamer, transforms only in his imagination and experiences compassion (however, unlike Agee and Muncy, Ormsby doesn't realize he strives for imaginative possession); the female drives him deeper into a waking dream by her ability to cause transformations in present human relationships through action. If one follows these moments of transformation as they parallel each other in the past and the present throughout the book, one may observe the conceptual control Morris exerts over his raw material.

II *A Ceremony of Transformations*

As spectator, Ormsby is able to evaluate his relationship with the Boy from a distance and to achieve the major recognition in the novel. Mother occasions Ormsby's moments of revelation regarding both Virgil and herself. For instance, the first preparation for these moments comes in a recurrent nightmare whose character Mother determines; for, even in sleep, he cannot escape her influence. In the dream, he is cut off from his son, even in death. But with Private Lipido, he improvises upon a father-son relationship which frees him from the nightmare images and unites him with his son in the image of the ship. Virgil has a temporary, human resurrection in Lipido for Ormsby's enlightenment. A dwarfed Texan, Lipido is a strange, ambiguous person. His disbelief in Mother helps Ormsby get a new perspective about her. Lipido (a pun on "libido") translates into reality what were probably Virgil's daydreams, for his behavior and speech are audacious. In a sort of catechism, he questions everything about Ormsby's and Virgil's relationship with Mother. It is as though the Boy has come back to hear from his father's lips an explanation of things that have long perplexed him.

When Ormsby first sees Lipido, the young man seems to be sitting on the eggs Mother is taking to Mrs. Dinardo. Eggs, symbolic of the birth-death cycle, reunite Ormsby through Lipido with the Boy. The eggs in Lipido's father's business turn up in Ormsby's own past when he, too, was in the business. Both Ormsby and Lipido's father feed the birds as "a form of worship." But in Lipido's family there is no confusion of parental roles. Exasperated with Ormsby's constant reference to "Mother," Lipido says, " 'My father . . . is *not* my mother.' " Lipido's effect on him confuses Ormsby regarding his own identity, and forces him to see himself, like Will Brady, as "nothing more or less than an impostor."

Generally, Ormsby's transforming imagination is nurtured in the isolation enforced upon him by Mother. Specifically, she drives him to the basement toilet and sends him to the attic; on the train he eludes her by sitting with Lipido. Out of this world, mystically reunited with his son, Ormsby talks until breathless about his own childhood, things he has not thought of in forty years. (His rural past contrasts with his present, overly urbanized life). But that morning, in the dark, dank basement toilet, the only private room in the house, Ormsby remembers the moment in Virgil's childhood when he realized that though buried alive together, they were at least father and son. "The first time the boy had turned up missing," Ormsby discovered that his own basement haven was also the Boy's. When Ormsby nearly stepped on him, the Boy said, " *'Et tu, Brutus. . . .* You think we ought to make one flush do, Pop?' " Although nothing more was ever said, "it remained their most important conversation—so important that they were both afraid to improve on it." The Boy had never before called him "Pop." Seated on the train beside Lipido, Ormsby is back in the basement toilet. " 'Have a seat, Pop,' " Lipido says. In the past Mother drove Ormsby and Virgil together; now, she drives Ormsby and Lipido together.

Preparation for the transformation Ormsby effects comes in the attic that morning. Sent there for Mother's suitcase, Ormsby encounters objects through which he communes with his son. Although they tell him, as the impersonal telegram three years ago could not, that the Boy is dead, he will not let the death of the Boy kill these things which provide "reasons for being alive." With a cliché expression that becomes one of the most evocative in the book, he grasps the truth. "Oh, it was one thing to be dead, but what was the word for describing what it was to have been not quite alive? Well, he knew. The words for that were *nipped in the bud."* He is a lily. Used ironically here as a symbol of modern man, lilies once symbolized chastity and romanticized fragility in women. He muses on the permanence assured the Boy by his heroism, for he had the good luck "to be known as Violet Ormsby's only son." Among some cobwebs, he finds the Boy's first, gold-filled wisdom tooth. If scientists can restore wholeness to the fragmented remains of a man who had lived thousands of years ago, whom he and the Boy had seen in a museum, Ormsby's transforming imagination will make of the Boy something permanent, "safe, you might even say, from time itself." But first he must improvise upon fatherhood with Lipido.

On the train with Lipido there is further preparation for the transformation. Lipido wants to know why Ormsby's plans for a trip with his son to Yellowstone did not pan out. Ormsby, desperately trying to explain, improvises upon one of Mother's favorite quotations: " 'The best laid plans—go phooey!' " Lipido dumps on his head the helmet he has been using as an ashtray. "From beneath it, like a cornered turtle, he peered out." As Virgil, he does two things with this Scanlon-like gesture—hides from Mother again and comments in general on his life with her. At the climax of his increasing irritation with what Mother has done to Ormsby and Virgil, Lipido chants, "'PHOOEY ON THE WORKS!'" Virgil himself went phooey. "'BUT AS FOR YOUR MOTH—'" Ormsby puts aside the lilies he is carrying to the ceremony, places "his right hand on top of Private Lipido's helmet, raised to his feet, closed his eyes, and pushed." He asserts his role as father; but he is still, he realizes, under the influence of Mother, who had once disciplined Virgil the same way. Lipido cries, Ormsby comforts him, the boy goes to sleep in his lap, and the passengers seem to think they are father and son. Everything he failed to achieve with his consanguinal son, he swiftly experiences on one train ride with a strange young soldier.

As they cross Brooklyn Bridge, Ormsby achieves his major transformation. During the last phase of a ceremony of his own upon which he has improvised all day, Ormsby sees a boat, presses Lipido against the window, and yells, "'There—!... there he goes!'" For Ormsby the specific boat means less than the idea: from now on *all* boats will give him the feeling that he is seeing the Boy; and, since the Boy seems to have come back in Lipido, all boys will be the Boy. "'No, *son* [italics mine]—his plans didn't go phooey.'" Lipido (as the Boy) seems to understand.

> *"The* Boy and *the Ormsby,"* he continued, which certainly meant nothing whatsoever, or considerably more than anything he had ever said. "There goes the Ormsby," men would say, just as he had always looked and said to himself: "There goes the Boy." . . . There was something impersonal and permanent about both of them, and this was why it had never worked to call him Son. *The* son, perhaps, but not just Son, or Virgil, or Ormsby. . . . There goes the *Ormsby,* men would say, without ever knowing, as he knew, how absolutely right it was. Without ever knowing that this was proof that his plans went right.

While other men have lost boys in the war, Ormsby has found or adopted one; and, in the same moment, he has "freed something." Da Vinci, who said that the ultimate in human sensibility is "to enjoy—to love a thing for its own sake and for no other reason," expressed Ormsby's feelings for the Boy.

In this moment of perception, Ormsby unifies past, present, and future; and he *momentarily* transcends his enslavement to Mother. On the other hand, like everything else in her life, Mother's later moment of possession is a transient thing. In a sense, Ormsby's imagination emerges victorious, free of captivity in the past or impalement in the present—he achieves, that is, a future, free of Mother's immediate governance. He frees the Boy from *her* ship, but otherwise he remains a captive himself in her world. Virgil, mortal and impermanent, is given symbolic immortality and permanence in the ship, in Ormsby's memory and in the recorded historical memory of the nation. (*What* Virgil did is not revealed as it is of no importance in the novel itself).

Just as he comes under Mother's spell, Lipido yells, " 'There she goes!' " If Virgil is a thing of permanence as a ship, the element in which he still moves is the sea; and Mother is Mother Nature herself.

III   *Mother As Bewitcher*

Years ago, Ormsby stood beside his young bride at Yellowstone Park, "waiting for Mother Nature . . . in the form of Old Faithful to show off." When a little boy asked Mother, " 'Why does it *do* it?' " her answer seemed for him to cover the ground: " 'Son, that's Mother Nature—Mother Nature, that's all.' " For Ormsby the answer applies to Mother herself. She suppresses certain energies and then finally forces them out. To Ormsby it seems only natural that the Boy should turn up something of a hero: "The boy would find a way, he knew, to fit into the master plan. Mother had a way of getting the best out of everyone"—including Lipido. But, just as Mother's influence operates mainly in a negative way, her son can assert his potency only in destructive acts.

In a complex way, the novel renders the process by which Virgil achieves identity. While Ormsby gives him spiritual identity, Mother's function is to give him physical identity. She "lost him only to find him, as the passage said. Closing her eyes she saw before her a nameless boat." This moment is one of the few indications of Mother's sense of connection with the Boy through the boat, which has no reality until she officiates over its christening, just as she was in control at the Boy's birth. The raw material has taken shape, but it awaits a transforming gesture from Mother Nature to give it life.

The christening of a ship in honor of the son she has dominated becomes an ironic occasion for Mother to triumph over an aggressive segment of the male world, the navy. What happened to Virgil happens to Lipido as Mother's control and transformation of events bewitches him and turns his audacity against her opponent. Thus, as Lipido, Virgil finally connects with his mother (but from a distance, as in the past); because she has affected Virgil, he affects others; and, through others, she is joined with him.

Mother's effect on Lipido illuminates for Ormsby his own relationship with Mother and Virgil, and her relationship with the Boy. The lobby of a train station, a street in a slum, and the deck of a ship are the settings for the three major moments in which Mother affects Lipido.

As a mischievous child, Virgil witnessed Mother's transforming power in a moment similar to the first of those in which Lipido witnesses it. "Just a little shaver," Virgil once walked in on one of Mother's parties with an explosive jar of spoiled food from the icebox, and went around showing it to the guests. Unlike most mothers, Mother "sat there with a charming smile on her face," and gave the women "the impression that this was something the boy was growing for himself. One of his nature studies, and that she was *very* proud of him." At the top of the escalator, Commander Sudcliffe is greeting Mother with dignity, when Lipido deliberately jabs her in the rear with a suitcase. "Except for yipping a little bit" she doesn't "bat an eye.... Who in the world but Mother would look in her purse for lifesavers and just as calm as you please pass them around?" She completely ignores Lipido. He is "stunned, for though it was Mother that had been struck, the full weight of the blow—as it always did—fell on someone else." She is like Dudley, who stepped calmly away from the wreck and bought a cigar.

Now Lipido keeps his eye on Mother and tells Ormsby when she is pointing at a bird or a place of interest as they drive to the East Side slums, where the second of Mother's natural, unrehearsed acts is performed. Out the car window Ormsby sees "tier on tier of fire-escape landings, all of them occupied like boxes at the theater." Commander Sudcliffe gets out of the car and removes his hat: "This innocent gesture brought forth a cheer from one side of the street. As Mother stepped out, gracefully, the cheer gathered momentum and seemed to rise, like balloons, from tier to tier." Ormsby glances at Lipido, whose "mouth was open, ... war or no war it was clear he had seen nothing like this." And "there at the top, in all that bedlam," Mother takes off her glove, waves it, and "then from her bare hand" blows them all a kiss. Ormsby on the fringe "would have died rather than leave the car." The status of the male is suggested by a small urchin who thumbs his nose at Ormsby.

Mother's third, final, and everlasting effect on Lipido comes at the ceremony. If a four-star mother is to be insulted by a silly male tradition of the sea which prevents Mrs. Dinardo from accompanying her onto the ship, Mother will leave. " 'Viva!' cried a voice, 'Viva!... VIVA MRS. ORMSBY!' cried Private Lipido. 'VIVA DINARDO—NUTS TO THE NAVY!' " But she remembers that the boat, according to custom, is hers and that it will not be the navy's until she gives it back in the ceremony of transformation (just as the Boy was hers alone until she drove him into heroism and turned him over to immortality). " 'Young man,' she said to Commander Sudcliffe, 'how do ladies board my boat?' " Mother, now that she is on deck before the whole world, is "perfectly at her ease." With Mrs. Dinardo holding a parasol over her, she improvises upon her famous "Consider the Lilies" speech, applying it to the navy and to men in general: "the text was familiar, though the application was original." Mother and Mrs. Dinardo, flanked by the navy, pass in review. Lipido's hoarse voice suddenly breaks the silence: " 'Here she comes!' he cried, 'Here comes Mother!' and rose from his seat in such a manner that Mr. Ormsby, like a man on a springboard, rose with him." And all the men on the pier rise, with the help of their wives, realizing that the real hero is Mother: "As men who knew what they knew, and felt no need to talk about it, they stood, as converted men should, piously in their pew."

By the end of the book Ormsby is an atrophied witness, having observed some of Mother's finest moments and the bewitchment of a new witness. He is too old, too close to Mother to benefit to any great extent himself, but the fact that Lipido is symbolically Virgil resurrected suggests that Lipido may benefit.

Although Morris set out "to bag this nocturnal prowler with the goods," one reviewer's description of her as a "vicious, bird-loving man-eater" is too severe. Harvey Swados comes closer when he affirms that "Mother achieves a strange greatness." Morris says of her: "She is our own invention—every detail shows the loving hand of the potter—and there is some indication that she serves us better than we deserve" (Hutchins, 2). To condemn Mother is far more to condemn Father: "Betrayed by Man (deprived of him, that is), woman is taking her abiding revenge on him... she inherits, by default, the world man should be running. Since only Man will deeply gratify her, the Vote and the Station Wagon leave something to be desired" (Letter).

Morris never really comes to grips with Mother's mentality (her sections are much shorter than Ormsby's); she surpasses all close understanding. Ambivalent toward her, he arouses one's horror of her "annihilating femininity," but by the end of the book one respects and admires if one doesn't like her. This ironic reversal is one of the achievements and satisfactions of the novel.

Morris is less interested in indicting either Ormsby or Mother than in rendering the intricacies of the relationship. However, his intention *is* to show that this unnatural male-female relationship is certainly unsatisfactory. James, in *The American Scene,* observes: "She has meanwhile probably her hours of amazement at the size of her windfall," and she must wonder at the "oddity of her so 'sleeping' partner, the strange creature, by her side, with his values and his voids, but who is best known to her as having yielded what she would have clutched to the death" (In *Territory,* 202).

IV   The Deep Sleep: *Resurrections and Revelations*

In *The Deep Sleep,* a 1953 runner-up for the National Book Award, Morris achieves a greater complexity of theme and technique; and, in dealing with this complexity, he achieves even greater refinements of style. In this, as in most of his novels, it is only upon a "segment" or "fraction of life" that Morris focuses. Funerals and such ceremonies are segments the richest in associations. The present spans one hot, humid summer day from morning until dawn. Preparations are made for Judge Porter's funeral, that is to take place the following day, but which the novel does not include. Through the mind's eye of each character Morris threads this single event. That is simply all, but Morris' finer vibrations are exceedingly fine at moments.

Experiences are rendered through the distinctly different sensibilities of these five characters, friends and family of the late Judge Porter: Webb, the artist son-in-law; Katherine, the daughter; Mrs. Porter, the wife; Parsons, the handyman; and the Judge's mother, called Grandmother. In that order, the point of view shifts from one character to another, but it returns about ten times to each. Webb observes "their strange predicament as fellow mortals," that each sees a different world. All during the day, the Judge's presence is felt as he watches from the front page of a newspaper those he left behind gropingly ponder the puzzle of his life and thereby the pattern of their own. Intricately, the novel renders a series of revelations and recognitions in some of the characters.

Just as the christening of Virgil's boat was a funeral, the Judge's funeral will be a ceremony of rebirth. In Webb especially, he is resurrected, he survives himself. As a kind of hero, the Judge affects his witnesses, but he is influenced himself by his wife. Ironically, through the Judge's effect on others, Mrs. Porter is the force, both creative and destructive, whose effect is most pervasive.

Since character relationships, developed in meaningful moments, are more important than narrative, one may best look at the novel through an examination of Webb, who is most profoundly affected by the events and whose own thoughts and acts make him probably the central character. First, a general impression of the house and its inhabitants may give a clearer focus on Webb himself. For Webb, the artist intent upon getting the well-composed picture, the Porter house "brought the conflicting forces together and gave them shape. It added up to more than the sum of the separate lives." As Morris moves his characters through the house, shifting from the basement to the kitchen to the bedroom to the attic and outside with the mobility of a movie camera, one feels that the inhabitants move inside a living thing, fleshed by their actions and thoughts. When he first came to the large but modest house in "the historic, haunted, big-name country" near Valley Forge and saw the image of the house gathered in the lens of a mirror, it "seemed to Webb, right at that moment, that he had gone abroad not to find himself, or other such prattle, but in order to return to this room and rediscover America." Fifteen years later, Webb is still faced with the challenge of making sense of the lives of the inhabitants of this house.

The rattle of the Grandmother's cane always wakes the visiting Webb and jars him into putting the past in focus. "A symbol of the strength of the Porter line," she appears first, eavesdropper on the present who seems to pass "an everlasting judgment" on the house and its inhabitants. For different reasons, Webb, estranged from the present American civilization, agrees with the verdict. Webb and Grandmother dislike each other, but he admires her self-reliance and respects her privacy. Although she is incapable of being changed herself by the day's reflections, she indirectly occasions several insights in Webb.

Parsons' life, "such as it was, was lived at the rear" of his house, especially after he went to work for the Judge thirty years ago. Tolerant of other people's mistakes, Parsons feels, like Purdy, "called" to take care of people who have everything, except the ability to take care of themselves. Only *he* seems to know that there is "any trouble in paradise." People who live in fine houses seem "to need competent outside help. A member of the family, and an outsider at the same time." As he senses Webb's deep affection for the Judge, Parson's dislike of Webb slowly wanes. Aware that their female-induced frustrations are similar, he slowly guides Webb into understanding and becoming the Judge; also, Parsons is the cause, directly and indirectly, of several of Webb's insights.

Judge Porter is certainly more a man than Ormsby, but his relationship with Mrs. Porter is not much different from the Ormsby-Mother one. Though cut from the same block of ice, Mrs. Porter is more fully developed than Mrs. Ormsby. She is "strange in a way that had warped the life of the family, . . . a force of some kind, as if the place were haunted, seemed to drive people from her house." Unable to live in it, Katherine and her father "worked out a way of doing their living somewhere else." The Porter house, too, is equipped with modern man's sanctuary—a basement toilet for the Judge, his son Roger (killed in the war like Virgil), Parsons, Webb, and even Grandmother—all refugees from the polar wastes of the pristine Mrs. Porter. Katherine has always considered the upstairs bathroom *her* room: "She had gone there the morning she had decided, as the note to her father declared, to take what she referred to as her own life"; but the force that drove her to it also influenced her to get into the bathtub to avoid making a mess. As Wylie says, " 'Mother knows best' has practically worn out the staircase to private hell" (195).

It is mostly through her effect on others that Mrs. Porter is depicted. Parsons, who has always been a conscious witness to Mrs. Porter's influence and the object of her unconscious, insidious tyranny, tells Webb that the Judge said "he'd run the country if the Missus would run the home." In a one-sided way, she is Parsons' spiritual wife; unlike the Judge, he follows all her rules and thus explains the fact that he's still alive. Their mutual wife was the bond between the Judge and Parsons. While tending the Judge during his illness, Parsons sometimes felt a third person in the room, "like he felt that the empty bed near the door was occupied." At the Judge's request, he moves the bed to where the dying man can put his finger in the loop of the bare mattress. "The Judge didn't want to be alone." With her in it, the bed gave the Judge little solace; not the wife but her cold, permanent imprint on the bed eases his dying.

The frustrations of attempts to know love that Morris describes seem inevitable; among his characters, many of whom lead lives of quiet desperation, only the furtive attempts seem to bear any fruit. Perhaps the only way to be contented with Mrs. Porter is to be her husband by proxy, vicariously—in and out of the relationship. But if she causes what is privately pitiable about him, Mrs. Porter, as Parsons tells Webb, made the Judge's public greatness possible. Early in the morning, Webb suspects that, if the Judge had been broken, "it had been on the wheel of his choice." Twentieth-century American males have brought upon themselves a deep sleep, analogous to the sleep into which God put Adam to create Eve. While they sleep, the Eves are not only born: they keep the males under a hypnotic spell. Most men never awaken.

Katherine, like everyone else, finds it unnerving to talk to Mrs. Porter. Some of the remarks her mother tosses off are innocently deadly, but some reveal that she hears and understands more than she is given credit for. All the characters grope futilely for means of communicating with each other; misunderstandings of tiny shades of meaning make conversation oblique. But Mrs. Porter, it seems to Katherine, is content to live "in a kind of phone booth"; looking out, her eyes convey an impression of serenity and depth, of an inner calm. In the evening, she admires her mother's subtle technique for keeping Webb, Grandmother, and a boisterous neighbor woman under control: "Somebody had to act *as if* everything was all right. Her mother did."

The conscious male-female conflict between Webb, the intellectual artist, and Katherine, the refined, educated, self-aware wife, contrasts with the unarticulated battle between the Judge and Mrs. Porter. The reader, who has encountered Webb and Katherine before in Muncy and Peg, finds the relationship amplified here. But the situation is reversed. They visit the *wife's* home place, and it is her father's funeral for which they prepare; Agee-Muncy as Webb is now the outsider. But, unlike Caddy, the Judge is a heroic influence upon both husband and wife.

V *Women, Resurrections, and Artifacts*

Certain other aspects of the novel, significant in themselves, help make Webb's moment of compassion meaningful and dramatic: his strong feelings about the nature of women; the resurrection of the Judge in him; and the realization that artifacts are a means of maintaining connection with the Judge.

Webb's reaction about women begins when his wife receives word that her father is dying, and Katherine makes the statement that her mother later repeats: " 'Well, I'm sure it's all for the best.' " Although she may be right, Webb wants to shout, " 'And just how the hell do you know?' " because "the way a woman would settle, when the time came, for the worst of all possible worlds, made him feel a real despair at the core of human life." To have another child, another lover, and to get on with life seems to be their biological view. Perhaps Webb's biological business is to insist on mulling it over until he understands the Judge's life so well that only his body is buried.

Webb tells Parsons that everything he is or hopes to be he owes to his mother, who died when he was very young; the beauty of childhood, he feels, is limited to those who have outgrown it. " 'No man can do enough for his mother, but he can always die.' " Although he ignores this remark, Parsons remembers that the judge's mother nearly drove her son out of his mind by banging on the door with her cane and by inquiring if he were still "poorly." On the verge of the grave herself, she sucked the life out of his body by the reminder that his life never accomplished as much as she had intended for it. Webb passes a mother and child tableau, mounted on a bus-stop bench. The image of the sweaty, fat mother possessively fondling her little son strikes Webb as a form of cannibalism, and it sums up "all the problems that he was powerless to resolve." The Judge's picture, smudged, looks up at him from the newspaper, as if he, "as well as Webb, had just turned his gaze from the mythic, hydra-headed mother and child. The pair of them drawn together by the same force that drew the salmon, leaping, up the river, and men, as well as lemmings, to some fatal rendezvous with the sea."

The likening of the characters, principally Webb, to the Judge enhances the theme of resurrection. Almost every time he gains an insight into the Judge, Webb does something that makes him feel like him, or that shows the reader or another character, mainly Parsons (even Mrs. Porter at several points), that he *is* like the Judge. When Roger was killed, the Judge wanted Webb to be the son Roger had never really been. The "triumph" of Webb's life would be "to have justified the Judge's love and confidence"; strangely, the justification comes in the end after Webb has become the Judge.

By midday, Webb is beginning to feel like a new Webb and a new Judge combined. If the Judge killed himself with suppressed feelings, they come out in Webb, whose name the Judge shouted a few months before he died. "It had been a command and a cry of woe at the same time," a command to Webb both to awaken from his deep sleep and to be compassionate. He awakens that noon, having found and drunk some whiskey the Judge had hidden in the cellar. When Katherine and Mrs. Porter punish him for being late by treating him as though he were a chauffeur, he rebels.

A sudden, simple moment of compassion for Parsons prepares Webb for the compassionate insight into Mrs. Porter's life toward which he has been moving all day. Coming up from the cellar, he passes the kitchen window and observes Parsons' abortive attempt to smuggle out a garden tool in the leg of his pants. Parsons turns toward the window, and Webb's face is enough like the Judge's to make the old man's heart stop beating. To cover up the feeling that he has invaded someone's privacy, Webb yells for Grandmother. Both Webb and Parsons realize, each from his point of view, that Webb is the one who seems to have the "guilty conscience. Yelling like that, he was showing more shame than Parsons felt." Webb doesn't really need to tell Parsons, who has been stealing things for some time, that he has a right to anything on the place. The artifact as a means of keeping up connection with the loved one and as a source of revelation about the characters is an important idea in the book.

VI *Moments of Compassion*

Elements presented through the points of view of the other characters enhance for the reader the process of enlightenment that Webb and Katherine simultaneously undergo. As the Judge's spiritual son, Webb is so engrossed in understanding him that he does not realize until the end that he has reached a deeper under-standing of Mrs. Porter which retrospectively alters all his previous judgments and throws light on his own life; and Katherine realizes that only recently has she given her mother's life serious thought. Every insight into the Judge's life reveals Mrs. Porter, both positively and negatively, to Webb and Katherine. They are pathetically unaware of the extent to which they share certain attitudes and responses, as the reader, shifting from his to her point of view, readily perceives. In the morning, Webb feels more than he under-stands, Katherine understands more than she feels, although they behave as though the opposite were true; in the end, they arrive at a balance.

In the mother role, as she sees fit to play it, Mrs. Porter, never having shown the need for understanding, never gives it to others. But she seems unconsciously to guide both Katherine and Webb to places and to objects which are sources of enlightenment about herself and the Judge. Thus Katherine experiences moments in the garage similar to Webb's in the basement and in the attic. Although the reader senses a curiously affectionate attitude underneath their behavior toward each other, a steady stream of sly, constrained innuendo and witty, sophisticated invective flows back and forth between Webb and Katherine. It grows worse as Katherine slowly becomes her mother's ally. In the world in the attic, where the Judge used to hide out, and to which Webb has been ordered by Mrs. Porter, he finds a number of revelatory objects, including a gold watch. Having drunk a little whiskey and smoked a forbidden cigar, he reaches a desperate, solitary climax to his daylong, random, improvised inquiry into the Judge's life. When Katherine nags him in his attic refuge, Webb delivers his last word on the subject of the American Home.

"The first Commandment of the House reads—Thou shalt not give a particle of gratification. Thou shalt drive from the Temple the man who smokes, and he shall live in a tent behind the two-car garage, and thou shalt drive from the bed the man who lusts, and he shall lie in tourist camps with interstate whores, and thou shalt drive from the bathroom the man who farts, and he shall sit in a dark cubbyhole in the basement, and thou shalt drive from the parlor the man who feels, and he shall make himself an island in the midst of the waters, for the man who feels undermines the Law of the House!"

This climactic speech contrasts sharply with his moment of compas-sion several hours later. When he falls into a final deep sleep on the cot in the cave-like gloom of the attic, his intelligence, like "the bulb in the ceiling," has "burned itself out"; when he rouses, his feelings will take over.

In the kitchen, Katherine has her own final moment of understanding. She is shocked when her mother begins to wash dishes. Speaking as though the Judge were still alive, Mrs. Porter replies, " 'Your father and I . . . can not sleep in a house where the dishes are dirty. There has not been a dirty dish in this house in thirty-seven years.' " Katherine begins to see the dishwashing ritual as a kind of baptismal ceremony: "A time when everything in the house that had been sullied—including the lives of the inhabitants—could be put through three cleansing waters and made pure again." Perhaps the spirit of the Judge and the reality of Mrs. Porter put Katherine and Webb through a baptism in the religion of the ordinary life. The younger couple have yet to create in their own way some such harmony, or illusion of it.

That night, Katherine sheds tears not for the Judge, but for her lonely mother, who, looking up at the stars, finally says, showing real remorse for the first time, " 'I'm going to miss your father' "; in the context created for her, this is probably the most passionate avowal of love possible. If Webb's "mania for the truth" once bewitched Katherine, she now feels "that *the truth* was just about the biggest lie of them all. . . . just a fancy way of covering up the facts." "Her mother, God knows, understood nothing, neither her husband, her son, nor her daughter, but perhaps it was not beyond reason to understand her. Perhaps *that* was just what her husband had done. Perhaps that explained what could not be explained about him." She believes that Webb will never be able to "puzzle out" the pattern of her parents' lives, to perceive that "the unjust thing was that it was just. The horrible thing was that it was not horrible. . . . the really senseless thing about it was that it made sense." In the flood of revelatory moments, the question of Mrs. Porter's culpability becomes meaningless.

In the conscious, intellectual act of trying to get the "picture," Webb is moved by Mrs. Porter (somewhat as Mother moved Lipido and Ormsby) to an imaginative act of compassion. Two of the Judge's watches become links between Webb and Mrs. Porter. The watch motif goes through a complex development, but the important thing is that Mrs. Porter causes Webb to find both of them. Hearing the dollar watch of the Judge's public life (which Webb has dropped into a wastebasket), Mrs. Porter searches for the exquisite gold watch of his private life. Ironically, after the time he had lost it on a birdwatching trip and she had found it, he had put it, under her influence no doubt, in "a safe place"—the attic, where

Webb finds it. In Mrs. Porter's developing reaction to the ticking of the dollar watch, Morris demonstrates a characteristic of his work that is particularly evident in this novel—the creation of rhythms of feeling.

On the cot on the screened-in porch, history and the points of the compass seem to meet in Mrs. Porter, the order of whose life places her in harmony with her universe. As mother and wife, she is the magnet that keeps the world in one piece for those who depend on her. How *she* feels about the world remains a mystery, and mystery is part of her devastating power and ability to bewitch. Webb himself sometimes feels the world "slipping away," but she survives, endures, at least outwardly, more ably than any of the others.

Perhaps because she feels strongly herself, she realizes that *someone* has to keep a grip on the emotions and refrains during the day from searching for the watch. Suppressing her own emotional need, she tries to keep the tension she senses in others from exploding, failing to realize, of course, that they are the way they are partly because she is the way she is. One's failure to sympathize fully with her only heightens the pathos of her isolation from everyone else, and enhances the dramatic impact of Webb's compassionate act.

Through the grill of the ventilator, Webb watches her wander in the dark in search of the source of the ticking that keeps her awake. "In her nightgown, peering around the room like Lady Macbeth," as though sleepwalking, returned "to the scene of the crime," she moves about as though directed by the current of Webb's rising sympathy. She pauses over the objects she finds in such a way as to reveal her common humanity with the others. She finds the dollar watch, but the one she seeks still eludes her, and she allows Katherine to take her to her bedroom.

Webb gropes through the "cave" to the porch and lies down "on the cot from where she had just got up," an act which is both an actual and symbolic expression of the nature of compassion—to feel *with*, rather than *for*, someone. But before he falls asleep, he puts the gold watch into the sideboard,

> not a very safe place but one where Mrs. Porter might come upon it. If she didn't, he would stumble on it himself.
>
> "Mother," he would say, "what in the world is this?" and he would stand there, with the case open, until she came toward him and looked at the watch.
>
> That was quite a picture, one that pleased him, and whether he heard the ticking or not, something kept him awake until he heard the Grandmother coming down the stairs.

As Morris has stated, "Webb's act reflects his respect for the forces that both salvage human life and destroy it: the pitiless compulsion that testifies in its appalling way, to the spirit's devious ways of survival" (Letter). But in a way, Webb, by secretly giving Mrs. Porter the watch, triumphs over her. He doesn't take petty credit for finding it. He has the enormous and mature satisfaction of providing a means of contentment for a woman who innocently brings so little—or so it would seem—to others.

The circle is complete: from ignorance, bitterness, and scorn in the morning to understanding and compassion the next morning, when the Grandmother rattles her cane, and reaches for the paper that has no further mention of the Judge. Gone from the public eye, he remains in the public heart. It has all been said, felt, transformed in those he left behind.

CHAPTER 7

Lighting Out for the Territory Ahead

THE HUGE SEASON (1954), *Love Among the Cannibals* (1957), and *What a Way to Go* (1962), though separated from each other by novels that return to the plains *(The Field of Vision,* 1956, and *Ceremony in Lone Tree,* 1960), have much in common. They deal, away from the plains, with the problematic question: How does one escape captivity in the past to live in the present? In these novels, the author develops attitudes and techniques for confronting the everlasting enigma of his Nebraska background. As such they may be looked at together before one takes a final look at the author's efforts to master the plains environment.

In *Man and Boy,* no single character is the author in disguise; Webb is an outside observer in *The Deep Sleep.* Thus, these two novels provided a transitional objectivity by which Morris gained confidence and stability in his craft. Until he had at least partially escaped the captivity of his childhood, Morris could not even approach the era of the enigmatic 1920's when he became a young man. In *The Huge Season,* his most ambitious book, Morris confronts this segment of his past that was almost as crippling as the plains.

In third-person chapters called "Peter Foley" in *The Huge Season,* Foley (a version of Webb) processes the raw material of the past (the huge season of the 1920's) and the present (the arid 1950's). In the Sunday newspapers in 1952, Foley sees a picture of his old friend Jesse Proctor, whom McCarthy has called before the Senate committee investigating un-American activities.[1] Monday morning, Foley sets out to visit Proctor and his mistress, Montana Lou Baker, at their apartment in Brooklyn. He spends most of the day wandering in Manhattan, killing time: he recalls his college years with Proctor and Charles Lawrence,[2] an audacious tennis player who committed suicide in 1929; and he encounters frightening aspects of present American civilization. At the Proctor apartment, an improvised party gets under way when Dickie Livingston, a friend of the bygone Paris days, arrives. The party breaks up when Proctor almost shoots himself. Going home, Foley sums up the meaning of his research into things past.

The "Foley" segments alternate with chapters called "The Captivity"; told in first person by Foley at a younger age, these narrate the events of his college years, including the brief time in Paris, exactly twenty-three years before the May morning on which Foley goes to visit Proctor. At Colton College in California, Lawrence, the hero and a sports major, "had his captive public": Proctor, modern literature; Ed Lundgren, science; and Foley, classics. Five pivotal events occur at college: Proctor spends Christmas vacation with Lawrence in Indiana, and on the return trip shoots himself in the foot with a Colt revolver; Lawrence pretends to have been robbed and beaten to avoid a college physical examination that would disclose he has contracted gonorrhea; returning from Indiana with Proctor after summer vacation, Lawrence wrecks his Bugatti sports car near the Mojave where Proctor shot himself; when Proctor moves out of the dormitory to find solitude for his writing, Lawrence takes Foley on long rides, during one of which Lawrence deliberately burns his hand in a smudge pot; one day Lawrence takes a drive alone, impulsively decides not to return, and turns up in Paris hospitalized with a horn wound received in an amateur bullfight in Spain. Proctor, Foley, Dickie, and Montana Lou are in Paris when Lawrence shoots himself. The "Captivity" chapters comprise a complete narrative of events; in a point-counter-point manner, the "Foley" chapters elaborate the meaning.

Three linked themes give form to *The Huge Season:* (1) the crippling effects of the hero-witness relationship cause (2) the witnesses to remain captive in the past, but Foley achieves (3) the imaginative, conceptual moment of truth by which one may escape into the territory ahead.

I   *The Hero and His Witnesses: A Gallery of Fossils*

Not since Dudley have we actually seen the male hero in action; but, unlike Dudley, Lawrence is a young public hero who affects other young men. Foley, not Lawrence, however, is "the latest transformation of The Kid"; Lawrence is, Morris stated in a lecture at Amherst, "the purest fiction, arising out of the need the imagination felt for [his] existence." He "must be seen from the outside, since it is his effect on the others, not his own personality, that is of interest." Nothing about Lawrence is presented except as it pertains directly to his role as hero.

Produced by the Midwest, Lawrence represents the American Dream and character. The audacity and tenacity of his grandfather, who built an empire in the barbed-wire business, came out only in Lawrence. Perhaps his failure to achieve physical and spiritual conquest over himself symbolizes both the failure of the past West and of the 1920's. Foley wonders: "Did they lack conviction? No, they had conviction. What they lacked was intention."

Lawrence is already famous as a tennis player when Foley meets him; on the wall of Foley's room in Chicago is a picture of Lawrence, along with Bebe Daniels, Sappho, and Charles Lindbergh in the cabin of the *Spirit of St. Louis* about to take off for Paris. Intact, with something insolent in his pose, Lawrence gives people the feeling of a lighted firecracker that has not gone off. When Foley tells Lundgren that Lawrence is their suite-mate, Lundgren says cynically, " 'Walk on water.' " That is what they all watch Lawrence attempt to do.

Lawrence, like most of Morris' heroes, does to his witnesses what a chipmunk does to Foley's cat. One day the cat appeared with the chipmunk in his mouth, set it down, cuffed it twice, then settled back to watch it dance. As this performance was repeated during the summer, Foley was inspired to formulate a creative evolution theory of his own: "The unpredictable behavior that lit up the darkness with something new.... The Origin of a species based on charm, on audacity, on the power of the dance, and the music that soothed whatever needed soothing in the savage breast." Through the years the witnesses retain the bewitching impression that this promising audacity was the spirit of the Roaring Twenties.

On the tennis court and in the bullring Lawrence audaciously pursues perfection in his own way. Pitted against Crewes, a fine player of professional caliber who lacks personality, Lawrence, a man of magnetic personality, lacks technique. With Crewes, one watches the tennis; but, with Lawrence, one watches Lawrence. Even his witnesses expect, and almost hope, he will lose. But, by refusing to adjust to Crewes's games and by playing the killing pace as much as the game, Lawrence eventually causes Crewes to fall apart. He wins with tenacity, will, and audacity rather than with technique. Proctor understands Lawrence enough to explain to Foley that, in trying to kill the bull the hard way according to the rules, the hero welcomes the risk to himself. On the court, "the only game he knew was between him and the ball"; in the ring, the bull is perfection, and the fight is between the imperfect and the perfect. A serious fool in competition only with himself, Lawrence is the bull he fights.

" 'Everybody copies somebody—why the hell is that?' " asks Montana Lou. Each of the witnesses is a carbon copy; however, Lawrence, an original, copies the image of himself he sees in others. But Lawrence " 'isn't human. How can you copy something like that?' " The pathetic dilemma inherent in the relationship is this: each wants to be what the other is, and in imitating each other, each cripples himself *and* the others.

Proctor, the most obvious witness and true to his name, gives the others excuses to move in orbits around the hero, creating the impression that they are a solid group. Lundgren, least affected, feels not only that Proctor helps to create the Lawrence image but that he also gives the hero his cues. When Proctor shoots a hole in his foot, Lawrence is cleared of the suspicion of having shot him, although symbolically he has. Having crucified himself—the wound appears to have been made by a nail—Proctor will never achieve his ambition of running the quarter mile in record time. Although Lundgren observes that he shows "a fine, promising talent for suffering," he gives Proctor credit for *doing* while he and Foley only *interpret*.

Lawrence's charge reaches Foley mainly through Proctor, just as Mrs. Porter affects others through the Judge. Proctor is the lovable fool who tries to imitate the real thing; Foley is the introvert who, charmed by the antics of the fool, expends his energy mulling over the significance of the fool's ambiguous acts. But that Foley also intuitively understands "the real McCoy" is indicated by the intensity of his subjective identification with the hero. When Foley takes up Proctor's task of writing Lawrence's papers, the Dean believes they now sound more like Lawrence.

Although Lawrence is attracted to Foley, the difference in their natures appears one night on a trip from Bakersfield in the Bugatti. When a cook in a diner announces that USC beat the Bears, Lawrence says, "Ha!" (Proctor's expression). No one beats the game, he says, no one wins. An argument ensues. Foley the arbitrator is ineffectual. Like Proctor, Lawrence seems to think the expression "bullshit!" covers the ground. On the highway, he wants to know if there is anything Foley, who is "so goddam calm," *really* likes. Lawrence, who admires what he cannot do himself, admires Foley for being able to take "the bullshit with the straw." When Foley asks what isn't "bullshit," Lawrence jumps out of the car, runs into a lemon grove, and shows him: he burns his hand severely in a smudgepot. Lawrence "could do just about anything he had a mind to, so he had done that." From Spain, Lawrence sends Foley a post card picture of Belmonte, the great torero, down on one knee facing a bull, with the message: "This is no bullshit, old man." Foley knows that his own achievement will be of a different nature—"The Moment of Truth" that springs not from action but from perception.

Minor witnesses are affected in differing ways by the hero. Even the cynical Lundgren gets "overcome with shock and admiration." Lawrence's effect on Montana Lou and on Dickie Livingston operates through Proctor. She is drawn to him because his life-long emulation of Lawrence has made him hopeless and helpless. Proctor has been transformed into the kind of man whom Dickie feels compelled, literally, to tease to death.

The hero's most fervent witness and his most indifferent one contribute to his only intention—to kill himself. Proctor cannot write the last chapter of his novel, *Querencia* (the place in the ring where the bull feels most at home), because he cannot decide whether to kill or to save the hero; killing him, according to Lou, who is translating the book into French, would leave Proctor without a *querencia* for himself. Dickie, Proctor's agent, pulls "the neatest trick of the decade"—without Proctor's consent, he publishes ten copies of the book minus its unwritten final chapter, the author's name appearing only in the dedication, the cover photograph showing Lawrence serving a ball. Probably, the book gives Lawrence, lying on his back in the hospital an apparent failure, the cue he has been waiting for. Knowing that he cannot live happily ever after (as none of Morris' heroes can), he puts the perfect end to an imperfect thing. Between the hero and the witness, who chronicles his attempt at perfection, comes the constant child, Dickie, for whom life is a prolonged prank and heroes are a source of resentment. Unable to understand what Foley expends a life-long effort trying to perceive, Proctor strives to resurrect the dead hero in himself. "The shot that killed Lawrence had crippled all of them."

Both in life and literature, the hero continues long after his death to spellbind his witnesses. By 1952, Foley, Proctor, and Montana Lou have written blighted masterpieces about Lawrence: "Unfinished, these books gave purpose and direction to their lives."[3] The picture of Proctor so vividly suggests the futility of Foley's writing a final chapter to his novel *The Strange Captivity*, otherwise finished long ago, that he almost burns it. (The novel constitutes the "Captivity" chapters of *The Huge Season*, which itself ends with its final chapter only implied.) But, because Foley himself is still captive in the past, the facts have not been transformed into fiction. The transformation occurs not in Foley's novel but in his mind as he possesses the past by re-creating it.

If in the 1920's, they were all arranged "like iron filings around a magnet," in 1952 what has become of the charge the hero gave off?[4] If they were once like Lone Eagles, they are "now a covey of Sitting Ducks." "What had taken more than twenty years to die was now dead. . . . Dead or good as dead." But "what mattered was that they were *his*. Foley's lifelike decoys." From isolated bits here and there, one learns what has become of the witnesses. Proctor is most important.

The *Times* states that Proctor, the witness, has now been cited for contempt. Foley studies the picture. "All the soft gentile topsoil, the non-furrowed regular guy, the comical Jewish clown, had eroded away." More a martyr now than a prophet, he is "throwing open his shirt front to show the public his wounds." He is reported to have said that if he were a good American he would be in jail (like Thoreau); even now, because either the cause has never mattered enough, or he has always hoped that the next one would matter more, he has not taken the greatest risks, not pushed himself to Lawrence's limits. Foley has kept in touch with the many enthusiasms and causes Proctor has taken up, or been taken up by. Laureate of the Bullshitters, Jewish importer of Jews, writer, radical, bohemian, Spanish Civil War veteran, he is currently "The Voice, now unmasked, of America." Foley feels unmasked himself, for his own "life—such life as he possessed—seemed to have begun with one Jesse Proctor and to have ended when *that* Proctor had given up." Proctor bolts life raw (like Wolfe); Foley intellectualizes it (like James).

Foley, uncommitted intellectual of Philadelphia's Main Line, is now a "bachelor, professor of languages of no practical value" on a "quiet calcified campus." Wearing clothes of the style of the 1920's, he seems a representative of the finer things of a better day: "The style had come back, in the last few years, but not the men who patented it." Both Foley and Proctor once tried to commune with the hero by wearing his clothes, but neither could create the same aura. Now Foley wears the hero's jacket around the house—always an armchair Lawrence. If the word that covers Proctor is *erosion, evasion* covers Foley. In him, Foley's mother, a Nielson, has charted to an anticlimax the course of the Viking explorers who once found, then lost, America.

"A fossil of some sort," looking like Garbo in the newspaper picture, Montana Lou has been sleeping with Proctor for years, having had other lovers of various nationalities. A true bohemian who does everything "for the time being" only, she has had many odd, legend-breeding jobs. Publishers continue to give her advances on her unfinished book, more because of the style of the person than because of her literary talent. "A raddled oracle," she insists that they were not "deceived." "They had been possessed by a truth. Perhaps by too many truths, as it happened, every other one a seeming contradiction." In the "modern corn-dance ceremony for making rain," her fellow witnesses can depend on Lou Baker to maintain the spell that blinds them to the blight.

Dickie, a durable, graying playboy, "a boy at heart," frankly anti-Semitic, talks about Proctor all the time. "The neatest trick of the decade had proved to be the trauma of two lives. Life seemed to have stopped, for prankster and victim, right at that point." Dickie hates and fears Proctor because he has never struck back. As for Lundgren, a man who neither acts nor imagines, Morris dispenses with him in a brief passage. Foley once ran into him while walking in Manhattan. A colonel, he wore the "set expression of a man who was beaten but would not give up."

Because the hero lived so bewitchingly in the present and killed himself when he saw he had no future as a perfect hero, the witnesses, fossils in the present, are captive in the past.

II   *The Burial of the Past*

In *The Huge Season,* Morris makes his first major assault on the past as determined by the demands of the present; however, not until *The Field of Vision* does he relate this aspect of the time theme to the familiar Nebraska store of memory. There are three main aspects of the confrontation of the past theme: (1) the time concept of the novel; (2) the contrast between the romantic ideals of the 1920's and the disenchantments of the age of anxiety, the 1950's; (3) the ceremony at Proctor's apartment in which the past (in the sense that it is dead) is buried and the captives reach the threshold of liberation.

The interfusion of past and present in the structure of the novel is relevant to the idea that Foley (and the others) is what he is because of what happened in the huge season. In the 1920's time seemed to flow with a fixed regularity; thus, in the "Captivity" sections events are presented in straight, chronological fashion. Since the past is inextricably bound up in the events of the present, for Foley today, time is ambiguous—it exfoliates; thus, his third-person reflections on the past in the "Foley" sections are almost free-associational in manner.

The first "Foley" chapter covers briefly the entire time span; and all the major events, characters, and themes are introduced (a typical Morris technique). Foley's slow journey to see Proctor provides the only sense of action progression in the present, and the ceremony in the apartment is the only *event.* Much of the experience the novel offers lies in perceiving the ramifications of the contrast between Foley's first-person objective rendering of the past and his present third-person subjective evaluation. As the memories contrast with the immediate data of the present, Foley thinks increasingly less of the past; there is a grand evaluation before and after entering the apartment where past and present contrast more dynamically among the characters assembled.

For Foley,—who thinks of himself as an example "of the pre-historic present, the persistence of the past" which renders the present immobile,—the times are out of joint. For his father, a Latin professor when the language was still more or less alive, time seemed contained in his watch, which still keeps *his* time, not Foley's. If this artifact of the past mocks him, so do the clichés of the 1920's. Ironically, Foley never does anything to justify the "striking resemblance [he] once bore to Charles A. Lindbergh, another fossil from the great Age of Flight." The resemblances of Foley and Proctor to Le Grand Lindbergh and of Montana Lou to La Grande Garbo effectively weld the nostalgic image of the past-haunted present.

In a world in which the past is both real and imaginary, Foley's is a sensibility trying to get a workable perspective: "Young men are a corn dance, a rite of spring, and every generation must write its own music, and if these notes have a sequence the age has a style." Lindbergh, a catalytic, real hero, performed with style an audacious deed "that had a wonderful resonance," and Gatsby, though fictional, just as forcibly represents the spirit of the age.[5] Morris' Lawrence is a blend of fact and fiction. To Foley, all three are a blend of discipline, innocence, and audacity. Absent from the present scene are men like Lawrence, who "forced on the frontiers exceptional accidents," and men who have Proctor's questing spirit. And gone is the group brotherhood. "Those who lay naked in the huge season arise all together and cry / that this world is mad!" (From the novel's epigraph from St. John Perse's Anabasis.) Their voices concert in Foley's. As his concept of the present evolves out of his evaluations of the past, one understands why he has preferred to remain a captive.

Having tried for fifteen years to comprehend in a literary way, Foley now lives the process of understanding in an inquiry that is a real dredging up of the past. His philosophical, sometimes simply emotional, reactions are presented in highly figurative, metaphorical terms. The pieces of the puzzle, re-introduced from various perspectives disjointedly, tend toward a pattern; the novel renders a process out of which concept evolves and emerges. In Manhattan various aspects of American civilization come at Foley swiftly. His thoughts become more telegraphic and jerky the further he penetrates the matrix of modern civilization; he moves as though through a very animated "scene in hell."

In the children caged on the playgrounds, in the old men playing chess, and in a family that radiates a Norman Rockwell-like glow, all living in an age of security against a backdrop of pushbutton doom, Foley sees something of himself, of the heroes and dreams of the 1920's that remain in the air. But now "in place of the Leader was the line," and one believes in "machine-made perfection—if anything at all." If the facts speak for Every-man in this world, they do not speak for Lawrence and for his witnesses, who once spoke for themselves. But Lawrence the Leader led only himself; Proctor the Follower followed only Lawrence; and Foley the Thinker thought only of the dance, while the real world quietly continued to fall apart. When faced with doom, death, and evil, men like Proctor turned their power to transform upon themselves instead of upon the world that needed transforming. But, if the stars were the limit then, the neons are today. Man lights up the darkness of his ignorance with a sudden, blinding flash: caught on a movie screen is the "symbolic Zero of Hiroshima," "as though the camera caught some miraculous birth"; on the asphalt the camera finds the faint "shadows of men in the light of their own man-made sun." At the white-hot heart of the inferno that is about to become a cold clinker, Foley pities himself and his kind. "The new man, the cybernetic marvel, opened his plastic jaws and said, *I am a fact finder*." He sees, as Fitzgerald did, "the contradiction between the dead hand of the past and the high intentions of the future" (*Crack-Up*, 70). "Under a cloud of unknowing, Foley arose," and, as though responding to a magnet, he crosses Brooklyn Bridge. His observations have put him in a fertile frame of mind for responding to the climactic events at the apartment where Proctor awaits him.

In *The Huge Season,* as in several of the novels, a kind of funeral is the central event in the present. On the anniversary of Lawrence's death, an attempt is made to bury him and the past. The funeral ceremony begins in the apartment, continues in Foley's mind, but is not quite complete when the book ends. Foley remarks that after all these years he has nothing memorable to say, but everyone improvises upon the act of reappraisal. All the horseplay and the pyrotechnics of wit in the apartment may seem gratuitous, but each touch comments on what has gone before.

Dickie, "aging juvenile delinquent" and wearing a coonskin cap, brings a matronly, ordinary woman because she just happens to have been in Paris during the 1920's. Announcing that he has a cure for all the troubles "that threaten the lives of us vanishing Americans," he produces the same Colt revolver with which Proctor shot himself in the foot and with which Lawrence killed himself. The joke is a dud because Proctor reacts calmly, though distractedly; and Lou is upset. The woman is right when she says, " 'It's always the empty gun that kills somebody' "—not the self-inflicted bullet but the prospect of emptiness within him killed Lawrence. Proctor goes to the bathroom. " 'You think I've given him the last chapter?' " asks Dickie. As Lou nervously flaps a towel in the air—the broken wing of a Lone Eagle—the sound of a gunshot comes from the bathroom. Smoking gun in hand, Proctor just looks at them. Dickie denies knowing the gun was loaded.

But Dickie does indeed give Proctor, as he gave Lawrence, the final chapter; however, today Proctor lacks the courage of his emptiness—the spirit of the 1920's fires a blank in the 1950's in Proctor's final abortive attempt to follow Lawrence. Lawrence's pure rebellion was contrary to Proctor's verbiage; it was meant to kill the bullshit with the bull, to create something permanent. When the party breaks up, Lou tells Dickie, " 'I think we *were* different.... They *say* it's been real, but we *were* real.' " Thus she provides an epitaph for hero and witnesses.

As Foley says goodbye to Dickie, who has given him a ride into Manhattan, he notices that "the eyes under the coonskin cap were those of a Space Cadet." Liberated from the past, even Dickie is beginning to live in the future. "Up ahead, toward the captive future, the lights changed from red to green," from the *stop* Lawrence's awesome acts incurred, to the *go* Foley gains through compassion and insight so that perhaps heroism is possible for *him*.

III   *The Moment of Truth*

In the final "Foley" chapter, Foley concludes his immediate confrontation with the past; and his insights amount to a liberating moment of truth. On the train, he has a brief Ormsby-Lipido kind of relationship with a young, drunken soldier that reminds him the huge season of youth is over for him. But his name will never join the roster of those for whom "the steady erosion of the liberal mind" ends in suicide. Lou Baker would say that Foley lacked, being only a thinking man, the guts. "He had the guts but he lacked the conviction, the habit of perfection, that would lead him to believe that even *that* settled anything." Lacking both the temperament and passion for despair, he didn't want to leave a mess, aside from the general one, for someone else to clean up. Through the train window, he throws the Colt into the river.

Another soldier on the train reminds Foley of Proctor. For no good reason he blows a comic bugle, much as Proctor once did at a football game. "No bugler, the sound that he [Proctor] made was not of this world. More like a shriek, a loon's cry in the darkness, so that players, umpires, and spectators wheeled to see what comet, unknown and unpredicted, crossed the night sky. As one had.

Perhaps, as one always would. Cruising around in the dark, in the void, just for the hell of it." But never for the point of it. Proctor was drawn by the magnet, Lawrence, himself impersonal as iron, but where and why?

With its youthful rites of vitality, the 1920's promised more than the individuals, even Lindbergh, could deliver, at least consistently. Those who felt the charge of such men were destined to be blighted because they lacked intention, were too full of energy and daring to focus on a center. Lawrence destroyed himself in an absurd gesture and habit of perfection; he realized "that he might be caught with perfection on his hands and still be discontent." Proctor's actions all these years have been affected, but not guided (as Camus' were) by an intuitive realization that there is meaning at the heart of the absurd; Foley, the only witness able to benefit, finally reaches this conclusion intellectually at the inception of a new day.

"Foley's whole effort," says Booth, "is ... to find an escape from the limitations of the heroic ideal without losing the imaginative transformations it could effect.... The danger of the heroic is that it can freeze the imagination as well as liberate it" (4-5). But Foley finally re-creates and transforms the past into the immediate present. The hero and the witnesses will live and achieve permanence not only in the captivity of Foley's memory but mainly in his imagination. Lawrence becomes, like a Keatsian figure on an urn, "suspended in time, like the ball that forever awaited the blow from the racket ... A permanent scene, made up of frail impermanent things. A lover like Lou Baker, a saint like Lawrence, a martyr like Proctor, and a witness like Foley." "The permanent is permanent by virtue of being outside of time," says Booth, "—and yet as human beings we discover it only in time, only in the world of impermanent things" (20). Foley's father's watch has stopped, captive time has stopped, "at two o'clock in the morning, the first day of his escape from captivity."

His imaginative moment of truth enables Foley to act. Today he has been *living* the last chapter of the huge season, the one he couldn't write; summoned to testify before the McCarthy Committee, tomorrow he will enter the final passages. The hero's charge will have positive effect on the witness, whose public testimony will, presumably, have not only conviction but intention as well. The past is dead, but resurrected. "How explain that Lawrence, in whom the sun rose, and Proctor, in whom it set, were now alive in Foley, a man scarcely alive himself.... with no powers to speak of." Foley has "picked up the charge that such powers gave off ... Impermanent himself, he had picked up this permanent thing."

CHAPTER *8*

Sex: The New Frontier

ALTHOUGH MORRIS, like D. H. Lawrence, deals with the works of love in all his novels, *Love Among the Cannibals* (1957) and *What a Way to Go* (1962) are the only ones in which erotic love is overtly important. The lovers do not go beyond the sexual level, where, Morris suggests, everything else begins. Sex is the new frontier, and the Greek and Cynthia are a new species of audacious female; they persuade the male that, on the sexual frontier, where one may start from scratch, "the real McCoy" is still possible.

Since separate discussion would lead to unavoidable repetitions, a break in the method necessitated so far is appropriate. At the risk of an occasional, slight distortion, these novels will be viewed as they parallel and, at times, contrast with, each other.

In *Love Among the Cannibals*, Horter, writer of cliché lyrics, and his teammate Macgregor, composer of sentimental popular music, are under contract to write a movie musical; they spend most of their time on Hollywood beaches, soaking up back- and foreground. One day on the beach Mac meets Billie, a blonde Memphis "cannibelle," and that night at a party Horter meets a sensual girl whom he calls "the Greek." Wanting to bolt from his present situation, Horter persuades the Greek, Mac, and Billie to take an auto trip to Acapulco, where they spend a couple of weeks in an unfinished villa, supposedly writing a musical with a Mexican setting. They have a fine time making love and lying on the beach. Finally, Billie cajoles Mac into marrying her, and the Greek bolts with an elderly biologist. In the end, Horter envisions a reunion with her. Characteristically, the tale is simple. Morris sets the scene; then he describes the roundup; the passage follows.

In *What a Way to Go*, Soby, an English teacher at a small college, takes a sabbatical trip to Venice for which, through a literary experience, he feels a great kinship. On the ship, Miss Kollwitz, herself a language teacher on leave, "adopts" Soby; traveling with her is Miss Throop, a just retired headmistress of the Winnetka

Country Day school. In Venice, they join Miss Throop's niece, Cynthia, who becomes the center of attention. On a junket to Greece in a rusty old steamer, packed with an assortment of "kooky" passengers, they have a series of adventures, out of which Soby and Cynthia emerge married. The events in both novels occur over a period of about two weeks.

Although all Morris' books contain strong elements of comedy and wit, the use of wit is most sustained in *Cannibals*, and the comic thrust is more vibrant in *What a Way to Go* and in *Cause For Wonder*. In all three, there are elements of literary and cultural satire and parody.

I *Cannibalism: The Impersonal Wisdom of the Body*

Morris seems to have created some entirely new characters in Horter and Soby. A closer look reveals Horter's resemblance to The Kid, back where he started from; his story is close "in tone and substance" to The Kid's. But both Horter (forty-one) and Soby (forty-seven) take their cues from young women, the Greek (twenty-three) and Cynthia (seventeen). Both girls respond to young, middle-aged, and elderly men, all stages in their development.

Intended to represent the real thing in women, the Greek and Cynthia are something less than real. A frank, sexual force, the ideal of pure sexual reality, the Greek is an archetypal female. Everything about her has an aura of origins; her name is Eva (Eve) Baum (German for "tree"). Though portrayed in more realistic detail, Cynthia is a less successful creation. She is encumbered by numerous Lolita-like details that testify to her bewitchingly awkward adolescence: "Soby noted the vaccination scar, the peeling arm, the vertebra along the spine like knuckles, the white line left by a halter, the green line left by a chain presumed to be gold." Unlike the Greek, she is unfinished, encrusted with resemblances to countless other females, past and present. When she was fifteen, the Greek almost died giving birth to a stillborn baby: "'They said I was dead and came back to life.'" Unable to have any more children, she tries to fulfill her essential nature, as she sensed it on the other side of life—to be a woman in every way and as often as she can: "'This life I have is a gift.... Why should I hoard it?'" As a governess, she delights in taking care of "little monsters"; as a lover, she makes Horter forget his age. Free of the past, which died when she was reborn, she is in the present, a whole person. Cynthia lives in the present, too. But of what does it consist except the pure fact of her living in it? Although she perhaps senses that most of the talk around her is phony, as an audacious debunker her constant wisecracking becomes tedious.

Faced with the problem of determining which—feeling or intellect—creates or reflects reality with the greater fidelity, Horter and Soby must resolve the conflict, achieve a balance. A reticent man, Horter at middle age, grasps "just one more chance" with the Greek. She teaches him that "the mind is in the body." To Mac, sex is sex, but the *real thing* has "to have heart, man!" Mac responds to Billie, the most cliché of women; she is sex as pretense and tactic; basically a prude, she is a grotesque of American insincerity. Mac and Billie counterpoint Horter and the Greek in every way.

Soby wears the stamp of a teacher as obvious as the frock on a clergyman. Cold to the advances of women his own age, he leans undecided "on the rail" between one life and another, "rather than risk an early commitment." He is engaged in life-long research on a book about "The Wisdom of the Body, as he humorously described it, its causes and its cures." He knows that "Beauty, the word made flesh," establishes "in man the two poles of his nature—to materialize or to spiritualize? To pass away in a delirium within sight of the beloved object, like Aschenbach [in *Death in Venice*], or to sit and stare like cannibals at the grape-stained lips."

The impersonality of love, developed in a familial context in *Man and Boy*, is developed in a sexual context in these two novels. When Horter asks her what she likes about him, the Greek frankly says that he arouses her desire. Her impersonal approach to sex keeps the affair as uncomplicated as possible. But Horter's thinking complicates his feelings; he thinks, for instance, too much about the other lovers she has had, now has, or may have. But, when she leaves him, he does not care who has her now. He takes pride in his own luck.

Soby was once married to a real Greek girl much like Horter's girl. She had "gazed at him . . . with a serene and impersonal affection, without sentiment or any interest whatsoever in what made Soby *tick*. So much for the spiritual, the immaterial side of their seven months together" (before she was killed in a foolhardy car accident). "Their most intimate relationship was the most impersonal. . . . What did love have to do with such forces, such nameless lusts?" Unlike the Greek, Cynthia, who seems abysmally ignorant of everything but such tricks as curling the hair in Coca Cola, does not *know* the wisdom of the body; but she is entrancing in her eagerness to respond to it. In her behavior as a sensual young woman, she responds readily to the numerous and various cues provided by whatever environment she happens to move in. The mind in Soby's eyes responds instantly to Cynthia, but his intellect requires most of the novel to catch up. He *knows* what must be done if Cynthia is to achieve the pure sexual impersonality his wife had, but his own *feelings* provide a very hesitant guide for her. "'I *used* to want to be so beautiful everybody who saw me would just fall down *dead,*'" she says. Soby does fall "down dead— in order to arise, like the phoenix, from [his] own ashes." In the end, both respond to the wisdom of the body, to the action of sexual tides.

In an impersonal relationship in which the wisdom of the body is the guide, it is sometimes necessary to start at a stage of cannibalism. "What a way to go!" Cynthia would declare, the expression stenciled on her bathrobe. By the end, Miss Throop can say, "'I'm sure we're *all* in full agreement.'" Clichés are vegetable; the body is cannibal. Most people are vegetarians; Horter becomes a cannibal with the Greek. In the love act, living in the flesh, lovers depend only upon each other; they don't need the inessentials of the cliché vegetarian world.

As a cannibal, Billie is different from the Greek. Her primly pleated but raw mouth—"so many sets of sharp teeth in a purse of flesh"—gives Horter "the weemies." The last night of lovemaking for Horter and the Greek affects Mac and Billie, who make love for the first time. But the result is that Mac's little cannibelle nibbles him down to marrow and matrimony. They become clichés: "stand-ins, perhaps, but not people, figures in a frieze symbolizing the eternal bride, the eternal groom, and the eternal deception they played on one another—being true to one another in order to be false to everything else." Because of the Greek, Mac will always know the real thing by its opposite.

But the Greek does partially transform Billie by making her aware of her body as a body, as more than bait, by forcing her to defend it against the Greek's animal violence. Just before she bolts from Horter, the Greek almost bolts Billie. Ripping her gown, she ties Billie from corner to corner on the bed, and rubs "the contents of the nightpot . . . like an ointment" into her. Horter is "struck by the beauty of her eyes now that she had looked at something through them." With "blood under her nails" and "the suntanned flesh of the Greek" on her lips, Billie is a true cannibelle at last.

Soby and Cynthia move closer and closer to the animal-encounter stage. Staring at her flesh, Soby wonders if what he feels is "desire" or "something more on the order of cannibalism." On the threshold of old age, Soby, who once glimpsed such primitive desire with his Greek wife, closes his eyes to it, as Aschenbach did. But Cynthia keeps the cannibal basis of the sexual encounter constantly before him; for instance, like an animal, she bites both Soby and Herr Holzapfel, a gigantic young German. The relationship between

Cynthia and Soby is paralleled by that between Miss Throop's cat and a Venice stray, whom she calls Aschenbach; but here the female is the shy one, the male the aggressor. The two cats come slowly together just as Soby and the girl do. Both are conscious of the parallel.

II   *The Immediate Present*

In a relationship in which one learns the wisdom of the body and achieves impersonality in love, sex is a thing of the moment in which only the present is alive. *The Huge Season* points out the direction *Cannibals* takes. Although in the contrast between present and past, the present as well as the past is found wanting, one must escape the "crippling thralldom" of the past and attempt to "make a stand" in "the shifting and treacherous sands of" Time Present, "in all its contradictions"(Amherst Lectures). *Cannibals* begins on this assumption. Morris' comments on that book may also apply to *What a Way to Go:* It "marks a fresh engagement with the present, rather than with the past, which has now been re-experienced. I am not, in any sense, through with it—*The Field of Vision* is the first act of organization—but I am finished with immersion. In the waters of my fathers I have been dipped. This may be the great American baptism, since all our writers of consequence have to go through it. In my opinion . . . damn few survive. Immersion is immolation." In his deliberate attempt to put aside the "familiar nostalgic pattern," "to shake the sentimental leaves from all those mythic limbs" (Letter), Morris, like Horter and the Greek, improvises upon the act of bolting, to start again from scratch in the territory ahead.

Nearing that territory, Morris found that D. H. Lawrence had made some inroads of his own: "there is another kind of poetry; the poetry of that which is at hand: the immediate present," where "there is no perfection, no consummation, nothing finished. The strands are all flying, quivering, intermingling into the web, the waters shaking the moon" (*Territory*, 230). Morris bypasses, for the moment, the problem of how to escape from the Nebraska past; the present is "castigated," but in the world in the attic the dust lies undisturbed.

Charles Lawrence's witnesses in *The Huge Season* were trapped in the past. But neither Horter nor Soby is encumbered by a past; thus, each is able to respond to the immediate present when a woman bodies it forth to him. For twenty years a captive of nostalgia, The Kid, as Horter, attempts to confront the present in the Greek in Mexico. Though it lures the present generation away from the plains, Hollywood is less the territory ahead than Mexico is.

Horter's Midwest background may condition his response to the immediate moment, but the past, for most of the characters in both novels, "lies buried somewhere behind them, or drugged to a disquieting sleep within them. . . . The day starts, as life starts, from scratch" (Lectures). The past is in the making *now*. Since nothing outside himself holds or acts upon him positively, it is from the emptiness of his present life that Horter bolts. Captive of the past only to the extent that the public clichés to which he is attuned refer to sentimental echoes of the past, he confronts the living present in a primitive context. Once he has experienced the Greek, who teaches him to live in the present without misgiving and without "bad faith," he possesses a *real* past: "Stripped down . . . to what we referred to as the essentials, I possessed nothing under that moon but my past. That much I could take with me, if I cared to, and I did." All that is given of Soby's past is a sketch of his brief marriage, near the end of which he approached Horter's final state.

Living in the present among such females as the Greek and Cynthia, one is always confronted with the disquieting but promising question, What Next? This is the title of a song in progress when Horter meets the living answer, the Greek. Academic in the beginning, the question is real now, since, free of cliché at the end, everything is possible for Horter. The pathos is that, being forty-one, he will have to hurry. But, if he cannot find the Greek again, he will look for a similar nature; and, transformed as he is, he will be able to recognize the real thing. A running motif in the Soby novel, What Next? is related to a question each man must answer according to his own nature and needs: "What did the law of the sea recommend?"

III   *Crossing Interior and Exterior Frontiers*

Some of the best conditions under which one may learn the wisdom of the body and connect with the living present are those which prevail in travel. New scenes arouse the impulse to "make it new!"

Just as Dudley improvised on assembling a carload of male fools, The Kid as Horter picks up women. "The car is the link between the mythic past and the intolerable present." It is a vehicle for flight either away from (as with Dudley) or toward something (as with Horter). "A fireman's-red dream chariot," the studio car lent to Horter is a character in itself, like the Marmon. It drops into a ditch much the way The Kid's did on the railroad track; but here the destination has been reached. The Greek's reaction is Dudley-

WRIGHT MORRIS

like—seeing the sea, she runs into it. "With full cargos both ships set sail for the Great Good Place. . . . across the dry places to the real McCoy" (Lectures). The Soby novel presents an actual ship of fools and phonies.

The sea, pictured as the origin of all life, joins the two novels. "If you like parallels," says Horter, "the beach is where we came in, and where we'll go out. Having crawled from the sea, we're now crawling back into it." The Greek is drawn to Dr. Leggett, "a friendly, disarming, lady-bug-shaped, ridiculous" biologist because he responds to the essence of the sea element that spawned her for him; a scientist, he sees her stripped to the facts, the genus. If it is not desire he arouses in her, it is her feeling for *his* unencumbered desire. The old man's passion "had undergone a transformation in the magnetic field of the Greek. His passive ooze had picked up her charge." Too late, Horter sees his own life warmed by the Greek's hands. She bolts with the biologist. One risks the effects of the scene one makes in one's travels—the emergence of the primitive, of suppressed desires. When one "peels down," then "peels off," on a Mexican beach, one runs the risk of getting burned; when one ventures upon the high seas, one risks losing the stability one assumes one had on dry land. Like the pioneers, one takes the risks in hopes that *somewhere else* life will be better.

The risks begin when one crosses certain frontiers; one is liable to become sick: "To bolt with a woman you've got to cross a line, a frontier, in your interior. You've got to burn certain bridges that won't be there in case you come back." Mac implies one kind of attitude: "'State line, man? . . . We cross a *state* line?'" On seeing the lights of Acapulco up ahead, Horter thinks, "Anything that is so right, that seems perfect, is followed by a state of apprehension, which reminds you how imperfect perfection really is." Horter's carload becomes nauseous on the food of the unfamiliar territory.

At sea, one risks throwing up one's indigestible old self; between intakes of passengers, the ship itself seems to eructate. The order in which Soby and his friends become seasick depends upon the degree to which the interior of each is susceptible to change. Miss Kollwitz first tries to protect Soby from the sickness at sea that symbolizes his release; then she delays his full acceptance of the change which does come over him. Just before Soby and Cynthia make the final leap together, a ceremony of seasickness joins them. *She* throws up, but "oddly enough Soby felt relief, as if the food had been on his stomach."

By land, Horter goes from the Hollywood beach to the Mexican;

by sea, Soby goes to Venice, where everyman's doorstep fronts the beach, and to Greece, to the archetype of all beaches where Nausicaä rescued Odysseus. Of the two beaches in *Cannibals,* the Hollywood beach enhances the theme of the phony present encrusted with inessentials; the Mexican beach, the theme of the real present, stripped to essentials. The passage from Hollywood to Mexico emphasizes the shift from Horter's immersion in a phony present to his emergence into a real present in an atmosphere that encourages the change. Horter and Mac change with the scene because of the women there; the Greek herself doesn't change.

In the "mobile world of Los Angeles," Uncle Dudley and The Kid sat on a bench near the beach. Horter lies on the beach itself. California "haunts the imagination and defies the effort to come to terms with it." Morris asks, "Where else but in the City of Angels does America bury its past and flee from its present on a network of speedways? Where else, so aptly, could an author who has buried his past confront the present in its most appalling form?" (Lectures). Los Angeles "has never ceased to attract, repel, and fascinate [Morris] as the laboratory of the future." All the inessential artifacts of the transitory moment are there: sun-tan oil, portable radio, swimming cap with simulated hair. Languishing on the Hollywood beach, Horter is, in a negative sense, more out of than in this world. "I'm the biggest fool in the world for pathos, and you can't beat the pathos of a beautiful world in which nobody, and I mean nobody, knows how to live."

Until he meets the Greek, he is too indifferent and tired to bolt from the fix he is in: mere existence in such a world. The Greek and the Mexican scene cause Horter to live positively. On the beach, "a strip of sun and sand where the sex is alert, the mind is numb," Horter is in *his* territory ahead, which he recognizes by the fact that he has not been to *this* Mexico before. One evening they all go down to the beach to talk over *what next?* But nobody cares. "Here on the strand, in the languorous air, we seemed to have found what we had come for"—a ceremony of natural love without cliché.

At sea "anything might happen. On occasion it actually did." On the ship, Soby learns that between strangers a sudden intimacy is possible, that a disinterested curiosity may come into play, which friendship or kinship forbids. "'You don't have to *know* people to *like* them!'" Cynthia tells Miss Kollwitz. She responds naturally and spontaneously to Dr. Hodler and to Perkheimer, both strangers and Germans. When language is a barrier, the freedom of travel allows animal magnetism and physical gestures to become modes of communication.

There are people who take precautions against the effect of the sea and new places, like Miss Kollwitz, who constantly (too constantly) peels fresh fruit,[1] and those who withdraw, like Mr. Lipari, in such terror that they gain a certain dignity. Miss Throop, on the other hand, surrenders to impulse: she attends the Bal Masque as Miss Italy, her costume composed of travel folders. At the dance, the effect of the sea transforms some of the passengers into "shadowy nightmare figures in a smoky bacchic frieze" that reminds Soby of Aschenbach's dream: "One might step from one wild scene into the other ... under the spell of the stranger God." For some the gangplank is a "roped incline where the dreams crossed ... the only natural habitat." Thus Cynthia becomes a mermaid singing to Prufrock, and she and Soby end as "a pair of cool fish, scared of drowning, but no longer so scared of each other." After this transformation, Soby comments: "there's nothing like a voyage by water, is there? A sea-change is the first and last change, isn't it? After all it was the sea, as you may remember, from where—" Miss Kollwitz remembers only too well. Sensing that "something evil" is transforming the people on the boat, she decides to disembark to prevent losing "something one could never recover"—one's thick skin of cliché. The unpredictability of Venice gives some a sense of freedom, and unnerves others. By the end, Soby has failed to straddle the opposed attitudes of the two old maids concerning the effects of travel.

Even on land, people and things seem to tip or tilt, conveying a sense of the sea's enduring effect. In Venice, "it was perhaps only natural that [Soby] believed himself somewhere at sea." If Morris is fond of likening the dry plains to the sea, making it a metaphysical landscape like Melville's ocean, in Venice he observes the intermingling of the two; he contemplates both the arid past and fluctuating tides of the present.

In Mexico, the setting is primitive; in Venice and Greece, the characters encounter three stages of European culture: Medieval, Renaissance, and Classic. To a great extent, both now exist for the sake of swarms of tourists, many of whom bring with them what they insist on seeing. They fail to perceive the forces of life that thrive beneath the encrustation of clichés; those for whom the scene answers an ontological need do see that here is a life more vital than that which the tourists left behind. For instance, the first visit to the Acropolis proves a disappointment both to Kollwitz and Soby; but, later, only Miss Kollwitz is thrilled to see it again in a book of cliché-pictures like the ones that drew her to Greece in the first place.

IV   Improvisation: The Cliché Transformed

The characters cannot experience the present in the immediacy of sex, nor know the wisdom of the body and the impersonality of love, nor respond to the effects of travel, if they have not yet come to terms with the clichés that flood their everyday lives, and stripped themselves down to the essentials. Since these two books are more concerned than any of the others with the process of improvisation in which the cliché is transformed, the reader might look more closely at this important element in Morris' work.

If one keeps sympathetically in mind the fact that Morris' unique style, grounded in the simplicity of Midwestern speech, depends upon his conscious improvising on the cliché, one is less inclined to be disturbed by his style. Clichés lured many men West; today, Western clichés are big business. In the barren environment of his childhood, Morris doubtlessly encountered the force of cliché; as Horter observes, "culture is a series of acceptable clichés." After Morris, a cliché is never quite the same—it is killed and resurrected in the same moment of usage. The cliché is symbolic of the dream defunct, and it is with this "dead" language that Morris depicts the sterility of modern life. But, in resurrecting the freshness of clichés in his use of them, he suggests, in his very mode of expression, that the dead past can be made to live.

A cataract of falsity blinds our collective vision of archetypal elements in our past. Norman Rockwell's illustrations, a prime example of the abuse of the past (see *Territory*, 113-29), give the real a phony, sentimental semblance of life. In the beginning was the cliché, and it is still there in the end; in his crippling respect for it, he is perhaps ignorant that a false archetypal image is projected. While Rockwell strives to give his graphic clichés the denotative force of the familiar, the tone of Morris' diction makes the cliché sound strange—it has an aura of having just been coined. It never loses the sense of wonder that gave it birth, the sense of the unique on which it first thrived. "Every cliché once had its moment of truth. At the moment of conception it was a new and wonderful thing."[2] Morris makes new a "diet of outworn clichés."

An artful control of the cliché performs a major function in Morris' works. With clichés he does three things simultaneously: (1) presents them, as such, with a fidelity that reveals their essential grotesquery; (2) presents his characters in the mode of the clichés by which they live and communicate; but in so doing he (3) reveals what is genuine and valid. Cliché serves the purpose of almost every technical device. For instance, the manipulation of cliché is basic to the effectiveness of Morris' unique humor.

In the same moment that the cliché works against itself it is transformed, and becomes, at times, both eloquent and significant.

In life, too, "it is the style that sets the cliché." What moves us is the "charm of the style": "Hemingway turning a phrase, the cowboy rolling a cigarette, the gunman slipping on or off a glove." It enables a mythic figure to "exchange his mortal life" for immortality: Lone Eagles like Garbo, Ty Cobb, and Lindbergh. The characters in *The Huge Season* had style in the 1920's. But today it is the cliché, not "the real McCoy," "that proves contagious": those who imitate Brando, Presley, and Oppenheimer merely "bear witness to the cliché." "We are left with a product rather than a process—a coonskin hat rather than Davy Crockett." This is a paralyzing quality, but "clichés, bless them, both destroy life—and make it possible." In their raw-material form, both character and cliché are "inflexible" and "appallingly predictable," but transformed in the character of Uncle Dudley, for instance, they are as resilient as Charlie Chaplin's cane, as unpredictable as that standby of all clichés—the weather.

For Rockwell, character is *presented* cliché. But for Morris, as early as *The Home Place,* "Character is revealed cliché." Muncy observes the way his Uncle Harry holds a baby in the barber shop, as though he were a Madonna with child. "On the one hand I knew that what I saw was unbelievably corny, on the other hand I knew it was one of the finest things I had seen." In his sensibility, both the cliché and the real thing blend in a moment of revelation.

Horter is the intellect dealing with clichés, transforming them into song lyrics for mass consumption; Mac, who cops his second-hand emotions from clichés "coined before he was," does the same with music. By profession, if not by temperament, Horter is immersed in the clichés of the submediocre mass media culture of contemporary America. "When the beach is crowded I listen for the up-and-coming clichés." He is painfully aware that "every sentiment had its own pitch, the way that every generation has its own sentiment. . . . The pitch we hear today, the phony pitch, is absolutely right for the phony sex, the phony sentiment. . . . The word for it is slobism."

Horter has become so saturated with clichés that he meets the Greek in Hollywood, where the phony pitch is strident, "the way a man meets his fate" in a movie romance. This "master of the cliché" cannot express the way he feels, "since he hardly knew, without the cliché, what it was he felt." To see if she were real, feeling unreal himself, Horter arranges a rendezvous. When he asks her what she would like to do, she looks him straight in the eye: " 'Is there anything else?' " Horter, affected already, says to the motelkeeper,

" 'We are in love . . . and want something good.' The freshness of the cliché disarmed him."

Morris has observed that one of the most obvious traits of the American character is the ability or the impulse to improvise: "the passion, sometimes the mania to *make it new*" (Lectures). As a massive culture, America is unique in history, remaining "as a *process,* changing its shape and its nature, daily, before the world's eyes." For the artist, improvisation becomes experimentation. But in his own photo-text technique, now abandoned, Morris learned that "the improvising flair is a tool, but not an end." The culture observed in *Cannibals* demonstrates the fact that "to improvise, however well, is to breed a form of incoherence, since everything must remain in a state of flux." Previous to meeting the Greek, Horter tried, in his songs, to "make it new" by improvisation, a continual process in the book. Now he improvises upon the process of transforming the cliché in his own life. By example, the Greek teaches Horter that the "first problem, surgically speaking, is to remove from the subject the encrusted cliché."

Having moved in a world of superfluity, Morris sees the need to strip down materially and spiritually to the essentials. The conflict between the real thing and the cliché is one between essentials and inessentials. The "shearing off" process leaves one in a "useless condition. A reassembling of the usable parts, of the functional experience, must begin again" (Amherst Lectures). The only character already stripped down when the novel begins, the Greek causes a stripping process among the others and teaches them "about loving and talking from scratch." Near-death has made her a non-dreamy realist who knows that "you can't ignore the basic things." Horter's need for *her* is basic. At the threshold of the motel cabin, she kicks off her high-heeled shoes. The room, like the beach, contains only the essentials: "A simple facing up to the facts." He feels no shame, no embarrassment. In Mexico, Horter is stripped, like the phony studio car, to the essentials; at the same time, he is in the process of becoming, like the unfinished house.

Like Dudley and The Kid, Horter cares nothing for his car and the "valuables" it contains because he realizes how inessential they are. On the trek across country in *The Field of Vision,* the pioneers drop both inessentials and essentials along the trail; and Morris grew up where everything was kept to the essentials. But the stuff Horter drops is transitory anyway, nothing like Muncy's grand-mother's cane bottom chair. Although the villa will become ultra-modern with all the conveniences, Horter and the Greek live in it now as though it were a primitive Mexican house equipped only with the essentials. But the closer to sexual nakedness and freedom from cliché Horter comes, the more inundated in cliché and propriety Mac, via Billie, becomes. She is upset to find the material inessentials of her life stolen from the car. " 'Ah will nevah even know what ah lost,' " she says, having lost nothing that was ever a genuine part of herself and therefore of value.

The end of Horter's sojourn in the Mexican garden of Eden comes one night when the Greek, nude, steps over the threshold of the villa with nothing more to kick off, except Horter, who is no longer essential to *her*. But when Mac says, " 'It's been real, man!' " Horter is profoundly aware of just how real it has been. For with the Greek, he has reached the point where he can cease to speak the clichés of romance which his intellect has always scorned. After her, Horter the essentialist will never again be satisfied with less than the real thing.

The characters in the Soby novel are engaged in a similar stripping process. All around Soby things are in a state of flux, being either stripped down or built up; for instance, he reminds himself to count the stars on the United States flag. On the ship, Miss Kollwitz, knitting a green sweater for Cynthia, uses Soby's long arm for size; in Venice, she knits *him* a brown one, and thus the two are symbolically related. Like the sweaters both Soby and Cynthia are in the process of becoming. Cynthia suspects that Soby admires her portrait because, like their relationship, it is unfinished. But he rejects the painter's fixed Botticelli image of her because it fails to capture "the somewhat elusive, still evolving, indeterminate" qualities. Finally, Soby is stripped to the point where Cynthia, her head audaciously rammed through the still wet portrait, asks, " 'Daddy-O, why yoh travel so light?' "

Perkheimer, the little German photographer, sees things in all their naked whatness. He accuses his fellow Germans of being under a curse: they will never succeed in becoming German *enough*, in perfecting the clichés about themselves. Thus Germans flood Greece "not to *see* Greece, no, no, Greece lay buried under their own fall of ashes—but to gaze into the Grecian mirror for the one perfect German." In a dispute about the German soul with the *Wandervogel*, especially Holzapfel, Perkheimer sets the style for audacity. If "the soul's cage was the body, so let them bare it, and see how matters stood." " 'My friends,' he said, 'what a small thing it is to take off one's hat to something. If one admires it—and is German enough—let him take off his clothes!' " He strips. Exeunt Germans.

In the Soby novel captivity in the cliché is caused by limitations of vision. The most irritatingly repetitious, but one of the most important, motifs is the lidding of the eyes when a character's equilibrium is upset. It begins with Soby and Aschenbach: "From the goings-on in the torchlight both the dreamer and the reader averted their eyes." When Cynthia looks at him out of an impersonal existence such as the dream conveyed, he avoids her eyes. If Miss Throop learns to lid her eyes with pleasure, Miss Kollwitz most often seals both eyes and lips against "evil." Unlike Miss Kollwitz, Miss Throop has "not come to Greece to look at ruins she might have seen on Long Island." Dr. Hodler, a freelance, imaginative archaeologist wonders, "What had ruins to do with Greece? Ruins had only to do with themselves. The living proof, not the dead reminder, the living flesh, not the mutilated marble-- for this one journeyed to Greece, or one was deceived. . . . It was Nausicaä one wanted, not tracks in the sand."

In Dr. Hodler, Cynthia recognizes a man free enough of cliché to respond to the dead past come alive in the living present—herself. It is because she *is* Nausicaä that she alone can return "the lenses' bold stare." Dr. Hodler lauds Perkheimer, a photographer, for his Schliemannian aspiration: to rediscover one of the earth's stars, Greece. Why explore the moon and the stars, which are lovely only when seen from earth, while Greece "lies buried under half a century's fall of photographic ash?" Some German cameras already come loaded with pictures of Greece. Perkheimer, "the first to bring light to the camera obscura," refuses to take any pictures if he cannot take one that has not been taken before. After the day's excursion on Corfu, he shows Soby four *empty* cameras—his way of penetrating the "layers of photographic ash." If one can't make it new, one should let it lie.

"If you live in a world of clichés, as I do," says Horter, "some of them of the type you coined yourself, you may not realize how powerful they can be." But Mac points out that the phony is all one has; it *is*, as opposed to what was or is yet to be; and one must make it real. The American impulse to "make it new" is an effort to reshape reality to the heart's desire. Horter attempts to make new the fluctuating clichés of American life. Soby and some of the passengers attempt to make new the clichés of our European heritage. If the process is successful, "the new element forged" is oneself (Lectures).

V *Life Imitates Art*

In a world of clichés, one may observe life imitating art, the relation between fact and fiction becoming ambiguous. But, if one responds to the past imaginatively, one lives most actively in the present. Attuned to the life of both fact and fiction and to one's environment, one may transform one's physical and human surroundings, and finally oneself in the process to achieve identity.

Although these themes are developed in *Cannibals,* they are most explicitly depicted in *What a Way to Go;* in fact, on a terrace in Venice, Soby evaluates at length the nature of the common experience, much as James's Strether does in Paris.

Perhaps the territory ahead, which Morris begins to explore most clearly in *Cause For Wonder,* is the realm of the imagination, where so much lies undiscovered; one may often recognize that he has not been there before. In "Man on the Moon," Morris impressively points out modern man's deficiency of imagination in dealing with the world he has made: "It is not a loss of nerve that confronts man, but a failure of the human imagination. The mind is not scaled to the facts it is obliged to face."[3] What enables one to see that from which the mind shrinks? "A wisdom of the eye, so to speak, preceded that of the mind.... the mind was in the body, and the wisdom of the body counselled the brain what to feel and think. It was the source of fiction, as well as what were known as facts." Venice is as dead in some ways as Lone Tree, but away from home, Morris seems to suggest, a non-crippling response to the past is possible. In Soby's imaginative field of vision, the dead, mythic past becomes fictional fact, given life by the girl.

At sea and on land, Soby's is the centralizing intelligence that perceives pattern amid chaos. On the ship, he observes that life is a Bal Masque. People have "an urge first to take their clothes off, then to put other people's on," as a way of both concealing and revealing themselves. James compared Venice to a mammoth bazaar; Soby sees it as "a tremendous opera," the costumes and the characters being of mixed styles and types, forcing one to face the question, Who am I? The Venetian is "a beautiful race that lives by its imagination," James wrote; for Morris, Venice itself is a result of self-transformation. "Had they not transformed—without divine intervention—a disaster to the city's eternal advantage? ... Soby loitered, gaping, as if waiting to be paged"—for his own transformation. James felt that "there is nothing left" for the visitor "to discover or describe, and originality of attitude is completely impossible."[4] If life looks to most people like "a series of unrelated gestures," Soby's ability to *see* facilitates his transformation.

In Miss Throop, Soby sees a specific example of the way life imitates literature. All the characters infect each other with the virus of suggestion, and Miss Kollwitz blames Soby, who lent Miss Throop Mann's *Death in Venice,* for the sudden effect upon her friend's "climacteric." The first to cross a frontier in her interior and to get sick, Miss Throop is the first to imitate Aschenbach. With her recurring, enigmatic wink, she lets Soby know that they understand each other. From the cabin boy, who resembles one of those men in Aschenbach's dream, Miss Throop does not avert her eyes. She tells Soby that "youth is wasted on the young," and feels, like Henry James's Strether, that "some of us are old enough to enjoy it." Next to get sick, Soby too, inwardly if not outwardly, imitates Aschenbach.

In minor ways at least, each character, responding to the past as it lives in the present or by imitating art, effects a transformation. He transforms either his surroundings or another character (particularly a love object) or both; in doing so, he risks transforming himself. Cynthia is the principal catalyst in this process. Wherever she is, Cynthia's freedom from cliché enables her to respond purely. In Venice and in Greece, she is in harmony with her ancient surroundings. For instance, when she passes the stones of Venice, they seem "to come alive"; and "at her glance the bronze men on the clock tower hammered their bell."

Where the real and the sur-real are almost indistinguishable, all time is one. Morris' interest in the archetypal reaches its fullest expression here. Dr. Hodler asks, "Were some things not always the same? . . . Things like voyages?" Are they not, each in his own fashion, "new actors for the old parts?" The beach where Nausicaä found Odysseus will always exist because it is a myth; and, unlike a natural or man-made wonder, it will not be destroyed by time or man. There, tomorrow, Hodler will supervise a re-enactment of the myth, setting in relief, momentarily, its timelessness: "No apparent time seemed to separate [Cynthia] from the voyages of Ulysses."

When the living make an imaginative response to the dead past, certain risks must be faced. For instance, there is no road to the beach; and, among the rocks, Dr. Hodler sprains his ankle. Holzapfel is not up to the risks posed by his role as Odysseus; Cynthia pretends to drown, lures the non-swimmer out to sea, and the mythic rescue proves more dangerous than was planned. But at the Acropolis, Perkheimer, competing with Holzapfel for Nausicaä, takes his cue from her and audaciously transforms the colossal tourist trap into a battlefield. In a wild chase, partly terrifying, partly a burlesque of the martial Greek past, they revive the Dionysian winesprings of the culture that has here turned to dust. When Soby revisits the Acropolis, Perkheimer's audacity merges with history in Soby's vision; for, absent in body, his spirit lingers.

Cynthia is transformed in the eyes of each beholder. "Everyman his own Pygmalion," Soby says. Although nature may imitate art, the good artist does not imitate nature: "Isn't the artist's purpose to present us with something new? Something more life-like, if possible, than life itself?" Amid the strange scenes of Venice,

Aschenbach, the fictional artist, turned Tadziu into a marble faun of flesh and blood; Signor Pignata turns Cynthia into a "gold-leafed Primavera."

The purpose of both the artist and the lover, roles joined in Pignata, is to transform the object into "a fiction, possibly a work of art, an image of the heart's desire." The face of Pignata himself has been the work of "several centuries of nature imitating art." In the streets of Venice, Pignata hails Cynthia as Botticelli's Primavera; faced with a living fact, a fictional product of her time, he relies on an image of the past to stand in for his failure of imagination. His concept of Cynthia, which he alters on the canvas as he encounters her various fictional guises, makes of him "a bird in his own gilded cage." An awareness of the risk is not part of his response. She becomes a siren of the rocks; the leer she wears is the one he himself conjured up in the unfinished portrait. As Soby remarks, the subject imitates the artist's vision of her.

On the ship to Greece, Dr. Hodler, no artist, hails Cynthia as Nausicaä, the living end to thirty years of research on the beach. He transforms her in the fire of an ancient historical image kept alive in the imagination. When he mates her with Holzapfel, he is the maker of the image. He is glad the question of whether Nausicaä or Odysseus ever existed remains a matter of conjecture. Each man, as Homer realized, is forced to "paint her for himself."

To Soby, Cynthia is alternately Lolita, Mona Lisa smiling mockingly at the old artist frightened of women, "a gift from the sea, a green-eyed sea nymph," a wild goose, "a lank-haired lady Godiva," and "Eve in a pair of soiled shorts," a smile on her mouth that suggests "her bite of the apple" is still in it. She audaciously wears a few outlandish costumes peculiar to her own age group, and she clownishly moves in and out of the costumes of those around her. Ironically, she thinks all along that Soby doesn't like her. When she tearfully asks if he liked *any* of the girls she's been, the reader sees that she has intuitively played all the roles she is cued to play. A little less than any one of them, she is more than enough for Soby. Married to Cynthia, Soby concludes, "Getting back to the Greeks has its hazards."

Aschenbach transformed his beloved, the boy Tadziu, "into a marble faun, but in so doing he was also obliged to transform himself," both his outward appearance and his inward nature. Cynthia affects older men the way Tadziu affected Aschenbach. In transforming her, they transform themselves. Pignata himself comes to wear the smile he painted on Cynthia. Her always evolving nature, from Madonna to Maenad, increasingly tears down his old world reserve until he goes on a rampage of insult and repudiation that Miss Throop wishes Cynthia could hear because she might now "adore him." Dr. Hodler has not read Mann's book, but he naturally, as a member of the *ancien regime,* turns Aschenbach's "illicit, bloodshot leer" on Cynthia; however, he consciously identifies with the historical Caesar, "the mature, seasoned man" whom such a woman as Cleopatra "held in reserve for these special legendary occasions." Perkheimer transforms himself by imitating Dr. Hodler to appeal to Cynthia. On the Lido, Soby feels the presence of Aschenbach in himself. In the relationship between Soby and Cynthia, there is the same slow pattern of coming together as there was between Aschenbach and the boy. The significant difference is that the modern lovers audaciously act on the wisdom of the eyes' mind. Soby does not turn his emotions into a plague that kills him.

Cynthia transforms herself when she strips off the roles she has played. Soby sums up the whole affair: "If it's something immortal you're after look behind the eyes, not at them. . . . However, if it's something mortal you're after—and I take it that it is—what you see before your eyes can be good enough. . . . the beloved is both named and nameless." She is an "*im*person," rather than a person.

In *What a Way to Go,* in which there is so little narrative action, and in which, instead of complexity of vision among characters, the author's brilliant observational powers race about like an eye capable of fantastic changes in speed and rhythm, the reader becomes too often conscious that style is almost all there is. The conception is impressive, but the workings of technique are all too clear. Even though there is more action in it than in most Morris novels, the character and event frame seems flimsy. Morris has such control over his style that he gives to each detail an equal ring of authority. Both these books make particularly extensive use of parallels and similes, but *What a Way to Go* seems one elaborate, often tedious, simile. That everything is like everything else may be a thematic point, but it is driven into the ground. Occasionally, *Cause For Wonder* approaches these stylistic excesses. The first person narrative in *Cannibals* serves the same function in Part One of *Cause For Wonder*—it checks the author's tendency toward self-indulgence.

Morris seems to have learned a great deal about style from Henry James. In James's passion for craft, the immaterial became, "in his hands, the material with the maximum density," and "raw material" often "literally dissolved into technique" (*Territory,* 96). This is a danger to which Morris' style exposes him. In *What a Way to Go,* Morris like Hemingway, almost falls "under his own spell."

Style threatens to substitute for raw material, and manner verges on mannerism. Every self-aware writer "sooner or later is confronted with the *dictates* of style." What Morris says of Hemingway suggests the dangers he faces himself: "The style, not the creative mind, dictates the range and nature of the experience, selects the cast, and determines what is permissible." Style dictates "the turn of the thought" and "gives it the ring of truth" (*Territory*, 138, 145).

CHAPTER 9

The Navel of the World

P ARTS OF A SINGLE NOVEL whose third part is yet to come, *The Field of Vision* and *Ceremony in Lone Tree* are probably Morris' finest works. In them, he attempts to resolve thematic implications presented in previous novels. He needed a design that would encompass, elucidate, and give new dimension to the several, though similar, designs that shaped the material before; a locale symbolic of the former ones; characters in whom the significant ones would be represented; and a way of ordering the scattered images, ideas, motifs, and themes. In *Field* and *Ceremony* he begins to arrange "familiar pieces in a new pattern.... It could not be done at all ... while I was trapped in my own material. In these self-dug graves lie the bearded giants—face down" (Letter).

Nostalgia often immolates the writer in his raw material. Morris discusses this problem in *The Territory Ahead:* "Nostalgia rules our hearts while a rhetoric of progress rules our words." Confronted with the present, the finest writers respond to the call of the territory behind, the mythic past: "The best American fiction is still *escape* fiction." The minor artist is content to abuse the past by merely indulging in it, by reminiscing, like Mark Twain; but the craftsman like James consciously conceptualizes, *uses* the past. The one never transcends autobiography; the other is art. To use the past is audaciously to destroy and create at the same moment of conception and imagination. This is what Morris attempts in his latest novels. "For Wright Morris," says Alan Trachtenberg, "the pastoral dream-lament has lost its integrity" ("C. of V.," 42).

In Mexico during the Christmas holidays, Gordon Boyd, self-exiled Nebraskan writer in late middle age, accidentally meets his childhood friends, Walter and Lois McKee, and takes them to a bullfight; during the several hours until twilight the present action of *Field of Vision* occurs. With the McKees is their grandson, Gordon, and Lois's father, Tom Scanlon. With Boyd is his analyst, Dr. Lehmann, and Paula Kahler, a male transvestite. In the past, Scanlon's father had led the pioneer trek West, Boyd had snatched Ty Cobb's pocket, had kissed Lois on the front porch, and had attempted to walk on water. In the present, Boyd squirts a bull with pop, a Mexican kid jumps into the ring, Lois faints, a matador is gored, and little Gordon himself goes into the ring.

The present action in *Ceremony in Lone Tree* occurs between twilight and sun-up toward the end of March of the same year, inside and around the defunct Lone Tree Hotel where Scanlon lives. A reunion in honor of Scanlon's ninetieth birthday brings together his children: Lois, Maxine, and Edna; and their husbands, Walter, Bud Momeyer, and Colonel Ewing. Also present are Etoile, Maxine's adolescent daughter; Calvin and Gordon, Lois's grandchildren; and their mother, Eileen. Boyd brings a pick-up whom he calls Daughter. Jennings, son of Will Brady, also appears. Most of these characters share the past presented in *Field*. While the McKees were in Mexico, Lee Roy, Bud's nephew, killed three boys with his hotrod; and Charlie Munger (patterned after Charles Starkweather, the Nebraska killer) shot twelve people; both are in jail. The main events in the present are the elopement of Calvin and Etoile and their raucous return to Lone Tree which provokes Lois into firing her grandfather's pistol, startling Scanlon and precipitating his death.

Each character's view of his place in time is conditioned by his place in the hero-witness relationship. Boyd and McKee, as hero and witness, represent two opposed sides of the American Dream. There comes a point when this relationship must end; the witness must wake from the spell, and the hero must free himself of dependence on the witness. Severance begins in *Field* and is accomplished, for better or worse, in *Ceremony*. Both McKee, when he impulsively sends the invitation to the reunion, and Boyd, when he impulsively responds, realize that disillusionment in Mexico was not enough; the break must occur on native ground.

I   *The Creative Eye*

In highly concentrated moments of consciousness each character *sees* his own life in time. "The eye," says Trachtenberg, "does not merely record, but ... creates. Vision begins in the head" ("C. of V.," 43). In *Field* none sees the same bullfight; none sees the common experience of the past and present from the same perspective or with the same attitude. Complications arise from the different ways each processes the common raw material. Some emerge from the darkness of these complications in the light of inconclusive discoveries and recognitions. In the present, the major event is psychological: the characters' effort to order the pieces of the common puzzle of their lives.

The viewpoint characters are: McKee, Lois, Scanlon, Boyd, and Lehmann. Why do they appear and alternate in that order? The McKees have made the present material world which Scanlon, ineffectual bridge between the pioneer past and the present, has refused to enter. With an artist's sensibility, Boyd tries to give meaningful form in his imagination to the worlds of past and present and to his own role as hero. Lehmann, the foreigner, provides an objective appraisal. His sections are general variations on elements in the lives of the three major characters; by pondering the world in universal, symbolic terms, he makes sense of the thoughts of the others even though he has no direct access to them. While Lehmann sees the possibilities and the built-in defects of human vision, his own sight is flawed because he spends too much time seeing through the eyes of hyperconscious neurotics like Boyd or mindless ones like Paula. Morris creates three kinds of distances from these views: his own third-person tone, and the implied consciousnesses of Paula (the vision of the inspired insane) and Gordon (the vision of the child). This rich complexity of vision enables the reader to become a participant who dynamically unifies in his own imaginative field of vision, in a conscious act of perception, the fragments of vision, and thus finally focuses Morris' concept.

The characters in *Ceremony*, ostensibly ordinary people in an extraordinary world, are intricately bound up with each other; and an intricately controlled design of motifs relates the vision of each character to every other, the past to the present, and Lone Tree to the outside world. *Ceremony* begins with Scanlon's viewpoint in "The Scene" as he contemplates the navel of the world, Lone Tree, through a flaw in the window. His vision merges, in the same section, with McKee's; the modern, grassy world of nearby Polk that threatens Lone Tree is McKee's world; he represents the new breed and has the most adaptable perspective on the present. "The Roundup" of the characters who are to appear on the scene begins, appropriately, with Boyd; if they are all trapped in Scanlon's past, they are also imprisoned, actually or symbolically, in the hero-witness relationship. Boyd's is the ambiguous view of the self-exile, the haunted iconoclast. Refracted through his view, we get a more objective attitude, that of Boyd's alter-ego, Daughter. She is caught in her own personal vision; while she heckles those who live in the past, she takes up with Boyd. In the material present world of Lincoln, McKee's view is first, followed by Lois's view of the world he has made for her; next comes Maxine's view of her child in that world; then comes Etoile's, followed by Calvin's view of the world the adults have created; Bud's is that of the child-adult; Lee Roy's is that of the child who goes beserk; and, refracted through his, is Munger's more extreme view. This section ends with Jennings' view, that of the sympathetic outsider. A man much like his father, Will Brady, Jennings is so intrigued, like Lehmann, with the mystery of life that he has no life of his own. He comes from Omaha to investigate a new style mystery, Lee Roy; but he encounters his milder counterparts instead. The rationale of viewpoint sequence in "The Ceremony," the longest section, is more complex. It is enough here to say that Scanlon, having no perspective on the present, remains on a cot behind the stove without a point of view. The book ends in McKee's vision, because his will prevail, Boyd and Daughter having closed their eyes in sleep.

It is interesting to compare the actual and symbolic settings for the interaction of fields of vision in the two novels. An accidental reunion brings the characters together at the bullring; a planned reunion assembles them at Lone Tree. In Mexico the transforming ritual of the bullfight, with its traditional ceremonies and artistic elements, is the actual setting and allegorical frame that stimulates the characters to relate present and past. In spirit the Nebraskans are back in Lone Tree and Polk, always as mysterious to them as Mexico. Hot, exotic Mexico is a violent atmosphere for stirring up old memories and suppressed tendencies; and the brutal bullfight ritual contrasts vividly with the seemingly mild incidents of the past. Consciously and unconsciously, they see their lives in a way that tends toward a critical moment that parallels the matador's moment of truth. In *Ceremony* American show business, with its improvisational element, is the *symbolic* background. Assembled in the lulling moonlight for a reunion ceremony in the home of the man (Scanlon) who personifies the past and most intensely acts a part, the characters force, by their present behavior, a violent confrontation of past and present. In *Field*, the characters are relatively immobile spectators; in *Ceremony*, they step down into the symbolic arena at the defunct home place, retaining their ability to see while in the midst of action.

With defective vision, the characters come under the power of illusion and of imagination, which sustains those who remain captives of the past. In *Ceremony*, the scene and all it evokes are preserved in Scanlon's imagination—land (fact) and water (fiction) blend. The creative hero and the creative witness perceive or make in their imaginations a blend of fact and fiction. When the railroad track bed cuts off their view of the town, Daughter says, in the parlance of magic: " 'Now you see it, now you don't.' . . 'Nevertheless,' said Boyd, 'You know it's still there.' " This recurrent expression suggests the magical ambiguity of the blend. The characters are inclined to see anything suggested to them; what is visual is no more vivid than what can be envisioned. Although the land and the tongue are dry, the eye and the mind are wet with romance. Lone Tree is like a ghost-town movie set, delivered in the night on a railroad flatcar. A movie house replaced the bank when the money failed to arrive from the East; "Visit the Lyric Tonite," the sign still reads. "And why not? If the call was wild enough maybe some of them would." Moonlight illuminates the romantic nostalgia of the past, but that moon is eclipsed by disillusionment and nausea in the present.

II *Unconscious Struggle for a Community of Vision in Time*

In *Field* the significant events occurred in the past, but in *Ceremony* the characters think almost entirely of the recent and immediate common present, while the distant, common past casts its crippling spell. At the bullring the movement of consciousness is away from the present toward a reshaping of the past. At Lone Tree, however, the movement is away from the past toward a more intense experience in the present as preparation for an uncertain future. Thus, through the minds of four generations in both books, the reader perceives character and event in the contexts of immediate action, memory, and the connected consciousnesses of characters intuitively striving for a communality of vision.

Considered in the context of all his works, Morris' chief purpose in *Ceremony* is to free his characters from the past in the midst of an actual conflict between past and present, under the threat or promise of the future. Most of the characters go through an informal ceremony of ridding themselves of the inessentials of the past by audacious acts, each according to his nature. In Scanlon's actual death and departure for burial, everyone witnesses the symbolic death of the heroic past. Presented in *Field*, the past is now buried with Scanlon. Nothing hints of a resurrection.

Ceremony conveys a sense of past and present in weird coexistence; living and dead "fossils" on the scene parallel immediate things. Lacking a mythic past or a folk tradition that sustains rather than cripples them, and lacking the creative hero that should follow an era of raw experience, the witnesses (and the defunct hero) are caught up in a complex problem of identity that is especially acute in *Ceremony*.

The prairie is now a dry sea where it all began. Aware that something is ending in Lone Tree, the characters wildly improvise on new selves. In the foreground is the innocent show-business image (past fiction), but in the background is the atomic-bomb image (present fact). *Ceremony* is rife with vaudeville, movie, circus, television and popular fiction allusions; the past is a grotesque shadow play enacted against a sky where at any moment a lethal man-made cloud may blossom.

Munger and Lee Roy exemplify themes and motifs that have less drastic counterparts among the other characters, most of whom identify with them. The aspiration to be *somebody* is part of the American Dream. Anybody can be President; anybody can be famous. If one is nobody and if the pain, the fear, the certainty that one will remain so is oppressive, what does one do? One shoots somebody, or other nobodies, and becomes notorious. Lee Roy stated that he wanted, like Munger, to be somebody. He wanted, like so many people, to be almost anybody but who he happened to be. Obviously, the Munger-Lee Roy audacity differs from that of the pioneer past.

In his personality and in his observations, Jennings synthesizes the show motif and raises the question of identity, couched in the language of a vaudeville routine. Lacking a strong self-nucleus, most of the men play roles whose styles are set in the past and patterned on fictional or "real" persons. The women depend less upon identification with current or outmoded famous figures; but, because the men fail to cause anything real to happen in the present, the women are often no more effectual than their unreal men. Almost everyone *is* somebody else. This process of identification both helps and hinders the characters in their unconscious search for identity.

The men are in a double deep sleep: they are under the spell not only of the women but of their own dreams of being heroes or of their persistent acting out of the past. The show-business routines, the bombs, and the trains wake them, lull them to sleep, or startle them to death. If one is to transform oneself, a balanced blend of past and present must be achieved.

III   *The Explosion of Suppressed Emotions*

In *Ceremony* more than in any other novel, Morris explores the problem of suppressed emotions, a legacy of the pioneer generations and a problem that strengthens the imprisoning power of the past. Fear of themselves and each other, of Munger and his kind, and of atomic annihilation, among other things, creeps among the characters in Lincoln and in Lone Tree. The Munger-Lee Roy killings are an immediate expression of the inevitable explosion of these suppressed emotions. Since the spirit of the times helped shape him and since all are part of a hostile society, Munger can kill anyone and get the right one. Lee Roy fastens on a group that directly antagonizes him. Etoile arouses his hopeless passion; Calvin and the "lucky" college boys arouse his envy; and some hoodlums, who mock his masculinity and ridicule his weird hot rod, finally arouse his cold, impulsive rage. A week later, Munger blindly slaughters 12 people he doesn't even know. "Repressed sexual energy" erupts in "the violence of impotence."[1] On the frontier plains, men ran amok after the solitude of herding cattle; now the solitude exists when among people.

A theme of wildness pervades the book. "The Scene" conveys a premonition of death and a sense of desolation, elements which have their spiritual correlatives in the characters. "Primordial violence" smolders beneath the placid surface. The bomb (symbol of the threatening world man has made rather than imagined creatively) that didn't go off in the desert proving ground explodes here; it is concocted of the suppressed emotional energy of the psychic community.

Stifled emotions would seem to be the usual situation. Back on the old frontier, almost everyone—even the quiet, the "normal," and the prudish—is desperately audacious as a kind of last stand. Each character gropes for his moment of truth, audacity, love, imagination, or of release from the past or from the hero by surrendering to impulse in word or deed, tasting freedom and wildness. Ironically, only Boyd and Scanlon fail to do something that is, in their terms, audacious.

One way to get a clearer understanding of the hero-witness relationship, the technique of vision, the dynamics of time, and the suppression of emotion is to focus on six of the main characters of *Ceremony,* the first four of whom appear initially in *Field of Vision*: Scanlon, Boyd, McKee and Lois, and Etoile and Calvin.

IV   Scanlon: A Fossil of the Past

The first charge was the one Tim Scanlon transmitted to his son, Tom. He put the story of the pioneer trek he led across country to Nebraska through one transformation after another. Tom failed to pass on the charge to his own children. Neither Boyd nor Scanlon has any hope of benefiting from what he is, but both feel that only in children is there any hope. Scanlon teaches Gordon that the shortest way to heaven is "right smack through hell." When the boy meets Boyd at the bullfight, Scanlon has already filled in the background. Representing opposed views, the two heroes make no connection with each other. In *Ceremony,* Scanlon, as hero, sleeps and awakens only to die.

Seated at the bullring or behind the flawed window, Scanlon provides a historical frame, acts as curtain puller on the drama of the old Midwest. Blind to the real bull, he sees only his symbolic bull. When he closes his eyes, the bullring becomes a desert. The sounds from the ring stimulate and parallel his remembering; for instance, although he doesn't see the bullfight, he and the matador become one; for, when the gored matador yells for "aqua," Tom, dying of thirst in the desert of his imagination, calls for water. From his bed by the window facing the tracks West, Scanlon likes the empty view as his father had before him. His imagination fills it.

Scanlon is the most vivid example of the fact that each character sees only himself, even when seeing others; for, in seeing his father, Scanlon *becomes* his father and loses selfhood. The proof of the superiority of the old breed is in the telling. And the more he tells the story to the boy as though the events happened to himself, the truer it seems. Just as his father victimized him, Scanlon victimizes his two grandchildren. He tries to make Gordon see through his blind eyes. Of his own accord, Calvin, Gordon's brother, desires to merge his vision with Scanlon's, to exchange his frustrating present for what he wrongly thinks is Scanlon's past. But each is saved by a woman: Gordon by Lois, Calvin by Etoile.

Scanlon's highly charged imagination effects no transformation in others because his father's acts made his own superfluous. He arrives at no moment of truth or compassion. When the boy, bewitched by Boyd, ignores Scanlon (old-type hero of the imagination), the old man, stranded in the wasteland of the present, recedes deeper into the better world of the past and transforms himself: he *becomes* the past. Scanlon had thought his father immortal. When Tim died, Tom was "in every sense that matters, just about as dead." In *Ceremony* he has become Buffalo Bill, thus raising his father and himself to mythic status and leaving completely the human realm.

Both Scanlon and Paula represent the paradox of self-transformation, as Trachtenberg points out. For each self-creation is also an act of self-destruction; and this act is seen as an American dilemma in Scanlon and as a more universal one in Paula. "In striving to know itself," the mind "runs the risk of knowing nothing else" (54). Unconsciously, Paula and Scanlon fail to overcome that risk, which Boyd consciously both faces and eludes. If Paula's catatonic sleep proves Lehmann's observation that there is "no mind if the lines to the past were destroyed," Scanlon is proof of what happens if all lines lead to the past. Paula dies as a male, to be reborn into an entirely feminine world, where she lives only in the present, having obliterated, with her sex, her male past.

Scanlon immolates himself as an individual by living immediately in the masculine past. The fly in the YMCA room that reminds Lehmann of the one Paula resurrected and that causes him to reflect on the common predicament of all living creatures (all need help) buzzes between the curtain and the window pane in the Lone Tree hotel, but Scanlon sees no such kinship. Blind to people of the present, Scanlon sees only mythic figures; blind to human beings now, Paula sees only her kinship with insects.

Looking at Scanlon, some of the others sense that they had better free themselves from the past. His mother named the town after "a lonely tree in the midst of a lonely plain"; Scanlon and the dead cottonwood are now one. His father opened the West, his brothers closed it, his children fled to the East. Like the rider backing out of the bullring, he backed out of the new century; it didn't face West. Since there was nothing he ever cared to live or die for, he is neither dead nor alive.

If the artifacts found on the heroic land were once holy to Morris, artifacts of both past and present are now observed in a negative context. Both the rural ruins and the urban houses, along with their inhabitants, are shells. A television antenna "like a giant Martian insect, crouches on the roof of McKee's house as if about to fly off with" it. From his window Scanlon sees flint arrowheads (wild past defunct) and rusted machinery (the promise of the future). If residents near the atomic proving grounds wear metal tags which indicate whether "the place is safe to live in or not," a similar test is unsystematically made in Lone Tree. It proves uninhabitable for life of the past; but it is fertile, due to modern methods of dry farming, for an agrarian life of the future. Materially, if not yet spiritually, a new era has come to the plains: "On the face of the moon the vapor trail of a jet slowly dissolved." The modern equivalent of the Western frontier is outer space.

As they crossed the frontier, the pioneers ritualistically stripped inessentials away, but Tim Scanlon and his son failed to build, materially or spiritually, anything for future generations. It seems that men who clear wildernesses can't live in the clearing, since wildernesses are what they really want. When Scanlon is unceremoniously buried, the past has come full cycle. His birthday is his death day, but it is also the birth of the present for several of the others.

Scanlon "seldom felt *much*, so any feeling threw him off." His children, especially Lois, take after him. Faced with the land, the pioneer life, and Scanlon, his wife shut her eyes to everything to keep from going mad. When she died, Scanlon worried about how the chickens would take it. For him, imagination watered by the monsoons of the past was a surrogate for emotional sterility in the present. Now he feels only hate.

V Boyd: Audacious Amateur

It is in *The Field of Vision* that the hero-witness relationship has its fullest expression. The flat, dry land makes a hero of Boyd, Morris' most effectively drawn hero, as arid regions have always produced prophets. Nebraska is "where the dance" is. "From that still point the mind rippled out." Like Tim Scanlon, Boyd needed a witness, but he needed one in the heat of the act. Since his youth, he has had no bewitched witnesses; in the absence of Lois and McKee, he has done nothing: "Profession: Hero. Situation: Unemployed." As a hero, he is superior to Scanlon, for his imagination reaches out; but, like the land, he doesn't pan out: "In the dream, that is, began the irresponsibility."

One of the most concentrated present moments in *Field* comes when a Mexican kid climbs over the fence into the ring, a symbolic event in which all the other moments are dynamically fused and clarified. Mainly, it is an illuminating elaboration of the hero-witness theme. Morris gives perspective to the relationship: a kid unconnected with the group becomes inspired by the matador to exhibit the "derring-do of the non-professional touch. The high waxed-winged flights of Icarus Boyd, audacious amateur." The spirit that lifted Boyd over the ball-field fence sets off the Mexican kid. In the ring, the matador, the professional, executes a brilliant pass and turns away, "as from a still life, an arrangement that would remain as he had left it, the scene transformed into a frieze of permanence. . . . Word into flesh, and the flesh itself into myth." In killing the bull according to the rules and according to the risks, the hero achieves "the power to transform." The moment of truth comes in the style of the performance, not at the thrust of the sword; following the moment of transformation, both man and bull are empty of the power that transformed them. But the bull, coming up from behind the matador, gores him. "The crumpled end of the hero's life." The ritual of the bullfight explains Boyd's own life as hero: "In the expectation of the goring the hero was made. As well as broken. A crumpled top hat with the rabbit bleeding inside."

Boyd caught a foul ball hit by Ty Cobb, the Georgia Peach. When he went out on the field to get it autographed (transformed), he dropped it in the crowd. But before the awed gaze of McKee, he tore the pocket from Ty Cobb's pants. In that act hero, witness, and pocket were one in a moment of transformation. Throughout his life, Boyd carries the talismanic pocket, but it has become "a winding sheet where the hero lay, cocoon-like, for the next twenty years. Out of this world, in the deep-freeze of his adolescent dreams." Boyd and McKee contemplate "the enduring nature of the aftermath."

In the bullring, the actual focus is on scorched sand, but over the metaphysical landscape of the mind the water rises. Columbus, the inspired explorer, walked on water. The pioneers set out in prairie schooners upon a dry land that resembled the sea. Scanlon's father discovered water in hell. Years later, Boyd tried to walk on it. He spilled *his* "blood" at the sandpit. What physical audacity failed to achieve, Boyd tried to raise to the level of art in his play version of the incident. But his problem is that he is too keenly aware of the conditions that produced him, and of his role as hero. Having set himself impossible goals early (as did America itself), he starts an endless series of anticlimaxes and failures. "If only the impossible seemed worth doing," Lehmann observes, "Boyd would end up doing nothing."

Although he understands and follows the bullfight, Boyd sees the ring as "that twilight zone on the porch where anything might happen and sometimes did." As Lois knows, Boyd has always put the later appreciation of the effect before the immediacy of the moment. The kiss "stymied" Lois; but the *idea,* the audacity of the act, charmed Boyd, who is more hopelessly bewitched than any of them. In *Ceremony,* as they part in Mexico, Lois puts her gloved hand casually, lightly on Boyd's arm, as though returning the charge of the kiss years later when his own current is weak. "Hardly a moment, but long enough to finish what the bullfight had started. After thirty years of exile Boyd was back where his life had begun," on the porch with "the only woman in his life." Afraid of the highly charged life, Dulcinea chose Sancho instead of Quixote; and that choice has bewildered the hero ever since. Boyd began slipping when Lois married McKee.

What does the hero think of his witnesses now? Lois is "a serene wooden Indian equally blended of fire and ice. The chaste virginal mother of three sons and nine grandchildren.... Husband and wife share the ice side together. The fire side, as Boyd could tell you, had long been out. He had been the one to blow it alive, then let it go out." They witness "the final goring of old Bullslinger Boyd."

Boyd, whose promise is now fifty-some years old, is less like Lawrence than like the ineffectual Proctor. Lawrence faced the bull alone and was gored; Boyd, flanked by his witnesses, merely squirts the bull with Pepsi-Cola, thus ending his audacious acts: "the gray-haired youth who slew the Minotaur with a squirt of pop."

But to what end? "His moment of truth?" Ironically, yes. He would like to have died at that moment, the crowd and the matadors cheering; but "like everything else, *that* too slipped out of his grasp." He has audacity, but he lacks intentions: "In his heroics a potential bungler, and in his bungling a potential hero. In him every man loved the hero in himself."

Lehmann reflects on Boyd's life as hero in the light of the mystery of Paula Kahler's; inarticulate Paula and articulate Boyd cause Lehmann to be perceptive about the human predicament. Almost too late Boyd finds that "the one cliché, stamped Success on one side, Failure on the other, rang hollow at both extremities." An "armor of clichés" has kept him from touching "the floating bottom within himself," or "from being touched." He finds, "at the heart of the labyrinth," "erosion in the mind." Having failed to fail, he went to Lehmann. He showed Boyd Paula, who, dressed as a woman, once killed a male molester with his male hands. But Paula has succeeded where Boyd has failed. Paula has transformed the word "love" into flesh. While Boyd asserts his maleness as hero, Paula rejects his. "The words that Paula Kahler had made into flesh . . . called for a further transformation, back into words again." Boyd, the artist, takes on the job.

Gordon Boyd's effect on little Gordon began with the boy's father. McKee named his first-born Gordon, but Lois knew that he *was* Gordon. When Boyd discovered that his influence on the boy had been negative, he deliberately disillusioned him. Like his mother, the boy bolted and married Eileen, whose father settled several thousand tons of beef on him; and then Gordon became like Mc-Kee. But he named his first-born after the hero. At the bullring, observing this latest version of Gordon Boyd, Lois thinks, "Nothing had changed. It made her flesh crawl just to think of it."

When the matador is gored, Boyd looks at the boy and wonders what he sees. Little Gordon is a jigsaw puzzle loose in its box; it is he who must create the pattern—his own life: "An endless sequence of changes, a tireless shifting of the pieces, selecting some, discarding others, until the pattern—the imagined thing—began to emerge. . . . In an age of How-to-do-it, the problem was how *not*. How *not* to be embalmed in a flannel pocket, how *not* to be frozen in a coonskin hat. . . . To keep it open, to keep the puzzle puzzling, the pattern changing and alive." All the trappings exist in the boy's world—emblematic hats, pants, baseballs—but the risk has been removed. "Along with the means, that is, the meaning dropped away from it." Thus, in the heroic world created by the market, the transformation to *end* all transformations has taken place. "To eliminate the risks, you simply didn't run them. You *were* something. You stopped this goddam hazardous business of *be-coming* anything.... The object was to *be* champ, not to *meet* him. That entailed risk," to one's milder notions of what one must become to be champ. The blight on the preceding generations is touching the boy. He is captive in Davy Crockett's coonskin cap, symbol of a past made phony, a false transformation. At least Boyd can stress "the real McCoy." This time he attempts a transformation.

The boy cries when Boyd takes his phony coonskin hat and places it on the head of the matador. " 'There's your goddam hat. Now shut up.... it's been on the head of a hero. That makes it real,' " for the matador in his moment of truth is "the real McCoy." But the boy does not yet see, because he has not yet lived, the point. " 'Your Uncle Gordon will now bring a dead coon back to life.' " He throws the cap out into the ring, and the boy retrieves it. Boyd, the dead coon, is brought back to life in the audacious boy. In that moment when he begets another hero and ceases to be one himself, he touches bottom and pushes off.

When McKee offers him a paper bull, the boy informs him that it is not a bull if one buys it. "Once a hero, the undulant fever remained in the blood." Boyd has raised the curtain on a great drama in the boy, but there is not much hope that Gordon will be able to resist the numerous false cues that will come at him from all directions, as they do in *Ceremony*.

In *Ceremony* the hero-witness relationship between Munger and Lee Roy, which operates swiftly and lethally, is an exaggeration of the negative aspect of the Boyd-McKee relationship; all four are "local boys who made or unmade good." Boyd has " 'everything to live for, everything worth living for having eluded him.' " McKee has lived his own meaningless life vicariously through Boyd. " 'First and last of the completely self-unmade men,' " Boyd is Uncle Dudley gone wrong, because he has always wanted to be, like the Midwest itself, more than he is, prompted by his witnesses; but between the promise and the real thing wavers bewitchment.

Doubling as the barker who lures spectators into the tent and as the main clown on exhibition inside, Boyd is now only "a friggin bore." Less shocking himself than he is shocked by the wild and grotesque behavior of the witnesses, he is unable and no longer desires to impress McKee. He observes that, as he loses his reality as hero to them, they become realer than he. Like the characters in Boyd's book, *Hope and Hopelessness,* hero and witness merge. In "The Ceremony" section especially, the characters seem hero and witness to each other.

At the bullring, "the sanded navel of the world," where each man has eyes only for himself, the McKees' vision shapes the physical world of the present that once ended in the Dust Bowl but that science now promises to resurrect. They "would feel and see what they had brought along with them," thinks Boyd. "The Passion of the Bullring as seen from the deep-freeze along the Platte." Boyd's vision shapes the imaginative world. But because he is encumbered by the clichés of the only real world he can relate to, McKee's, and because McKee makes only a dim response to his lead, Boyd can get neither the world nor himself in focus. Like Agee and Muncy, Boyd can almost transform the American Land and Dream into art, he can impose upon the past a semblance of order and meaning, but his shaping imagination is stunned by the senseless fragmentation of the present.

Lost in the labyrinth of the past at the bullring, McKee repeatedly asks Boyd, " 'Don't it take you back?' " Boyd knows "sure as hell it did. But to where? And when? And for chrissakes why? . . . Always taken back. Never ahead." But stimulated in *Field* to enter the temple of the past, he makes, like Agee and Muncy, a pilgrimage to native soil, the territory behind, to confront the Nebraska present directly, to find out "if it's there, or all in my mind," and perhaps to throw a few bricks at the temple.

All his life Boyd, "the fellow who merely thought and thought and thought," has moved toward meaningfulness, always having and giving into impulses, trying to stay awake while men like McKee sleep. En route to Lone Tree, Boyd stays in a motel near the atomic proving grounds in the desert. The motherly owner, eager for Boyd to see the great show, writes WAKE BEFORE BOMB beside his name. Boyd wonders: "How did one do it? Was it ever advisable?" Since neither past nor present is creatively alive, what is lost if one doesn't wake? Does it do any good? In the world man has remade, is it best to sleep in the past or be awake in the present, to let one's emotions sleep or to rouse them? When the bomb of the past explodes, its light may reveal the extent to which Boyd (and the American Dream expressed in him) has failed.

At a gambling joint nearby he meets a young woman, just divorced, who smokes, drinks, and curses. Neither young nor old, living in the immediate present, and talking jazz lingo, she is the spirit of youth and of female freedom that Boyd (like Horter) craves. From her, the present, Boyd absorbs life as he journeys into the past. He pretends she is his daughter. Since the present eludes Boyd, only the past has pattern; things "coming toward him seem to break into pieces, and things that receded into the past seem to make sense." Daughter suggests that he has always been scared of the present; should the past explode now, it might scare him to sleep. "The past, whether one liked it or not, was all that one

The Navel of the World

actually possessed. . . . The present was that moment of exchange—
when all might be lost. . . . Why not sleep on the money in the
bank? To wake before bomb was to risk losing all to gain what
might be so little—a brief moment in the present, that one moment
later joined the past."

Lone Tree is a fossil bed, "a burial site for dinosaurs," a hole
in the map on the lobby wall where artifacts are stored, a point in
time (mythic past) rather than in space (territory ahead). In the
lobby Boyd finds an old newspaper with the headline: LIND-
BERGH OVER ATLANTIC. Unsmiling, he wonders whether Lindbergh made it, because among the youth of the present there is no
trace of his example. Where, then, is he? "Over the Atlantic was
where he belonged"; and Ty Cobb's foul ball is over left field.
Drugged by dreams in youth, the characters are under the "narcosis
of nostalgia" years later. "Up there, as in a deep freeze, THE
SPIRIT OF ST. LOUIS was suspended, a star of Bethlehem over
the stable of Lone Tree. In this manger the dreams were crossed."

Past and present confront, merge, and explode: "the heat and
light of that moment illuminated for a fraction the flesh and bones
of the present. Did these bones live? At that moment they did.
The meeting point, the melting point of the past confronting the
present. Where no heat was thrown off, there was no light—where
it failed to ignite the present it was dead. The phoenix, that
strange bird of ashes, rose each day from the embers where the
past had died and the future was at stake." Boyd, looking worse
than he ever has, says, " 'The past is dead, long live the past' "—the
old past is dead, long live the new past now in process. It is not
clear who gains, who loses; but the implication is that the ground
is cleared for the future.

Scanlon wakes from sleep, faces himself, dies. In waking the
others, at least momentarily, for the bomb, Boyd faces himself in
them and falls asleep. At the end, Boyd, an imitation of himself, is
asleep at the feet of the corpse; but at the reins, McKee, self-made
man, creator of the uncertain future, coolly offers the bohemian
a business opportunity and prestige in the Polk Chamber of Com-
merce. Having found that the past gives off no charge in the
present, Boyd had better start improvising. Free of the past, he
anticipates no real future. Perhaps in Polk, Boyd can find a new
kind of sandpit. Bolting from his final failure, he would do well
to start from scratch.

Prior to the explosion of the symbolic bomb ignited by Lois,
Boyd ignites a verbal bomb of his own. He does not speak until
they have all sat down to dinner; each character is a leaf of the
same table—no food is mentioned, but in a sense they eat each

other. His subject is Nebraska. " 'A predictable percentage of the women go mad ... and Mr. Charles Munger, celebrated gunman, is a native son.... The state emblem, a stiffly pleated upper lip, symbolizes the spirit of its people resolutely carried forward into the new age.' " When asked to speak, McKee defers to Lois (he speaks a great deal when she is not present). Etoile wants to know why a person can't say what he thinks. " 'Your feelings would be showing,' " says Boyd, who taunts McKee, typical of his countrymen, for concealing his.

When McKee points out that not everyone wears his feelings on his sleeve, Boyd asks where one does wear them. " 'Boyd,' said McKee, 'I hope you didn't come back just to stir up old feelings.' " Boyd, who thinks of himself as the one who has feelings, says, " 'Or is it new ones, McKee? Not the past but the present. In the good old days we both had feelings. How is it now? On good authority I have it that you and Mrs. McKee couldn't be happier. You couldn't be, so you haven't been, happier. What scares you pissless is not the fear of death, but the fear of exposure. The open fly of your feelings. You know why? You might not have any." McKee somewhat crushes Boyd's upper hand by saying, "You have to make a fool of yourself since you've made such a mess of your life." But one thing is clear: the nature of the future depends upon the way the arsenaled emotions of the characters and the dead fodder of the past explode.

VI *The McKees: Key Witnesses*

McKee, like Babbitt, keeps the faith; he does not question anything, especially his own life. The bullring reminds him of the Texas dust bowl, of the ball park, and of the theater where he saw Boyd's play. The details of the sandpit and of the ball park incidents accumulate mainly through his viewpoint.

McKee's lack of connection with the ordinary world of the plains may explain his need for a hero who promises a mystical connection with eternal things in his freedom from the trivialities of the moment. Perhaps the Boyds make the material success of the McKees possible, for the witnesses' impractical impulses are absorbed in the hero's magnetic field. When Boyd failed to walk on water, something in McKee failed, too; but the attempt left him almost as awed as if Boyd had succeeded. But of the men in *Ceremony,* McKee, already partly free of his role as witness, seems least constrained by the past, least inclined to play a part.

Boyd transmits the hero's charge directly to Lois in the kiss on the porch. She refuses to admit it to McKee, but the ring reminds her of the porch: "What it meant was that they were still all out on that porch." The details of that incident accumulate through her point of view. In Boyd's play, the hero kisses the girl, then goes off and drowns himself, "not intentionally, but with the full understanding that if he failed to walk on the water, which he naturally did, it would prove that he was not truly worthy of her." Had he succeeded, he would have returned and run away with the girl. He doesn't know that in her sleep Lois unlatched the back porch screen to admit her dream lover, whose weight in the dream caused the cot to collapse. But in the moment of wooing her to the highest pitch her sexual passions would ever reach, Boyd's kiss sounded the alarm of caution; prudence won out; and she married "thick and solid" McKee, who would slave to put comfortable shoes on the feet Boyd would only have kissed. She never suspects that Boyd ever felt "very much himself." Just as he really did drown himself, she fails as a woman. According to Etoile and Maxine, Daughter is everything that Lois would like, in lesser degree, to be. Oversexed, Daughter is the opposite kind of failure from Lois; but, if the one is habitually audacious, the other becomes impulsively audacious.

McKee has always missed the meaning of the events in his life. The kiss on the porch was just another of those things that no one else in his right mind would do. Always in his right mind, he knew that Lois would have been shocked had he, her fiancé, kissed her. He never tried to improve on the thrill Boyd gave her. He feels about Boyd the way Nick felt about Gatsby: "If personality is an unbroken series of successful gestures, then there was something gorgeous about him, some heightened sensibility to the promises of life. . . . An extraordinary gift of hope, a romantic readiness. . . " McKee prefers the mystery of Boyd's influence to understanding it. Boyd reduces the sandpit incident to essentials—a bare stage and talk—but his play reveals nothing to McKee, who believes what he sees, who recognizes the real thing only by its outward trappings. In the play the boy drowns—the imaginative act processes the life out of the literature. Although he is always comparing things, McKee sees neither the pattern nor the meaning that emerges from it.

Anything connected with Boyd seems as though it has just happened, but not until he comes to the bullfight does McKee remember the time he shot a hog on his Uncle Dwight's ranch. The killing of the bull with sword and cape, an ideal encounter of man and animal, contrasts effectively both with Boyd's squirting of pop and with McKee's shooting of the hog. McKee's other claim to fame is that he and his uncle started the Dust Bowl. He blunders into the future, and all the phony lures he puts out to attract and master life turn out, as did the hog incident, to be jokes on himself.

Suspecting that the new era of prosperity killed Scanlon, McKee wonders whether he welcomes the future himself.

In *Ceremony* McKee accidentally finds in a slot behind the hotel counter a letter from Boyd to Lois dated 1927 which symbolizes the message the past has for the present: a blank sheet of paper. It was Boyd's speechless reaction to the marriage of Lois and McKee. McKee feels as though he is going to die (a moment similar to Boyd's sensation of imminent death at the bullring). He never opens the letter, but his fear that Boyd may have made love to Lois is groundless. Lois feels that neither Boyd, the dream-caster, nor McKee, the prairie-tamer, "ever had her"; if Boyd thinks he and McKee have always been counted out, she regrets that they've never counted enough. The window glass Lois rolls up at the end of *Field* to shut McKee out of the car is one expression of their conscious lack of connection.

As the strange behavior of the characters in Lone Tree testifies, the emotions McKee's generation suppressed do not go away in time, but erupt in the generation McKee is so frightened to observe. By helping to produce the Mungers, it is the meek McKees who shake the world. Maxine is right: the killings and the threat of "the bomb" testify that " 'we're all stark mad.' "

Lois's exaggerated response to meeting Boyd in Mexico and especially at Lone Tree indicates the extent to which she has all these years suppressed the sensuality he aroused. But secretly, she indulges in a form of cannibalism that releases her impounded feelings. Not as reticent with children as Mrs. Ormsby or Mrs. Porter, she would like to lick the hot little body of her grandson, the most important person in her life, as a bitch licks its pups. She is the female who turns from the inadequate adult male to the male child, with whom she comes close to sexuality. Having castrated the weak adult, she subjects herself to the dominance of the child; for she fears losing him to the adult male world that offers her nothing. When she sees that the males are corrupting him with their own weaknesses, she finally asserts the traditional authority of a grandmother. Thus, female domination is forced upon her.

As Scanlon affected Lois, Gordon's emotions are affected by the adults around him; the bad habits and characteristics of the whole family and of Boyd seem to come out in him. Jennings tries to tell him about Santa Claus; but he is more interested in guns. Lois reluctantly indulges him in toys of violence. Going around "shooting" people, he is often linked with Munger. Lois herself feels that you can't "play at killing people without sooner or later killing them." But it is she who turns out to be the one most affected by the power and perils of the daily identification and imaginative association with guns.

Just as her mother did when Lois was a child, Lois often lies awake, stiff as an ironing board, waiting for something to happen, and McKee pats her shoulder to pacify her. What worries her, however, is that after waiting so long, nothing ever will. She desires that the future be something more than a puny imitation of the past. She waited long ago for Boyd or McKee to do something that would make sense; now she waits for the killer to reveal himself. "Then she would do what she had put off doing, what they had all put off doing until nothing they did made any sense." Ironically, Lois, who helps create the Mungers of her world, imitates him when she fires the pistol; however, the most inhibited of the characters, she can control her Munger-like impulses through imagination.

When Calvin and Etoile rage into town in the mule-drawn wagon with its bizarre cargo of Bud and the arrow-pierced dog, Lois knows that the killer has revealed himself: the mythic past gone beserk in the present. "Had her father's madness caught up with her?" Lois's firing of her grandfather's Colt, an event focused through several points of view, is, of course, the most concentrated moment in the book; in it the pieces of the puzzle come together like the sudden meshing of gears. For instance, Lois and Etoile appear more alike than either realize. Earlier, they are linked in the concentrated moment when Etoile appears dressed as Samantha (Scanlon's mother) and Lois falls into Boyd's arms. It is Etoile who provokes Lois into firing the gun by enticing Calvin into marriage and by causing the uproar of their entrance into town.

The charge Lois picked up from Boyd finally has its effect and his presence helps ignite the bomb in her that kills the past and causes them to focus on the present. But Lois's surrender to impulse is more purposeful, in a way, than Boyd's. His habitual, but now predictable, audacity lacks surprise and spontaneity. But for the witnesses, sudden one-shot improvisations can result in meaningful alterations in attitude. Lois wants and needs the incident for self-realization, not Boyd-like fame. From the ceremony of death it is the women who will salvage something for the living. In control, the women will build on the ruins caused by the sleeping males.

In that audacious act, Lois not only rouses herself from emotional torpor, but also causes a chain reaction among others. The shot brings out courage in McKee, stymies Boyd, unclogs Calvin's verbal stream, and startles Scanlon out of a deep sleep into the final sleep. She becomes a hero to Gordon, who gave her the Colt and the bullet; he obeys her for the first time; where Boyd and Scanlon fail, she succeeds: he will not be blighted by their influence. Symbolically, she kills Boyd as hero, Scanlon as fossilized repository of the prehistoric past—the two poles are demagnetized—and something in everyone else. The death of Scanlon, in turn, causes a series of changes in all the survivors of the past.

Lois does not admit her motives to McKee because his whole world, built around his idea of her, would fall. She pretends that she went to the window like a sleepwalker and that the shot was an accident; and McKee assumes that the events of the day have stirred her up (as when she unlocked the back porch screen). "On the contrary, she had never been so wide awake." She is like Lee Roy. The policeman assumed he lost control of his car, but Lee Roy declared that for the first time in his life he was in control—to be in control, de-control others. But neither Lois nor the others change completely. Her father newly dead, she retains her icy reserve.

VII *Etoile and Calvin: Birth of the Present*

Many of the younger generation are not asleep in nostalgia, and they rebel against the lack of emotional connection. While the others are trapped in each other's past, Etoile views (like the Greek) only her own present; she is waiting for, but also hurrying toward, the future. Much that has been emotionally and sexually wrong for many years in the male-female relationship is obliquely reflected in Calvin and Etoile.

Consciously but wholesomely sexy, Etoile, like Dudley, is an audacious debunker (she is an anticipation of Cynthia). In her physique and personality, she is a combination of most of the women in the novel. Without his knowing it, Boyd is a hero to her. A brief look at her parents gives a clearer perspective on Etoile. Maxine is closer than the other women to what an archetypal mother should be, but her marriage is lopsided because of Bud, who will never grow old, because he never grew up. His joy is his mail route because he can read up on other people's lives and talk to people: "In some strange way those other families were his own. Their problems seemed to be the ones he could help." Since his mail bag urges him to move on after every father-confessor intimacy, people often show him sides their actual kin never see. Someone gave him a bow and arrows. Killing destructive cats and finally Edna's dog, thrills Bud but, like Virgil Ormsby, he doesn't claim his acts for what they are. Used to living vicariously, he is Robin Hood when he kills; and he thus disassociates himself, as a mild person, from violence. He is a good example of the combination of the weird and the humorous that creates such a strange atmosphere in the novel. But the aura of quaintness fades when we realize that Bud is a grotesque, both bizarre and pathetically drab. The comedy proves as disturbing as it is amusing.

From her view of the world at the kitchen sink or the cook stove, Maxine sees the shed where two of Munger's victims were found. And "that piece of garden hose, kinks and all, through which flowed more than she could keep under control, was her life. When she tried to shut it off at one end, it just broke out somewhere else"—in Etoile who sprays herself with the hose. Aggravated by Bud, Etoile, and the others, Maxine's suppressed emotions finally explode in revolt.

Calvin resembles Boyd in some ways, but mainly he is witness to his great-grandfather, and thus is trapped in a mythic role. He prefers to be alone because he stutters, and he feels most at home on his horse or in the open country. Exemplifying one trend among the young, he takes to the open road of flight from Etoile and sex, and from his mother, Eileen, whose frank sex talk perhaps inhibits him and contributes to his stutter. Calvin goes through the hell of other people, in contrast to the natural hell Tim Scanlon went through in the canyon. While Munger and Lee Roy try to assert their selfhood among people, Calvin, like Scanlon, symbolically kills them by refusing to live among them. Lee Roy uses the machine; Calvin rejects it. Calvin flees to the territory behind; Munger and Lee Roy, to the zero regions of an emotional deep freeze.

If aggressive Etoile castrates Lee Roy by failing to recognize his masculinity, she rescues shy Calvin and herself from the sexual restraint that prevailed in the past; however, like her ancestors, she chooses a hopeless, helpless man. Etoile is like Lois but in reverse—with Boydlike audacity, she lures Calvin into an erotic union and breaks the emotion barrier. As though continuing the relationship that had once existed between Boyd and Lois, Calvin experiences with Etoile what Boyd failed to experience with Lois. The kiss on the porch (quaint American adolescent cliché) becomes seduction in a wheat field. Now Boyd is as "stymied" by Lois as Calvin is by Etoile; perhaps he always was. Lois, who waited, willing, for him that night, suspects that Boyd was as scared of her as McKee, that his audacity was mere camouflage.

Although she shunned him, Etoile now understands Lee Roy. She declares that "nobody wants to know" *why* he killed. Through the exhausts of his hotrod he released repressed impulses and tensions; when the boys ridiculed the exhausts, he aimed the car at them. In Lincoln, Maxine, who wonders if there is "anything so bad some good didn't come of it," knows what is on her daughter's mind: if the men didn't cause something to happen that would "change the world, she would do it herself." Maxine, Etoile, and Lois *do* act.

The real reason for the reunion is to create a situation in which Etoile may capture Calvin. Just when she is trying desperately to get him to elope so they can get on with the future, Calvin hires a wagon and some mules to enact a constant image in Scanlon's past, to transform Etoile into Samantha. Later, when Calvin leads the mule-drawn wagon out of the barn in such a way that she is reminded of Scanlon, Maxine wonders, "With her father dead, was it all to start over again?" Intending to see that it doesn't, she begins by finally declaring her own thoughts about the good old days. Although the women have always had their say, they have allowed themselves to be silent accomplices to the male fictions about the past, entrapping themselves with the men. It was one way of keeping them under control. But all the women have come to a new point in evolution, and Etoile is a new species—the fire that Maxine's mother hoped to find when she got up in the night turns up in Etoile. But it must be controlled, and Maxine begins that task, too: she disciplines little Gordon, "stymies" Boyd, and castigates Lois, as well.

Etoile throws Calvin's cowboy hat, symbol of a bygone style of manhood, over a schoolhouse and into the wheat field, just as Boyd throws little Gordon's coonskin hat into the bullring. Stopping the horses Etoile caused to run riot, Calvin tries to keep the wildness in her under control. He makes love to her in the green wheat where the present fructifies. Unconscious when they were naked together in the bathroom (as Lois was asleep when Boyd seduced her in a dream), Etoile "wants to know what happens" this time. Thus, she rejects the state of narcosis in which most of them live. Back at origins where everything has ended for the others, where the past dies with Scanlon, the present is born in Etoile and Calvin.

What is the benefit for the witness of exposure to the hero? The hero causes a moment in the life of the witness when he is most alive because he feels part of something that, compared with everything else, is real and permanent. The ability to generate love is the most enduring quality of the hero; Boyd is the cause of any love McKee and Lois ever felt. Everyone loves the hero, but is he capable of receiving love? Perhaps he wanders in search of a truly reciprocal relationship. The closest he ever comes is the hero-witness bond. None of Morris' characters is capable of achieving the ideal state through all three ways of self-transcendence: love, imagination, and the heroic.

"The heroic," says Booth, "can never be an end in itself; it is only a means to the imaginative transformations it can effect, the moments of truth it can yield. . . . The insight itself is what is important" (6). *Field* develops the theme that the hero-witness relationship may result both in transforming and in transfixing the hero, as well as the witness. Boyd's trouble is that his acts always give off more heat than light, and what has beguiled his witnesses is their hope that the hero will someday make the light they feel hopelessly incapable of making for themselves. When the witnesses realize that, because of the hero's acts, they are, like Scanlon, trapped in the past and unable to function, they back out of his magnetic field. The world may love a fool but to remain bewitched by him can mean paralysis; the past may be alive, but the present is dead. The present reality, offering only what one can know, *sans* glorious promises, is all one has to work with.

In the drama of the American Dream, the Western frontier has played the leading role. In the Midwest, dream and reality joined in an agricultural way of life that was an ideal and a promising complex of creativity and materialism. The old ways of the plains, once the Great American Highway of emigration, a transient area, *should* pass over to something better, something that manifests the creative elements in the American Dream. This land, whose inhabitants provide an index to American civilization, symbolized the promise of all America, the union of the romantic vision and the realistic plan. Lone Tree once symbolized that fuller promise as its physical ruins now symbolize spiritual failure. The West met the East on the Pacific Coast, and the East lured the best of the young to its machines, leaving a Great American Desert in both the factual and the imaginative sense. Technology has debased the maker; imagination has fossilized the dreamer.

In measuring the extent to which the dream has failed to materialize, Morris has depicted its nightmare side. The gates of the imagination open on a psychological frontier upon which Thoreau long ago challenged Americans to venture. It may be said of *that* frontier, however, that the dust on the westward trek presaged a dust bowl over which the clouds still release their dry rain. Yet out of the ashes, Morris seems to hope, the Phoenix will rise reborn. He wonders for all Americans what kind of strange creature it will be.

If the great trails of exploration have vanished, Morris blazes new ones into interior landscapes. His characters explore, says Frederic

Carpenter, "the primitive places" of "the human psyche," tracing "new contours of this undiscovered country."[2] Their minds are like Lehmann's view of Acapulco at night: "a labyrinth of lights . . . a loom of light where each impulse left its mark, each thought its ornament, each sentiment its motif in the design." The reader experiences "emerging and dissolving patterns of meaning."

Morris' epigraph from Milton suggests the mind's capacity to transform: "The mind is its own place, and in itself/Can make a Heav'n of Hell, a Hell of Heav'n." Afflicted with limited sight, the characters learn very little about themselves. As Robert Louis Stevenson observed, "sickness of the vision" is "peculiar to these empty plains." Out of each character's ignorance of himself in relation to others arises the conflict. But, as variously motivated, they ponder the same questions from different perspectives, they often arrive at the same kinds of discoveries and insights; and they commune unawares in a common psychic realm, achieving, as fractional creatures, a collective ethnic identity. The failure of perception is moving because one sees that the human being is capable of knowing himself. In *Field* particularly, the paradoxes, ambiguities, ironies, and fallibilities of human perception prove to be the dilemma of the human condition. Clear vision would require a combining and focusing of what each sees separately— an impossible solution. Can whole vision be achieved only as a blend of unconscious and conscious community, each man adding by a kind of mystical osmosis his unique vision to the miracle of human society, achieving a vision the wholeness of which only the artist and his viewers can approach?

A man who speaks in a broken language that "he made himself," Lehmann re-establishes broken connections. He is an intellectual who cleans up other people's messes. He keeps things in pre-historical perspective by contemplating the forms that make life permanent and meaningful. He perceives, for instance, that when man and his symbolic bull meet and merge—"the archetypal man growing out of the beast"—man enters the realm, at that moment at least, of the mythic. Real man and bull meet before Lehmann's eyes: "Would he go winging off like the flying horse?" Probably he will, but for how long, and what happens to such a man when he must come down again? But, for a moment in the transformation when both are bewitched, man and animal are one, dependent upon each other for that moment in which they transcend in a permanent instant their common predicament as transient creatures. "Man *and* Bull had both been shot down—Lehmann would tell you—at the moment of flight. Resolving and not resolving the anguished dilemma of human life. . . . Bull into Man was followed, too often, by Man into Ghost. The horn of the dilemma... was that it led to flight."

According to his nature, man is obliged to exceed himself, to throw light on why things are so seldom what they seem, to discover why it is that they are not meant to be. Man needs help because in reaching for more light, he risks what light he has. The crowd in the bullring yells for *luz* by which to see clearly what no two of them see in the same light. When the light comes on, the spectators applaud themselves as though *they* had made it; and, within limits, they have. What of the future? Lehmann applauds the dead bull as it is dragged on a tour of the ring. Boyd laughs. "'It iss nod for the bool, which is det... but for Lehmann, who muss go on lifink'"—in the territory ahead, if possible.

One can not understand some critics who feel that Morris denies the human being his dignity. In the light of what reality do they assert man's innate right to dignity and Morris' obligation to show it? The vision of Morris' characters projects his own vision of the human predicament. The collective vision is so ambiguous that there is neither good nor evil—the two are interdependent. Morris chronicles, as Baumbach says, "the moral erosion of our sterile and sterilizing civilization," where "evil is potent, good impotent" (56).

If art is not only comment on, but just as importantly and perhaps most appropriately, an artistically shaped concept of the human condition, Morris joins Joyce in rendering life in all its "unresolved and unresolvable ambiguities." The pure artist's task is to show his semblance of life and that, in a sense, should be task enough. One must not lose sight of this view of Morris as the intentions behind his novels, aside from considerations of pure art, are discussed.

CHAPTER 10

Time and Space in the Creative Vision

C AUSE FOR WONDER (1963)[1] provides a rather full sum-
mation of major elements in the works of Wright Morris. The
hero-witness relationship, audacity, improvisation, the phony and
the real, the American Dream, the revivification of the cliché, the
importance of ceremonies, the effects of travel, imaginative transformation, the impersonality of love, fact and fiction, the evocative
quality of the artifact, the community of vision, and the resurrection
of the hero in one of his witnesses are recapitulated with varying
degrees of importance. The achievements and shortcomings of all
his novels may be traced in large measure to the way in which
he deals with the problems of time and space that his conception
of his raw material raises. In *Cause for Wonder,* his concept of
the synthesis of time and space in the individual creative vision
seems a major advance in the author's controlled struggle with his
fictive world.

In *his* re-experiencing of the past, Warren Howe of *Cause for
Wonder,* a middle-aged television script-writer, is more deliberate
than any of Morris' characters. In Part One, "Time-Present," Howe
tells of a roundup of people who were guests with him thirty years
ago in a strange castle, Schloss Riva, in the Wachau district of the
Austrian Lower Alps, a three-hour drive from Vienna. Howe's
attempt in the present to persuade his Uncle Fremont to attend
with him the funeral of the master of the castle, Monsieur Etienne
Dulac, fails. Nor does Charles Horney, Howe's college friend, who
did not visit the castle before, accept the invitation. But back in
Los Angeles, Howe finds a willing co-traveler in Sol Spiegel, dealer
in junk. In this first third of the novel, in Howe's remembrances,
all the events of the past are recounted in miniature and all the
characters soon to appear are introduced, including Katherine
"Kitty" Brownell, Howe's "almost" girlfriend; Wolfgang Prutscher,
Howe's Austrian friend; and George, Riva's eccentric caretaker.

In Part Two, "Time-Past,"[2] told in third person through Howe's
point of view, the scene and the ceremony of return-reunion-revela-
tion are depicted. Howe and Sol discover that Dulac is still alive,

though ill. Wolfgang is there, an accomplice in the joke. Surprisingly, Kitty appears, accompanied by her grandson, Brian Caffrey. They all go for a walk, and Dulac deliberately stumbles down a cliff-side. He recovers enough to invite them to dinner at Spitz. (Such dinner scenes are almost obligatory in Morris). They mull over the past, then return to the castle and bed. Later, George's wild antics rouse them all; and, in the midst of the melee, Dulac dies quietly in his sleep.

I *The Oneness of Time and Space*

Time-present? Time-past? The announcement of Dulac's funeral services tells Howe the past is dead, but as a concept "the past" is ambiguous. Once Morris' concept of Time, as Howe perceives it, is clear, the titles of parts one and two become interchangeable, ironic. " 'You think I should go back?' " Howe asks Horney, who replies, " 'Have you ever really got away, Warren?' " If Howe lost both an athletic Fraulein and the vampish Kitty, he has not lost the fabulous *time* in which he met them. Seymour Gatz, Howe's agent, provides him with a good excuse to attend the funeral. A client who has put money on Howe's script, "No Place to Hide," may turn it down, but the fiction has so convinced him that he wants the locale—as a place to hide.

At the prospect of returning, Howe faces certain questions. "How determine one's proper time and place?" Just what is *now* and *then*, *here* and *there*? The present, he knows, has "a way of dissolving into the past." Uncle Fremont's mention of the pork they ate on the Texas farm "brought its taste to my mouth." Back at that other important place in his past, Riva, the way the doors slam consecutively as someone comes to answer the knock at the gate seems the same this summer as it was thirty years ago, and Howe hears again the hiss of snow on the roof that always landed on the person who had knocked—himself, more than once.

The past persists in frozen images evocative of the whole Riva experience: Dulac, before the snows, shaking apples from a tree—"a landscape with figures. . . . in time, or out of it," like a Breughel painting. Even forgotten moments of the past are able to usurp the supremacy of the present. Howe is suddenly smitten with the image of himself as a boy, skating on an ice pond in Kansas City. It was an uneventful episode; but with startling clarity, he realizes that he is not recalling the experience "*later*. Not that particular piece of time. It was right there, cold and sparkling, in bed with me. To be reasonably accurate, *I* had changed, but that night had not." Time-past, place-distant, preserved in ice.

Human perception has another dimension: space. On the open road, straddling the center line on the blacktop highway at sixty miles an hour

> time and space seem to wind on the spool beneath me. Or within me . . . Dimension of time: I see it rushing toward me, worming slightly, then I see it unraveling behind me. A stretch of time? A piece of space? Or one and the same, weaving together. At the wheel of the car, at sunrise, with the dawn light behind me, the road opening out before me, I sense a dimension of Time that otherwise escapes me, the spool of tape being myself, Warren P. Howe. . . . Inside the car, past and future seem to merge; the present is the wavering needle on the dial. . . . Time. The spool of it that spins under my seat. That reappears in the shuttle-like loom of time in my head.

For Howe, "Time exists in space."

Reared where the 98th meridian intersects the 42nd parallel, he feels "that time, like space, has a point of departure and a direction." For Uncle Fremont, "the past lay to the east—from where one had come. The future lay to the west, where one was going. In *my* time," Howe says, "these directions were reversed. The past—the mythic past—lay to the west, the beckoning, looming future lay to the east." It is for this reason that "a sense of direction does not come easy to Americans." But Riva, an imaginative creation, was never fixed, either in time or in space; Howe has always been bemused with the impression that Riva was not "truly part of this world." Because of the way the characters respond to experience, clock time and the geographical concept of space are junked.

A carefully controlled design of parallel motifs keeps this concept of the oneness of time and space focused. Working on the farm with Uncle Fremont, he had earned $25 a month and his "keep," a particularly apt word, for he has *kept* the experience alive. Although his Riva sojourn has, in a sense, lasted thirty years, Howe imagines that his return visit may last even longer. He spent about the same amount of actual time on the farm as he spent in the castle—four months. He has recently revisited his home place in Girard, Kansas, which is similar to the Texas landscape. The castle in the Wachau mountains and the shack on the plains of the panhandle "had certain things in common. A place to hide? . . . one thing seemed to prevail: the snow and the wind." On the return trip, Howe sees that the Blue Danube is no bluer than the Missouri at Omaha, loaded with topsoil. The Europe-America parallel is suggested also in the characters: Wolfgang is Horney's European counterpart; Dulac, Fremont's. He encounters a plowman napping under the apple tree, just as he had encountered an old man napping in an old-world sled: thus, Riva-past and Riva-present are conjoined. Many ice, sled, and snow motifs relate the plains to the mountains. He returns in September. "The snow had melted; otherwise little seemed to separate them from the buried past." But George, the wild caretaker, is slowly, haphazardly painting *everything* white, covering the present Riva as Howe goes deeper into the past through memory and events that parallel those of the past. The paint is a comic objectification of the persistence of the snow-bound, zany past that is kept alive by George, who remains, like a ghost, unseen.

Certain artifacts enhance the time-space theme. The American scene and its inhabitants—past, but mostly present—are presented through objects in Part One. Freeways, mobile homes, and fall-out shelters (one is being built next door to Howe) testify to a "nation-wide movement to find a way out." In his Salvage Enterprise, Sol Spiegel makes a killing on both shelter supplies and artifacts salvaged from great movie stars of the past. The new gold diggers, armed with geiger counters to detect uranium, have erected a typical modern city, Quartzite, Arizona, whose 38,000 people live on wheels. "In the desert light it is often hard to tell if they are putting up a town, or tearing one down." A beginning or an end, in or out of this world? Sol declares that when the Europeans put up a castle they had many centuries in mind. If his store contains the junk of American history, Dulac's castle contains "the debris of centuries," including some bizarre American artifacts: a wooden Indian, a plow seat, an early Iowa barber's chair.

Through Howe's intelligence and sensibility, Morris projects "a troubled vision of life, of time"—the two are inseparable. It is in its effect on the other characters that Howe contemplates the *human* nature of time-and-space. Both Uncle Fremont Osborn and Charles Horney claim to live in the present, Osborn on wheels in Quartzite, Horney as head of a progressive school situated in a kind of fall-out shelter; but Howe sees that both are captives, un-aware, in the past.

A "serenely detached, disturbingly self-sufficient" man whose temple of worship is Carlsbad Caverns where the architecture is forty million years old, Fremont invented the dust bowl near Here-ford, Texas. He has gone from the ark-like shack on the empty, windy plains to a mobile home in the rapidly filling desert. But "in the creases of his shoes, and his body," Howe anticipates, "there would still be Texas dust."

" 'Warren, what would you say your time was?' " Fremont asks. Howe's reply that part of it was Fremont's is not quite correct. The

Riva episode had meant little to Fremont, and even the Texas era is less important to him than to Howe: "From the seat of the same tractor the past looked a good deal different." Fremont does not believe that one can live in the past: "'If he's dead,'" Dulac died, as all men do, "'in the present.'" But as he speaks "out boldly for the *present*," Fremont's "hook-and-eye shoes" are "firmly planted in the past." "In what *here and now* did he think he lived?" In front of his trailer, a piece of petrified wood (past) sits like an eye in the center of a tiny patch of grass (present). "A reasonably fearless man, he [Fremont] feared the phantom past. It was the past, not the freeway . . . nor strontium, nor polio shots, nor fallout that he warned me against."

Stimulated by Howe's presence, Fremont resurrects his sister Grace. When Howe says he isn't sure he wouldn't want to live in the past, the present being what it is, Fremont points out that Howe's mother had hated and turned her back on the past, wanting "to live—right here and now." It is the first time Fremont has ever mentioned Howe's mother. Howe himself did not know her: "With my beginning, my mother had made an ending." Grace used to shoot the insulators off the telephone poles; today "'she would be shooting at the moon!'" Time has not "blurred the image before" Fremont's eyes. "To see what he lacked the words to describe he closed his eyes." Howe wonders: "What past were we reporting on? For my uncle the past ended when my mother stopped shooting at bottles." For Howe, it began. Thus, he shares no past with his Uncle Fremont.

But his uncle, he realizes, shares the Dulac image. Howe has seen neither in thirty years; and Fremont, also, has been recently ill. Both the new and the old world, as young Howe knew it, were presided over by madmen. In both places, Howe ran for his life. In both, he engaged in seemingly senseless labor: Dulac's mania was the excavation of a deep, rock-filled pit, where he hoped to find remnants of the ancient past; Fremont's was a hopeless effort to grow wheat where no rain had fallen in seven years. In his Ford V-8 coupe, that now resembles a desert reptile, Fremont had once lived on his Pecos homestead—a situation no more fantastic than Dulac's seclusion in a castle. Just as Dulac, of noble birth, was once a streetcleaner (a reverse of the American success story), Fremont is now a handyman in a tourist court. Howe recalls that both men liked to put their guests, "me in particular, to the test. To prove what? God only knows." Though they had more than temperament in common, they disliked each other on sight, as did Scanlon and Boyd.

In a kind of McKee-Boyd relationship, Charles Horney complements and contrasts with Howe. For years, Howe set the example for Horney. He made an attempt to resist Howe's influence: "If I recommended it highly, Charles could not bear to do it." But without realizing how directly, Horney did pick up Howe's charge, so that now he sets the example for his students; the year Howe made his excursion into the European past, Horney took a job in a progressive school near Los Angeles. " 'You made an impression on people, Warren,' " he says.

Horney claims to live "from day to day." " 'If you live in the present you can't help but be ahead of your time.' " The past is past, he declares, because it is useless: " 'Anything that has proved itself useful continues to exist in the present.' " But he neither sees nor lives the full, imaginative implications of his own wit. Moreover, he deludes himself. The first thing he says when Howe enters after twenty years, is " 'Remember the old 78 Air for the G String? I've still got it.' " Howe asks, " 'If the past is dead why the hell live in it . . . like you're doing now!' " From his office window on ground level, Horney can look across the golf course at Colton College, site of the "good old days." Close up, he rationalizes, the past is not nostalgic. But he preserves their teacher, Percy, by copying his gestures. Howe experiences a sensation common to him "of once more being back where I had come in"; Percy had said that both men are blighted: Howe by the past, Horney by the present.

Under the pretext of wanting to collect stamps, Horney had asked Howe to write to him from Europe. He asks Horney what he really wanted, and the answer startles him: " 'Just a postcard, Warren— saying how much you missed me.' He paused, then added. 'I had the money, you know. I really wanted to come.' " Only now does Howe learn that Horney is jealous of Spiegel, who turned up "in the space once reserved for" Horney. The past that haunts Horney is the one he missed with Howe at Riva. Deeply hurt, he took up the present with zeal. Now Howe offers him a chance to make up for thirty years of balking, to see he was right all the time. " 'If the past is dead,' " he challenges Horney, " 'Let's bury it!' " Horney in fear and trembling, declines.

Both Seymour Gatz and Sol Spiegel are junk collectors who salvage the past. With one foot in the new and the now, and the other in the mythic past, Seymour is that rare man who can hold opposed ideas in the mind at the same time and still retain the ability to function. He "has an instinct for the sure thing about to fold." With Sol, who is a romantic, Howe now shares "an impersonal, salvageable past." He worked for him at the California orange-juice stand at the Chicago World's Fair; later, Sol joined him at Riva. The motto over Sol's door reads: "If you don't see it, forget it";

anything that hasn't survived into the present is worthless anyway. His "formula for success is" that "no one in his or her right mind can resist somebody else's junk," somebody else's past. At his side there is always an empty chair, because some fool will soon fill it, as Howe does. "'I don't see what's gone,'" he says of obituaries; "'I see what's left over!'"—what is salvageable from the dead past. At Riva he is on the lookout for objects to sell to "kooks" back home.

Kitty Brownell, whose gift for bizarre remarks, unpredictable gestures, and impulsive behavior used to horrify him, is symbolic of what Howe, "too clean-cut to bleed," missed in the actual past. He told Wolfgang that just because it was cold he wasn't going to miss seeing the castle. But because Kitty warned him she had a cold, he didn't even kiss her. When she recalls their missed opportunity, Howe brings up her warning. "'A cold!' she cried, her voice hoarse. 'You were afraid to catch a cold? It wasn't even worth a measly little cold?' Howe said nothing. Nothing." Howe has always been embarrassed by the word "love." "What did one mean by it?" "Like" seems a less-committed term for what Kitty made him feel. He is glad for a moment that he didn't have her, for he is spared the regret he would feel seeing her today, a grandmother whose grandson calls her "Katherine" to ward off the specter of age. But, having lost her contact lenses and her composure in a fall, she looks attractive. She assures Howe that she hasn't returned "to the scene of a head cold." Having turned down Howe's dare to come, she took Dulac's; moved by Howe's description of Riva, she visited the castle the weekend after he had left. Howe thought Wolfgang had her; Wolfgang thought Howe had her. Now they realize why she returned from Riva "a different woman." Dulac had her.

What these characters have in common is the uncommon Schloss Riva and its "Miester of Nonsense," Monsieur Etienne Dulac. They have kept in touch. "With *what?* The untouchable remnant on the bed?" A magnet.

Dulac's death is an end for both Dulac and Howe; but, in Kitty's grandson, both make a new beginning. Experiencing what Howe experienced before, Brian is in the process of focusing an intelligence similar to Howe's. Generating the imaginative force that gives a charge to the boy's impulse, Dulac spans both extremes: old, he is the past; but in the present, he behaves like a child with a future.

In an effort really to know Dulac, Howe began (as did Foley) a novel, *Run For Your Life;* it is unfinished, like the events themselves. Dulac "could hardly wait for the book you were writing," Wolfgang says. "It helped to keep him alive," just as the books being written about Don Quixote helped spur him on. In the 1930's

Dulac seemed rather Dada; the current term is "far out." When Wolfgang tells Howe, " 'I'm afraid he's not been with us for some time,' " Howe asks, " 'Was he ever?' "

In an old World War I army overcoat Dulac often took walks in snow storms. To exercise the dog, he explained: "No, it was more to exercise the inhabitants below and cause the guests to wonder." He first came to the castle because it made no sense; with the same absence of reason he married Madame Dulac, the most freakishly ugly woman in Europe. No reason—therein, lay the appeal of both castle and wife. " 'You know,' " says Spiegel, echoing Blake, " 'When you push that, it begins to make sense.' " In the castle, Dulac "seemed to think the past was where he was living," and he ran it on the medieval plan, both when he harbored Jews and when he forced the Nazis to besiege the walls. Pretending to be a Jew, he was taken away with the others. Victimized? Howe can't picture that. But he can believe that a madman like Dulac can "turn time endwise, bottoms-up. . . ."

The first barrier Howe and Sol pass is a time barrier. From a distance, the castle conveys the illusion of being a quaint cliché-relic of the old world; but, standing over the ancient moats, the quiver in one's legs is real. "Nothing betrayed its unreality," in another sense. In the winter, the snow's effect is like that in the glass balls that used to "set on the sewing machine": shake the ball and the snow conceals the castle until it settles. Dulac's "loony bin" is a stranded ark, "a refuge from the floods now inundating the world. A place to wait it out."

The guests were always off guard because their captivity "seemed imaginary." One problem with Howe's book has been that nobody would believe it. But at the heart of the trouble is the question: Was Howe running *for* or *away from* his life? It is the quality, force, and willingness of one's imagination that determines how captive or victimized one is. They are all part of Dulac's obsession—Riva—and Howe is the most willing accomplice to his acts of lunacy.

George is an extension of Dulac-Riva. *Then,* he shoveled snow on the guests; *now,* he paints them. Subjected to George, "Howe had almost lost his mind, but never his disquieting sense of affection." George tries to drop paint on Frau Dulac from high in the castle: "Familiar as if he had heard it that morning, Howe listened to the wheezing laugh." George's antics conjure up the haunting past.

Dulac is a kind of hero who transforms his witnesses in an atmosphere conducive to transformations. One of the most complete impressions he ever made was on Kitty. He "had eaten of the apple denied to both lover (Wolfgang) and liker (Howe). . . . How else explain why she was here. . . . Katherine would surprise you. Had she surprised Monsieur Dulac?" Surprised at first that Dulac even remembers him, Howe decides that "what he remembers is the same as what I remember. Not the impression I made on him: the one he made on me." Sol remarks that " 'when you get away from here you won't believe a word of it.' " Perhaps that is why they have all come back—to re-experience the unbelievable, to be given cause for wonder.

Exactly half-way through the book, Howe discovers that Dulac is not dead. " 'Not him!' " says Frau Dulac. " 'We are all dead before *him!*' " Although symbolically she is more nearly correct than she herself knows, he is all but dead when the reader meets him. Awed by him years before she married him, Frau Dulac brought him back to the castle after the liberation; only George had remained. When Dulac speaks, the sounds are "like those projected by a ventriloquist," sounds projected from the living past. A travesty of youth, he wets his bed. But his reflexes are quick; he deftly swipes Howe's cigarettes. A constant show-off, craving attention, he suggests a certain degree of awareness of what is going on when he winks at Howe.

As he prepares for one of his unreasonable walks, one leg paralyzed, his crutch resembles a piece of armor, and he looks like Don Quixote. In the confusion on the ramp, Howe pretends to go back for Dulac's cap. Actually, he is running. *From* or *toward* something? Shaken as he is at the prospect of reviving the past, this question is urgent. At the moment, he appears to be doing both.

Like "pallbearers," the guests march down in single file. When he falls off the edge, Dulac makes a cut on the hillside as neat as a "zipper." Expecting him to be dead, Howe tries to feel a sense of the tragic, "but he felt only the lightheaded swoon of a farce. The errant Knight of Riva, his lance beside him, once more unhorsed." Just "half dead," as Sol says, "he took on life from the eyes that focused on him." Mainly, Dulac wants little Brian nearby. "Neither strictly in this world, nor as yet in the next one, Monsieur Dulac presented something of a problem." He seems "accustomed to returning from the dead." But he has enough life in him to have planned the whole episode as a way of getting down the mountain to transact a little business. As a gesture of admiration for their ability to play their parts, Dulac gives each a plant from Riva; symbolically, each will plant in his mind his image of Dulac.

Neither Wolfgang nor Frau Dulac believed anyone would respond to Dulac's fake funeral announcements. He falls off the mountain to complete the joke. Wolfgang argues that Dulac is just as sensible as ever, just as mad, that is—perhaps madder; nor is he senile. He has been putting on an act: "Play dead—and then wake up immortal," *in them.* Actually, Dulac's announcement is not incorrect, since 1962 has four months yet to go, and he has arranged to have them present when he does die.

The height of the fun Dulac has been having with them comes when they return to the castle after dinner. Fresh paint tracks made by a large bare foot delight him. On Kitty's bed he has draped the skin of Fido Dulac, the "surreal dog." Exhilarated by her shocked reaction, he imitates Fido. " 'In the wings of the scene,' " says Wolfgang, " 'an old man suddenly starts barking. Woof-woof-woof.' " He points out that it helps if Howe can see the joke. " 'It's not unusual to turn fact into fiction, Warren, but not many have turned fiction into fact.' " Dulac beats the game—he is not in, he is out of the nuthouse (the world). He runs his own, and his guests display an inspired lunacy. And "to bear in mind" what they experience—"what was that but the gift of life?" Only a madman like Dulac can "put time in its place. What place? The madcap round of his skull. To this extent they were all, like him, time's cheats."

Under the influence of Dulac and his castle, the natural impulsiveness of certain characters comes out. Katherine screams at the sight of her green, bug-like car painted white and of Fido's hide draped over her bed; but, when a bat, painted white, invades her room, she surrenders to impulse. She stands before her window as though she doesn't know that in the wind and the moonlight the shift she wears reveals her body; and her vibrant presence elicits from reserved Wolfgang several reckless sexual innuendoes directed at her. "The eyes she turned on them had a madcap luster. A touch of Riva lunacy? She seemed to see better at night." Now it is she who wants to take a foolhardy walk.

Sol is even more beguiled by this trip than by the last one. Guarding his car from George and his paint brush and with Sinatra tuned in on the car radio and with a cigar in his mouth, he seems content. Even after George succeeeds in painting both him and the car, Sol declares that he is thinking of buying the castle himself. Seymour Gatz shows up, takes one look, and goes back down the mountain "to where the time of the day could be plainly read on the clocks."

Dulac seems asleep, lullabied by the racket on the ramp below. When they yell down to Sol that Dulac is dead, it seems "a simple statement of fact," but "like an echo from the moat the answer came back to them, 'Dead, eh? You sure?' " Dulac is "now out of time's reach." Sol goes down "to report the death, as had been done so many times before, of Monsieur Etienne Dulac." He is only one manifestation, as is Don Quixote, of an immortal impulse.

"Life fading and life blooming" are symbolized by the old man's white hair and by the kid's carrot-red poll. Brian is an egg-shaped little prodigy, his "large head capped with a blue dink, like a nipple," his eyes "disturbingly impersonal." Until the moment Brian enters, Howe has not questioned "that the center of the scene was himself, around which these other centers were arranged, and over-lapped." Now Brian "neutralized with a glance the lines of force in the room. His center out-centered them." Dulac, too, senses a center conflicting with his own, an object as strange as himself. They look at each other, "a pair of odd ones at the opposite extremes of life. Juvenile and senile—they seemed contented to bask in the confrontation." Howe's impression of the boy is that "nothing, no nothing was missed. The pile of new, unused material between those ears soaked up what he saw like a blotter. To hell with under-standing. First one soaked it up," sowed seeds in "the seed-box head." "The understanding would come, if at all, years later," on canvas or between the covers of a work of fiction.

As they start for a walk down the mountain side, they pause on the ramp. Looking down from a window above the disorganized group, Howe feels that he is losing "his point of view," something he takes for granted:

A confused overlapping impression of a man at the window . . . seen from the angle of the boy on the ramp, had been imposed on the scene he had just that moment viewed from the window. A double-exposure. . . . At that point where Howe's glance inter-sected that of the boy the scene was open, a point of view did not close it, the apparent overlapping did not blur it, and something faintly suggestive of the scene itself might be said to exist. Inclu-sive rather than exclusive. An event without a beginning, as such, or an ending. Where his glance intercepted the boy's a current from the past spliced to the present; the future would consist of this sound overlapping sound.

Dulac stands with his withered hand resting on the boy's head:

Through Dulac's hand, as through a cable, Howe sensed the flow of an alternating current. The past into the present, the present into the past. What had died of the past was dead, or more accurately put, was past—but what had persisted was now being taped, in some cryptic manner that would need decoding, in the head of the boy. From the old, the charge was now being passed to the new. *What* charge? That was what one never knew. The new, unused heads, like empty deep-freeze cartons, would not give up their meaning . . . until thawed. The present would prove to be whatever proved to be unexpendable. Good or bad. If it existed it had proved itself. But was it by accident or design that the old man toyed with the current? Now turning it to flow into the boy, now into himself? Had he sensed that what survived of Monsieur Dulac would prove to be what remained in the head on which he leaned— on such terms that neither of them would understand? In the present, as in the future, the past would lead a life of its own, the predictable elements being those already dead. As a pallbearer, the boy carried the future, or nothing at all.

Brian as camera is another important metaphor. "At some future time" the scene by the cliffside where Dulac has fallen "would unroll as if filmed from the rim trail, where the boy, in silence and wonder, made it his own." At dinner, it pleases Howe to think that the behavior which emerges from the intricate pattern of relationships among them is being photographed and soundtaped—impersonally recorded by The Kid. That night, during the final fracas, Howe thinks: "For a moment they stood, without movement, as if the voice behind them had cried, 'Camera!' and a scene that had long been in preparation was being shot. Behind them, shooting it, was the boy."

The relationship between Brian and Dulac is similar to that between little Gordon and Boyd at the bullfight. As Dulac, like a crippled guide, leads them through the ruins down the mountain, Brian is at his heels. With tall, skinny Katherine in the picture, they make a grotesque trio. When Dulac falls, Howe concludes that he neither slipped nor fainted: "In what way could he leave a more memorable impression on the boy who had stood there beside him? On the future, that is. He was now secure in the boy's past. Senility had not deprived him of the wisdom of his folly. A dead man, he returned to life in the boy." As Dulac's body dies, the boy, at the old man's request, is at his side. "How sell or lease this dispersed piece of property?" Howe wonders, remembering his excuse for coming. "The largest active holding freshly staked out in Brian Caffrey's mind."

Brian is making his own time, just as Howe now realizes that, since Riva thirty years ago, "the time that he observed was his own," not some other notion of time, such as the clock's or the calendar's. In the past Howe had to pass a time barrier—an old man asleep in his sled, waiting for the snowfall so he could get his load of lumber down the mountain. "Time had changed right at that point. What he had brought along with him—the time on his watch, the time better described as time-passing—that time, whatever it was, seemed inadequate. As he passed the old man time-present seemed identical with time-past." Today, the closer to the interior of the castle he comes the shorter his memories become; past and present episodes begin to blend; and the present becomes as farcical as the past. Reunited with his friends, he wonders: "Did they shuffle ... between the past and the present so easily? All of them? Bold lovers one moment, old fakers the next?" At Riva one has, in depth, "the illusive, delusive time of one's life."

For Howe, Riva shares with the ice pond in Kansas City (where nothing really happened) "a world where the snow never melted, impersonal, impartial, and out of the time he lived in himself. . . . neither before nor behind, neither past nor future, since time itself was absent, perhaps what the present was like if one could ever lay hands on it." From many angles he views the question, What time is it? "Skull time," he concludes. "Howe's non-melting pond of ice. No thaw would reach it. In the round of his skull *that* time had stopped." He perceives again the unity of time and space: "As for the ocean of time, it was there on his eyelids, the curve of space." In the time-less skull of the boy "order reverted to disorder, the flux out of which new order would emerge." The usable past is "the here and now." Thus, "at any moment such time as there was was present."

II *Imaginative Vision*

Riva is a "symbol, suitably haunted, of the mind." Riva (and thus the mind), like the castle in the glass ball, is both in and out of this world. The glass-ball image was the only description that conveyed to Howe's friends the keen impression of Riva that he carried in his mind. In the past, the quilt of snow, like an imaginative transformation, "ended up revealing more than it covered up." In the present, "now that everything was revealed he seemed to see less." It is the timelessness of the imagination that enables Howe to keep the past alive in himself, making everything seem "only yesterday." A scholar who visits the castle declares that because he is "unable to look out so well," due to enfeebled eyesight, he looks *in* and sees much better the countries he once visited.

The creative memory does not merely resurrect, it reconstructs. Howe is an old-fashioned romantic, Horney insists, because he remembers " 'what never took place. You write and talk about it in order to believe it yourself.' " Wolfgang elaborates: " 'Don't we invent what we choose to remember?' " Symbolic of Katherine's own imaginative investment in the past is her loss of her contact lenses; having no contact with the present, she moves within her exaggerated re-creation of the past. But the past one *is to have* must be forged, as Brian's is being forged, in the fires of the immediate present. In this process, the eye and the object collaborate: "Was the wonder in the boy or in what he saw?" It is an effect "due in part to the shimmering light, in part to the onlooker."

For many people imaginative vision is a rare experience. As Wolfgang says of the tourists who stumble on Riva, " 'If it's not on the map, they don't believe it.' " One is inclined to doubt what one sees anyway. Is the castle actually there, "or on Howe's eyeballs?" To achieve imaginative freedom one must develop the ability to subject oneself profoundly to the absurd. Last year, Brian found Disneyland too tame; Riva is the Unreal-McCoy. Living in no-time, situated nowhere, the mind is free. Dulac walks in blizzards, marries a freak, and makes love to Katherine because he is a fool who persists in his folly. When Howe invites Uncle Fremont to go with him to Riva, his uncle asks, " 'You in your right mind, Warren?' " Right mind for what? To live imaginatively one has to be a little *out* of one's mind. "Where you begin or you end is pretty much a question" of how you imaginatively transform the experiences you have.

The creative imagination rebuilds the world. America may be demolishing itself in peace, as Europe did in war; but in the country of the imagination no bombs fall. A friend once took Sol to see his home town in Indiana; a freeway lay where the town had been. Howe looks at the *new* corner where the rooming house in which he lived with Wolfgang once stood. As if bombed, it has vanished "into thin air." But in Howe "the details of the room were now stored." He can bring it out of storage and behold it as though preserved on film: "In the not-so-thin air a room seemed to materialize."

The nature of the imaginative vision suggests many of the paradoxes of human experience. For instance, although Howe cannot remember how his friends looked "back then," he sees suddenly the face of a man he cannot remember ever having seen before. " 'Somebody took that snap shot when my back was turned. It isn't something I dug for, having buried.' " Along with the Kansas City ice pond, it has been in the developing solution in Howe's brain-pan all these years. What enables some men to see the past so intimately? A certain impersonality, objectivity, non-involvement. As one of his macabre practical jokes, Dulac once caused Howe's horse to throw him. Howe saw the event as though he were no part of it himself. The selective but impersonal camera eye preserved the scene. "What had it been like? The memory of it was clear although it was quite unlike a memory, he saw it so well." In the instant of imaginative vision, memory and immediate perception, time and space, are one.

As Morris' heroes leave unfinished situations behind on the flat, arid, safe, and defunct frontier, it may appear that Morris has gone on to the problem of living in the immediate present as though he has solved the problem with which he has been preoccupied throughout most of his novels—the uses and self-abuses of the past. How as an artist is he to render and conceptualize the feelings he has about his own past? That he has continually sought new ways of dealing with this problem and always returns to it from novels less personally concerned with the Nebraska past suggests that he has never solved it to his satisfaction. "Art can ... inform and lead into new places the flow of our sympathetic consciousness," says D. H. Lawrence, "and it can lead our sympathy away in recoil from things that are dead" (in *Territory*, 8). It was Lawrence who "defined" for Morris "the serious predicament of a man coming to terms with the present and using the past, not abusing it in an effort to make this imaginative act possible" ("P. of V.," 45).

No other writer of his time and country has been able to look as profoundly as Morris has into the nature of the past and its effect on people. His latest books are not meant to show the superiority over the past of the present and the incipient future. If he is exhorting his readers to adopt the Lawrencian banner that bears the rising Phoenix, he does not attempt to prove the attractions or advantages, beyond showing the inadequacies of living almost solely in either the past or the present. While he demonstrates the desirability, even the dire necessity, of escaping bemusement with the past, the problem of time in all its dimension is a greater concern. How to live both in and out of this world is a question that must be answered in the act of living in time, in the tensions among all its dimensions. *Cause For Wonder* brilliantly comes close to an answer.

One of the criticisms of Morris as a major, serious comic novelist has been that he seems to lack interest in the immediate social problems of American society. He is not as *engaged*, some critics contend as his contemporaries—as, for instance, Saul Bellow, Herbert Gold, Paul Goodman, Harvey Swados, James Baldwin, Norman Mailer, and Ralph Ellison. "It is assumed books are written to provoke discussion," says Morris. "Actually, they are conceived to make discussion irrelevant" (Letter). Though he *is* concerned with the nature of the common man and his experiences, Morris has not directly stepped into the battle royal of controversial issues. This aspect of the American scene is *in* Morris, but as a force operating in the background of individual crises of a universal character. He is *engaged* in the art of writing novels.

There are flaws in Morris' vision. When the raw material is thin—as many critics claim it too often is—the brilliant style and technique frequently call attention to themselves. Philosophical reflection, no matter how well blended with the *life* of a novel and no matter how appropriate to the perceiving character, may weary the most sympathetic reader, and only blur what he has probably already been clearly *shown*. Although given dimension in various evocative contexts, some of Morris' characters verge on flatness. The fragmentary approach has its riches, and within the scope of the short novel much can be conveyed; but his most sympathetic readers await with an eagerness close to impatience the great American novel they feel only Morris has the raw material and conceptual potential to produce. It may have the brevity, the poetic condensation of *The Great Gatsby,* or it may have the epic scope, the symbolic grandeur of *Moby Dick.* But it is to Morris' field of vision that they look for it.

Wright Morris' achievement is that he has been able to project upon the literary firmament a many-faceted, serio-comic view of the American Dream, landscape, and character. In vision and content, he is, I believe, the most thoroughly American contemporary writer. Although he has nominal affinities with a number of American writers, past and present, Morris has little in common stylistically or thematically with most of his immediate contemporaries. He alone, it seems, has maintained a constant, though always refocusing, view of his characters and of the world they inhabit throughout a large body of work over a relatively short period of creativity.

In dealing with the vast raw material of America, he has avoided journalistic Realism, esoteric experimentalism, and subjective immersion. He has conceptualized and processed that raw material, using modern techniques and attitudes which he has assimilated and made uniquely his own. He has forged a flexible style that can probe as deeply into the serious as into the comic; in its use of the cliché and the idioms of contemporary speech, that style has no counterpart in current literature. While the themes with which he deals may not be unique, the combinations in which he develops them, the ways in which he conceptualizes them, and the techniques he employs to discover them create an impressive body of work that has magnitude, complexity, and significance. In his finest novels— *The Works of Love, Man and Boy, The Deep Sleep, The Huge Season, The Field of Vision, Ceremony in Lone Tree,* and *Cause for Wonder*—one sees unforgettable characters and landscapes, one hears an authentic American voice that speaks with authority, one feels a firm technical control. And some readers and critics believe that these are touchstones of excellence in modern fiction.

Notes and References

Chapter One

1. *The Future of the Novel,* ed. Leon Edel (New York, 1956), p. 50.

2. Stanley J. Kunitz, ed., "Wright Morris," *Twentieth Century Authors,* First Supplement (New York, 1955), p. 692.

3. *Holiday,* XXIV (July, 1958), 142.

4. Edited by Edmund Wilson (New York, 1956), p. 69.

5. *The Frontier in American History* (New York, 1920), p. 1.

6. *The Great Plains* (Boston, 1931), pp. 8-9.

7. "Ended: the 400 Year Boom," *Harper's Magazine,* CCIII (October, 1951), 111.

8. For a fuller discussion of the historical background to Morris' work see my essay "The Great Plains in the Novels of Wright Morris," *Critique,* IV (Winter, 1961-62). In addition to Turner and Webb, Henry Nash Smith's *Virgin Land* (New York, 1957) is an excellent interpretive history of the plains.

9. "National Book Award Address by Wright Morris, March 12, 1957," *Critique,* IV (Winter, 1961-62), 73. Hereafter referred to as "NBA."

10. *Crumbling Idols,* ed. Jane Johnson (Cambridge, Massachusetts, 1960), p. 12.

11. For a good, brief survey of Midwestern literature see John T. Flanagan, "A Soil for the Seeds of Literature," *The Heritage of the Middle West,* ed. John J. Murray (Norman, Oklahoma, 1958). See also Flanagan's "Writing in the West and Mid-West," *Critique,* II (Winter, 1959), 28-29, containing pertinent remarks on Morris.

12. *Love and Death in the American Novel* (New York, 1960), pp. 471-72.

13. A stimulating and original book, *The Territory Ahead* may be read as a companion piece (brought up to date by the inclusion of twentieth-century authors) to *Studies in Classic American Literature* by D. H. Lawrence, to whom the book is dedicated. I discuss this book, in what is primarily an examination of his novels, only as it provides some insight into Morris' own novels. For a brief critical analysis of the book in relation to Morris' novels see Carpenter's "Wright Morris and the Territory Ahead," *College English,* XXI (December, 1959), 147-56. After repeated readings, I am convinced of the efficacy of Morris' description of the problem, but his prescription for a remedy is too brief

to be satisfactory. Although new aspects of the argument are introduced with each author discussed (Thoreau, Whitman, Melville, Twain, James, Hemingway, Wolfe, Fitzgerald, Faulkner, Lawrence, Eliot), the book is almost negligently repetitious and, after a while, its pattern is too predictable.

14. Sam Bleufarb, "Point of View: An Interview with Wright Morris," *Accent,* XIX (Winter, 1959), 36. Hereafter referred to as "P. of V."

Chapter Two

1. From the Amherst Lectures. On October 22, 27, and 30, 1958, Morris delivered three lectures at Amherst College under the general title "Made in U. S. A.": "The American Character," published as "Made in U. S. A.," "The Origin of a Species: Time Past," and "The Origin of a Species: Time Present," unpublished. Hereafter referred to as "Lectures."

2. "The Cars in my Life," *Holiday,* XXIV (December, 1958), 45. While living in Chicago, Morris and his father spent a year on the road, seeing America first. They made two trips to California; on one return trip they abandoned their second-hand Marmon touring car in the Mississippi flood of 1927; they finished another trip full of mishaps in a motorcycle side-car. At fourteen, Morris took over the driving of his father's car. "The sleeve-valve motor was my baby, and looming on the horizon was my age" (47).

3. For a fuller discussion of this theme in relation to the plains background and in relation to Joseph Campbell's *Hero with a Thousand Faces* see my essay "The Great Plains in the Novels of Wright Morris," *Critique,* IV (Winter, 1961-62).

4. *Sewanee Review,* LXV (Summer, 1957), 147-56.

5. "Made in U. S. A.," *The American Scholar,* XXIX (Autumn, 1960), 483. Hereafter referred to as "Made."

6. *Critique,* IV (Summer, 1962), 41.

7. She is modeled on Morris' own audacious mother, Grace, who died shortly after his birth. In 1956, he learned that on buggy rides to town she "would sight down the line of telephone poles and shoot insulators off the crossbars," but he has been writing as though he knew it all along. See the National Book Award Speech and *Cause for Wonder.*

Chapter Three

1. For Crevecoeur's answer to this question, see *Letters From An American Farmer* (New York, 1957), pp. 39-40.

2. "Privacy as a Subject for Photography," *Magazine of Art,* XLIV (February, 1951), 51-55. Hereafter referred to as "Privacy."

3. "The Craft of Vision," *Critique,* IV (Winter, 1961-62), 55.

4. Richard Ellmann, *James Joyce* (New York, 1959), pp. 87-88.

5. From a letter dated December 7, 1957, to the author from Wright Morris. Hereafter referred to as "Letter."

6. One of the epigraphs for the book is by Rilke, who claimed to live in *things*. In a mystical relation with them, one may be conscious of the presence of God in things. A *thing* lives because it stirs the emotions. In his poems and his letters an esthetic doctrine of *things* is formulated.

Booth has observed of Morris that "Eliot's language now permeates his own." Images, ideas, phrases from other writers and artists whose thought has influenced Morris are woven into his works. For instance, the phrase "touch bottom" from James's *The Ambassadors,* is expanded into a central image in Morris' *The Field of Vision.* In Morris, echoes of the following authors may also be heard: Cervantes, Blake, Crevecoeur, Melville, Milton, Twain, Whitman, Thoreau, Keats, Arnold, Lawrence, Camus, Joyce, Sherwood Anderson, Fitzgerald, Faulkner, Hemingway, Woolf.

7. Morris suspects that these photo-text experiments complicated his effort to establish himself as a novelist; reviewers tended to regard him as primarily a photographer.

8. In this discussion of ritual and gesture I have been greatly influenced by the thinking of Suzanne K. Langer. Consult the index of *Philosophy in a New Key* (New York, 1962).

Chapter Four

1. William H. Morris was a railroad station agent and one of the first men in the Midwest to go into the egg business on a large scale. A "self-made" man, he moved with his son through the whistle stops in the Platte Valley. For five years they lived on the North Side of Chicago near Lincoln Park. The density of these years—formative years in a sense that Nebraska was not—is evident in the way Chicago appears in, or dominates, many of the novels, particularly *The Works of Love.*

2. *The Teachings of the Mystics* (New York, 1960), pp. 27-28.

Chapter Five

1. Harvey Breit, "Talk with Wright Morris," New York *Times Book Review,* June 10, 1951, p. 19.

2. In "Technique as Discovery," Mark Schorer discusses "the primary importance of technique to subject" and "their indivisibility" (26). To speak of technique is to "speak of nearly everything. For technique is the means by which the writer's experience, which is his subject matter, compels him to attend to it; technique is the only means he has of discovering, exploring, developing his subject, of conveying its meaning . . ." (19). He goes on to say that "technique alone objectifies the materials of art; hence technique alone evaluates those materials" (15). "The modern novelist—from James and Conrad down—" perceives "not only that technique *contains* intellectual and moral implications, but that it *discovers* them" (16). Reprinted in *Forms of Modern Fiction,* ed. William Van O'Connor (Minneapolis, 1948), pp. 9-29.

Chapter Six

1. *Generation of Vipers* (New York, 1942), p. 185.
2. John K. Hutchins, "On an Author," New York *Herald Tribune Book Review*, June 3, 1951, p. 2.

Chapter Seven

1. In *The Huge Season, Love Among the Cannibals,* and *What a Way to Go* the social context is much wider than are the family and the home, but Morris does not construct a social environment except as his characters reveal it. Proctor as a Communist is meaningful only by virtue of Morris' interest in him as a human being who reflects certain facets of human nature and American character, not as a comment on communism itself.
2. In 1930, a grandfather provided Morris with money for an education at a Seventh Day Adventist college on the West Coast, five weeks of which was sufficient for Morris. He moved on to Pomona College in Claremont, California, where Professor Leon Howard, to whom *Cause for Wonder* is dedicated, encouraged him to develop his talent for writing. He left Pomona for a year's *Wanderjahr* in Europe.
3. The complexity of viewpoint suggested here may be seen in Conrad's Marlow stories in which he is so insistent on the value of the hero-witness relationship that he creates a four-level connection.
4. This magnet concept comes perhaps from a rather casual line in Fitzgerald's "The Rich Boy": "I don't think he was ever happy unless some one was in love with him, responding to him like filings to a magnet, helping him to explain himself, promising him something. What it was I do not know." *Babylon Revisited and Other Stories* (New York, 1960), p. 187.
5. Fitzgerald's influence on Morris is confined mainly to the concepts of *The Crack-Up* and *The Great Gatsby*. Unlike Wolfe, Fitzgerald made of nostalgia "a work of art," says Morris in *Territory*. In *The Great Gatsby*, "and I think only in *Gatsby*, the mythic vastness of this continent, the huge raw material banquet that Wolfe bolted, received its baptismal blessing and its imaginative processing." In several novels, Morris refers to Jay Gatsby as a powerful symbol of the spirit of the American Dream. The relationship between Lawrence and Foley is similar to that between Gatsby and Nick Carroway. However, Morris' rendering of the college environment differs from Fitzgerald's. Morris delayed re-creating that period until both his art and his personality had matured.

Chapter Eight

1. Miss Kollwitz, one of the most interesting characters, is an example of Morris' tendency in this novel to carry his characterizations too far. Sometimes the characters seem to be a set of grotesque, in-

genious dolls, each with a stock of invariable mannerisms; in the absence of human beings, each doll turns the key that sets another off.

2. Unless otherwise indicated all quotations in this section pertaining to cliché are from "Made in U. S. A."

3. "Man on the Moon," *Partisan Review*, XXIX (Spring, 1962), 245.

4. *The Art of Travel*, ed. Morton Dauwen Zabel (New York, 1958), pp. 387-88.

Chapter Nine

1. Jonathan Baumbach, "Wake Before Bomb: Ceremony in Lone Tree," *Critique*, IV (Winter, 1961-62), 62.

2. "Wright Morris in the Territory Ahead," *College English*, XXIII (December, 1959), 156.

Chapter Ten

1. "No Place to Hide" was a working title for this novel. Morris wrote a novel called Madman of Ranna soon after his European *Wanderjahr*, using a cartoon-text technique; several unpublished novels set in Nebraska also use this technique. The Texas farm element in *Dudley* is more fully developed in *Cause for Wonder*, and several of the album entries in *The Man Who Was There* anticipate it.

2. "Time-Past" and "Time-Present" are the titles of two of Morris' Amherst lectures (1958).

Selected Bibliography

PRIMARY SOURCES

With the exception of juvenilia, all the published work of Wright Morris known to the compiler is listed chronologically below.

A. Books

My Uncle Dudley. New York: Harcourt, Brace and Company, 1942.
The Man Who Was There. New York: Charles Scribner's Sons, 1945.
The Inhabitants. New York: Charles Scribner's Sons, 1946.
The Home Place. New York: Charles Scribner's Sons, 1948.
The World in the Attic. New York: Charles Scribner's Sons, 1949.
Man and Boy. New York: Alfred A. Knopf, Inc., 1951. London: Gollancz, 1952. Turin, Italy: Einandi, 1954.
The Works of Love. New York: Alfred A. Knopf, Inc., 1952.
The Deep Sleep. New York: Charles Scribner's Sons, 1953. London: Eyre and Spottiswoode, 1954. Stuttgart, Germany: Goverts, 1957. Frankfurt, Germany: Fischer Bucherei, 1960 (paperback).
The Huge Season. New York: The Viking Press, 1954. London: Secker and Warburg, 1955. Stuttgart, Germany: Goverts, 1958.
The Field of Vision. New York: Harcourt, Brace and Company, 1956. New York: New American Library, 1957 (paperback). London: Weidenfeld and Nicolson, 1957. Milan, Italy: Feltrinelli, 1962.
Love Among the Cannibals. New York: Harcourt, Brace and Company, 1957. New York: New American Library, 1958 (paperback). London: Weidenfeld and Nicolson, 1958. Milan, Italy: Feltrinelli, 1958. Stuttgart, Germany: Goverts, 1959.
The Territory Ahead. New York: Harcourt, Brace and Company, 1958. New York: Atheneum, 1963 (paperback).
Ceremony in Lone Tree. New York: Atheneum Publishers, 1960. New York: New American Library, 1962 (paperback). London: Weidenfeld and Nicolson, 1961. Munich, Germany: Piper Verlag, 1962. Milan, Italy: Feltrinelli, 1962.
What a Way to Go. New York: Atheneum Publishers, 1962.
Cause for Wonder. New York: Atheneum Publishers, 1963.

B. Short Stories

"The Ram in the Thicket," *Harper's Bazaar,* LXXXII (May, 1948), 133, 182-94. First sixty-one pages of *Man and Boy.* Interesting version of the book that appeared three years later.

"Where's Justice?" *Cross Section*, 1948, ed. Edwin Seaver. New York: Simon and Schuster, 1948, pp. 221-30. A strange story set in the South.

"A Man of Caliber," *Kenyon Review*, XI (Winter, 1949), 101-7. Segment of a version of *The Works of Love*. Will Brady in the egg business in Calloway, Nebraska.

"The Lover," *Harper's Bazaar*, LXXXIII (May, 1949), 118, 175-80. Early segment of *The Works of Love*. Will Brady arrives in Calloway, works at hotel, involved with prostitutes. Interesting version of the book that appeared three years later.

"The Sound Tape," *Harper's Bazaar*, LXXXV (May, 1951), 125, 175-77. A study in the conflict between thinking and feeling in the American character, scrutinized in grotesque relationships in a suburban family. Reliance here, as in several of his short stories, on an overcharged macabre atmosphere; surprise ending resulting in a kind of shock seldom encountered in his novels. The stylistic control is superb. Related to *Man and Boy* and *The Deep Sleep* background.

"The Character of the Lover," *American Mercury*, LXXIII (August, 1951), 43-49. The confusion between fact and fiction. Life imitates art. Anticipates *What a Way to Go* by eleven years. By giving him *The Great Gatsby* and one of his own books, an author named Hodler (one of many elderly German males in Morris) sets the style for the behavior of a susceptible young man.

"The Rites of Spring," *New World Writing #1*. New York: New American Library, 1952, pp. 140-45. A young boy's initiation in the ritual of hog-butchering. Anticipations of Walter McKee's encounter with the hog and of Mrs. Ormsby's encounter with the Gudger boys. A version of Dudley's Texas farm is the setting.

"The Safe Place," *Kenyon Review*, XVI (Autumn, 1954), 587-99. Of hope and hopelessness. Seven years later, this story, one of Morris' finest, appears, abbreviated, with a different ending, near the close of *Ceremony in Lone Tree*. Boyd tells the story as part of a novel he is writing.

"The Word from Space—A Story," *The Atlantic*, CCI (April, 1958), 38-42. Reprinted in *The Magazine of Science Fiction*, XV (September, 1958), 111-18. Morris' first attempt at "science-fiction"—not bizarre, but whimsical. Theme of stripping to the essentials.

"The Cat in the Picture . . .," *Esquire*, XLIX (May, 1958), 90-94. Weird, almost fantastic, story of the effect of a stray cat on the lives of a retired Captain and his wife. When the wife and the cat exclude the Captain, certain emotionally stunted aspects of their marriage become apparent. Shock ending (see comments on "The Sound Tape").

"Wake Before Bomb," *Esquire*, LII (December, 1959), 311-15. A version of the early part of the first "Boyd" section of *Ceremony*; interesting variations. Boyd's name is Conley here, a name used symbolically in the novel. Conley is estranged from his wife; Boyd has no wife. Not much point in itself, but the characters and the idea are interesting.

"The Scene," *The Noble Savage, #1* (1960), pp. 60-75. From *Ceremony in Lone Tree*. Opening segment of *Ceremony*, almost verbatim.

C. *Articles and Book Reviews by Wright Morris*

"The New Criticism," *American Scholar*, XX (Summer, 1951), 359. Impatience with some of the inner-sanctum snobbishness of the New Critics. Letter.

"An American in Paris," New York *Times Book Review* (December 9, 1951), p. 28. Review of H. J. Kaplan's *The Spirit and the Bride*.

"The Violent Land—Faulkner and Expressionism," *Magazine of Art*, XLV (March, 1952), 99-103. A perceptive discussion of the correlation between Faulkner's stylistic techniques and the expressionism of Soutine, Munch, Roualt, Van Gogh, and Kokoschka, all of whom express a crippled rage. Compare with Morris' comments on "rage" as the signature of Faulkner's style in "The Function of Rage" in *The Territory Ahead*. That Morris himself has done some painting perhaps explains the fact that his characters Agee and Webb are artists.

"How Come You Settled Down Here?" *Vogue*, CXIX (April 15, 1952), 74, 117, 119. A year after taking Morris' advice to See America First in a jalopy, a young man returns to ask, "How come you settled *here*?"—in Wayne, Pennsylvania, in a ranch house. Some autobiographical material about Morris' Chicago years, his wanderings alone and with his first wife; much of the background of *My Uncle Dudley*. In life, as in art, one must make a choice from an abundance of possibilities.

"What Was Missing in the Fireworks," New York *Times Book Review* (September 1, 1957), p. 3. Review of Sean O'Faolain's *The Vanishing Hero: Studies of Novelists of the Twenties*.

"Norman Rockwell's America," *The Atlantic*, CC (December, 1957), 133-38. A version of a lecture delivered at a prep school. Appears as "Abuse of the Past" in *Territory*.

National Book Award Address, March 12, 1957. Reprinted in *Critique*, IV (Winter, 1961-62), 72-75. Contains biographical information, comments on *The Field of Vision*, and attitudes toward his work. Quoted extensively in the text. See index.

"The Territory Ahead," in *The Living Novel: A Symposium*, ed. Granville Hicks. New York: Macmillan, 1957, pp. 120-56. Much of this selection is reprinted in Part One of *Territory*.

"Our Endless Plains," *Holiday*, XXIV (July, 1958), 68-69, 138-43. Lyrical images of and comments on Nebraska plains environment, past and present, from an autobiographical point of view. A sketch of passages used in "The Scene," the opening segment of *Ceremony*.

"Henry James's *The American Scene*," *The Texas Quarterly*, I (Summer-Autumn, 1958), 27-42. Version, with some variation, of "Use of the Past" and "Objects and Places" chapters of *Territory*.

"The Cars in My Life," *Holiday*, XXIV (December, 1958), 45-53. Autobiographical view of people and events in the author's life as seen through the windshield of various cars. Nostalgia refined by wit. The makings, from various incidents, of *My Uncle Dudley*. Also, car elements in other novels: *Love Among the Cannibals, The Man Who Was There, The Home Place,* and *The World in the Attic* (i.e., such a car as Miss Caddy probably drove).

"The Ability to Function: A Reappraisal of Fitzgerald and Hemingway," in *New World Writing #13*. New York: New American Library, 1958, pp. 34-51. With some variations, this article becomes "The Function of Style" and "The Function of Rage" chapters in *Territory*.

"Mexican Journey," *Holiday*, XXVI (November, 1959), 50-63. Witty, vivid, imaginative travel chronicle. Presents much of the background for *Cannibals, Field,* and the first Boyd section of *Ceremony*. His travel pieces *suggest* another affinity with D. H. Lawrence and Henry James.

"Nature Before Darwin," *Esquire*, LII (November, 1959), 64-70. Comments on audacious people, cats, and birds; Morris' works compose a cat and bird sanctuary. Compare with pp. 159-70 in *The Huge Season*. The girl referred to in this essay appears in various guises in the novels. Compare with the style of Loren Eiseley (author of *The Firmament of Time*), to whom *The Works of Love* is dedicated.

"Lawrence and the Immediate Present," in *A D. H. Lawrence Miscellany*, ed. Harry T. Moore. Carbondale, Illinois: Southern Illinois Press, 1959, pp. 7-12. Reprinted from *The Territory Ahead*.

"The Open Road," *Esquire*, LIII (June, 1960), 98-99. As a traveler of the highways, Morris encounters aspects of the American scene expressed in various kinds of signs. An amusing response to the cliché.

"Made in U. S. A.," *The American Scholar*, XXIX (Autumn, 1960), 483-94. Excellent discussion of the peculiarly American ability to improvise and of the nature of the cliché in American character and language. Quoted at length in the text. See index.

"One Law for the Lion," *Partisan Review*, XXVIII (May-June, 1961), 541-51. (On Hemingway.) The man, the legend, the works are one, and explain both the genius and the failures of Hemingway. Subtle suggestions of Morris' debt to the master. Compare with "The Function of Style" in *Territory*.

"Conversations in a Small Town," *Holiday*, XXX (November, 1961), 98, 100, 103, 107, 108. A disappointing account of a return to the scene of the author's childhood as it figures in the Nebraska novels. Compare with barber shop scenes in *The Man Who Was There, The Home Place,* and *The World in the Attic*.

"Man on the Moon," *Partisan Review*, XXIX (Spring, 1962), 241-49. Especially provocative comments on the failure of modern man's imagination, subjected to the bomb, outer space, and Eichmann.

D. *Text-Photography*

"The Inhabitants," in *New Directions in Prose and Poetry*, 1940, ed. James Laughlin. Norfolk, Conn.: New Directions, 1940, pp. 145-80. Variations on "epiphanies" used in *The Inhabitants* six years later. Includes a few photographs not used in the book. The coupling of the "epiphanies" with the photographs is not always the same as it is in the book. Connection between text and photograph is even less obvious here. Pictures on the left, prose on the right—opposite arrangement used in *The Inhabitants*. Some pictures printed in reverse of their appearance in the book.

"White House," in *Twice a Year* (Fall-Winter, 1940; Spring-Summer, 1941 [Double Issue]), p. 116. (Published in New York by the Twice a Year Press.) Appears in the midst of Harlan Crippen's "Fields and Years," an essay about the Great Plains. Printed in reverse of its appearance in the book.

"The Inhabitants," *Direction*, III (November, 1940), 12-13. Pictures and text.

"Landscape with Figures," in *New Directions in Prose and Poetry*, 1941, ed. James Laughlin. Norfolk, Conn.: New Directions, 1941, pp. 253-77. Description of *New Directions*, 1940, applies here, except that this segment is divided into sections: The Country, The Village, The City, The Frontier.

"The Inhabitants," *Photography* (London), (July-August, 1947), pp. 26-29. Pictures and text.

"The Inhabitants," in *Spearhead: an Anthology*. Norfolk, Conn.: New Directions, 1947, pp. 191-201. Same as New Directions, 1941. Reprinted, shorter version.

"The American Scene," New York *Times Magazine* (July 4, 1948), pp. 14-15. Pictures from *The Home Place* with commentary not used in the book. Defines what the home place is; comments on the importance of going back to rediscover it.

"An Author Remembers His Home Place in Nebraska," *Life*, XXV (July 26, 1948), 8-10. "Speaking of Pictures" feature. A picture review of *The Home Place*.

"Home Town Revisited," New York *Times Magazine* (April 24, 1949), 24-25. "Scratch a big man, you often find a small town." Echoes of *The Man Who Was There*, *The Home Place*, and *The World in the Attic*. Dangles between excruciating nostalgia and compassionate nausea. Eddie Cahow pictured here, but not in the books.

"The World in the Attic," *Photography* (London), (September, 1949), pp. 17-26. Pictures and text.

"Summer Encore," New York *Times Magazine* (November 13, 1949), pp. 26-27. Echoes of prose used in the novels. Uncle Harry pictured, facing front, in shadow. Visual theme: soft focus on Indian Summer. Images: hammocks, leaves, piled pumpkins, graveyard, a road in a glade, corn shocked in an enclosure. Pictures not used in other books.

"Built with More than Hands," New York *Times Magazine* (December 25, 1949), pp. 12-13. The American spirit shows itself in the *look* of its many mansions. Churches pictured, in New England (Cape Cod), Nebraska, New Mexico (Morris once lived on a mesa near Gallup). In these pictures one can see Morris' selective principles at work. While the photographs are as fine as his others, they are not right for the conception governing the books.

"Guest of Honour—No. 12—Wright Morris (U. S. A.)," *Photography* (London), (July, 1949), 14-15. Pictures and text projected for "The World in the Attic," with brief biographical comment on Morris.

"The Home; Echoes from Empty Houses," in I, No. 3, *The Nation's Heritage*. New York: Heritage Magazine, Inc., 1949, no page numbers. Generous selection of the best photographs from *The Inhabitants*. Impressively mounted. Book measures about 1′ ½″ x 1′ ¾″. Inept captions, probably not Morris'.

U. S. Camera Annual, 1949, ed. Tom Maloney. New York: U. S. Camera Corp., 1949, p. 30, photograph, with comment by Lewis Mumford.

"Out of Shoes Come New Feet," New York *Times Magazine* (June 11, 1950), pp. 20-21. Some photographs not used elsewhere. Passages and echoes from the books. Focus on a child's feet. He moves among the artifacts of summer: egg, wheel, pump, trees and clouds, whiffle-tree with mint, flooded creek. Nostalgic transformation of the cliché.

"Privacy as a Subject for Photography," *Magazine of Art*, XLIV (February, 1951), 51-55. Excellent essay on the element of privacy in photography as it relates to the nature of the art. Includes photographs, and a revealing discussion of Morris' selective principles. Quoted at length in the text. See Index.

SECONDARY SOURCES

A. *Biographical Material*

BLEUFARB, SAM. "Point of View: An Interview with Wright Morris," *Accent*, XIX (Winter, 1959), 34-46. Excellent interview; extremely important for biographical information and for the author's comments on the development of his work.

BREIT, HARVEY. "Talk with Wright Morris," New York *Times Book Review* (June 10, 1951), p. 19. On the occasion of the publication of *Man and Boy*. The author comments on his craft and on his preference for the short novel form.

BUSCH, ARTHUR J. "Fellowships for Photography," *Popular Photography*, II (October, 1942), 22-23, 82. Pertains to his photo-text projects.

HUTCHINS, JOHN K. "On an Author," New York *Herald Tribune Book Review* (June 3, 1951), p. 2. On the occasion of the publication of *Man and Boy*. The author comments on his craft.

"Main Line Author of the Month," *Main Line* (June, 1951), pp. 24,

41-42. On the occasion of the publication of *Man and Boy*. Interesting information and comment by the author not found elsewhere.

WARFEL, HARRY R. *American Novelists of Today*. New York: American
Book Company, 1951. Biographical comment and description of
his work through *The World in the Attic*.

"Wright Morris," *Twentieth Century Authors,* First Supplement, ed.
Stanley J. Kunitz. New York: The H. W. Wilson Company, 1955.
Valuable statements by the author on his life and work.

B. *Criticism of Morris' Works*

ALLEN, WALTER. *The Modern Novel in Britain and the United States*.
New York: E. P. Dutton and Co., 1964. Brief general discussion of
later works.

BAUMBACH, JONATHAN. "Wake Before Bomb: *Ceremony in Lone Tree,*"
Critique, IV (Winter, 1961-62), 56-71. Excellent analysis of
Ceremony.

BOOTH, WAYNE C. "The Two Worlds in the Fiction of Wright Morris,"
Sewanee Review, LXV (Summer, 1957), 375-99. Finest criticism of
Morris to date.

————. "The Shaping of Prophecy: Craft and Idea in the Novels of
Wright Morris," *The American Scholar,* XXXI (Autumn, 1962),
608-26. A reappraisal of Morris' work, with comment on several
books not discussed in the previous article by Booth: *Love Among
The Cannibals, The Territory Ahead, Ceremony in Lone Tree,
What a Way to Go*.

CARPENTER, FREDERIC. "Wright Morris and the Territory Ahead,"
College English, XXI (December, 1959), 147-56. Cursory description of the works. Rather vague criticism of Morris' failure to
practice what he preaches in *Territory*.

EISINGER, CHESTER E. *Fiction of the Forties*. Chicago: The University of
Chicago Press, 1963. Excellent analysis of Morris as "The Artist in
Search of America." All the books are discussed.

FIEDLER, LESLIE. *Love and Death in the American Novel*. New York:
Criterion Books, 1960. Brief, but perceptive comment on *Man and
Boy* and its "Momism" theme. Also, a discussion of Morris' posi-
tion in contemporary literature as a "nay-sayer."

HASSAN, IHAB. *Radical Innocence: Studies in the Contemporary American
Novel*. Princeton: Princeton University Press, 1961. Brief general
comment.

HOWARD, LEON. *Literature and the American Tradition*. Garden City,
New York: Doubleday and Company, Inc., 1960. Links Morris
with Wallace Stevens, Faulkner, and Hemingway as a writer who
believes "in the creative power of the human spirit to endure and
prevail and to exist in the meanest and queerest of individuals."

HUNT, JOHN W., JR. "The Journey Back: The Early Novels of Wright
Morris," *Critique,* V (Spring-Summer, 1962), 41-60. Fine demon-
stration of the importance of Morris' early novels.

The Idea of an American Novel, eds. Louis D. Rubin, Jr., and John Ries

Moore. New York: Thomas Y. Crowell Co., 1961. Brief comment on and excerpts from *Territory*.

KLEIN, MARCUS. *After Alienation*. Cleveland and New York: The World Publishing Company, 1964. A fine 50 page discussion of all Morris' works.

LINDEN, STANTON J. and DAVID MADDEN. "A Wright Morris Bibliography," *Critique*, IV (Winter, 1961-62), 77-87. Reviews of the books listed.

MADDEN, DAVID. "The Great Plains in the Novels of Wright Morris," *Critique*, IV (Winter, 1961-62), 5-23. The relation between the Great Plains environment and some of Morris' themes and techniques.

————. "The Hero and the Witness in Wright Morris' Field of Vision," *Prairie Schooner*, XXXIV (Fall, 1960), 263-78. Sketchy introduction to the themes, techniques, and style of the novels through *Cannibals*.

TRACHTENBERG, ALAN. "The Craft of Vision," *Critique*, IV (Winter, 1961-62), 41-55. Excellent discussion of the element of vision in Morris' craft, relating the photo-text technique to the thematic vision of *The Field of Vision*.

WATERMAN, ARTHUR E. "The Novels of Wright Morris: An Escape from Nostalgia," *Critique*, IV (Winter, 1961-62), 24-40. General discussion of the theme of time in all Morris' novels through *Ceremony*.

"Wright Morris," *A Library of Literary Criticism*, ed. Dorothy Nyren. New York: Frederick Ungar Publishing Company, 1960. Critical profile by means of excerpts from reviews.

Index

Index

The World in the Attic, Preface, 44, 48, 49, 51, 56, 57-63, 81

Mumford, Lewis, Preface, 29

Muncy, Bobby *(The Home Place, The World in the Attic)*, 22, 52

Muncy, Clyde *(The Home Place, The World in the Attic)*, 19, 23, 32, 48, 51-63, 81, 85, 95, 122, 123, 144

Muncy, Peg *(The Home Place, The World in the Attic)*, 52, 54, 60, 62, 95

Muncy, Peggy (daughter), *(The Home Place, The World in the Attic)*, 19, 22, 52, 54

Muncy, Will "Chicken" *(The Home Place, The World in the Attic)*, 20, 58, 64

Munger, Charlie *(Ceremony in Lone Tree)*, 132, 134, 136, 137, 143, 146, 148, 149, 151

Murdock, Nebraska, 67, 72

Mysticism, 20, 45, 46, 50, 55, 56, 65, 71-75, 80, 86, 146, 154

Mythic elements, 20, 21, 26, 28, 47, 60, 63, 65, 81, 96, 117, 122, 126, 127, 131, 135, 138 ff., 145, 149, 151, 154

National Book Award Speech, 27, 29, 30, 92

Nausicaä, 22, 25, 119, 125, 127, 128

Navel of the world, 18, 29, 30, 65, 133, 143

Nebraska, Preface, 18, 19, 25, 29, 30, 32, 40, 47, 48, 51, 65, 69, 71, 101, 107, 116, 132, 140, 144, 146, 170

Newcomb, Gussie *(The Man Who Was There)*, 18, 21, 42, 43, 45-47

Nostalgia-nausea, Preface, 31, 33, 42, 44, 47, 57, 58, 60, 61, 63, 81, 82, 116, 131, 135, 145, 150

Oakley, Annie, 21

Odysseus, 25, 119, 127, 128

Omaha, Nebraska, 21, 64, 67, 134, 158

"On an Author" (John K. Hutchins), 83, 91

Ormsby, Mrs. (Mother), *(Man and Boy)*, 18, 20, 23, 79, 80, 83ff., 93, 98, 148

Ormsby, Virgil *(Man and Boy)*, 22, 23, 83, 85 ff., 150

Ormsby, Warren *(Man and Boy)*, 22, 23, 24, 79, 80, 83 ff., 93, 98, 110

Osborn, Uncle Fremont *(Cause for Wonder)*, 18, 20, 21, 80, 156 ff., 169

Osborn, Grace *(Cause for Wonder)*, 44, 59, 160

Osborn, Grandfather *(The World in the Attic)*, 59

Osborn, Grandmother *(The Home Place)*, 53

Panza, Sancho, 34, 141

Paris, 18, 42, 43, 101, 102, 109, 126

Parsons, Carl *(The Deep Sleep)*, 21, 92 ff.

Percy *(Cause for Wonder)*, 161

Perkheimer, Herr *(What a Way to Go)*, 25, 119, 124, 125, 127, 129

Permanence and impermanence, 35, 41, 45, 50, 52, 53, 56, 67, 68, 74, 82, 87, 88, 89, 111, 140, 152, 154

Perse, St. John, 108

Pershing Square, 18, 33, 73

Philadelphia, Pennsylvania, 18, 19, 21, 83

Pignata, Signor *(What a Way to Go)*, 25, 128

Plinski, Manny *(The Works of Love)*, 22, 69

Point of view, 78, 79, 97, 133, 146, 147, 149, 166; time-viewpoint technique, 78; multiple points of view, 79, 80

"Point of View: An Interview with Wright Morris" (Sam Bleufarb), 14, 18, 170

Polk, Nebraska, 133, 134, 145

Porter, Grandmother *(The Deep Sleep)*, 23, 24, 92 ff., 99, 100

Porter, Judge *(The Deep Sleep)*, 21, 22, 24, 92 ff., 100, 104

Porter, Millicent *(The Deep Sleep)*, 18, 23, 77, 83, 92 ff., 104

Porter, Roger *(The Deep Sleep)*, 22, 93, 96

The Portrait of a Lady (Henry James), 17

Privacy, 17, 54, 96

Proctor, Jesse L. *(The Huge Season)*, 20, 21, 101, 102, 103 ff., 109 ff., 141